COLLECTED POEMS
ONE 1968–1997

for Sue

PETER FINCH

COLLECTED POEMS ONE 1968-1997

EDITED BY ANDREW TAYLOR
FOREWORD BY NERYS WILLIAMS

Seren is the book imprint of
Poetry Wales Press Ltd.
Suite 6, 4 Derwen Road, Bridgend, Wales, CF31 1LH
www.serenbooks.com
facebook.com/SerenBooks
twitter@SerenBooks

ISBN: 978-1-78172-670-9

A CIP record for this title is available from the British Library.

The publisher acknowledges the financial assistance of the Books Council of Wales.

Cover artwork: Image by kind permission of Bentu Design

Printed in Bembo by Pelikan Basim, Turkey.

CONTENTS

On Criticism – 1984

from Reds In The Bed – 1985

from Selected Poems – 1987

from Make – 1990

The Cheng Man Ch'ing Variations – 1990

Poems For Ghosts – 1991

FOREWORD – NERYS WILLIAMS

The task of bringing together the first thirty years of a poet's work into one volume requires considerable oversight and care. Poet and editor work as curators presenting a life in letters, highlight the artist preoccupations at different yet connecting points of an artistic trajectory. It is an absolute pleasure to welcome Peter Finch's *Collected Poems Volume One 1968-1997*. On a practical level this volume provides access to works – chapbooks, broadsheets, special limited issues – which are either impossible to source or, in today's global marketplace of small press ephemera, prohibitively expensive to collect. This volume offers us a much-needed timeline of artistic activity. With customary charm and wry humour, Finch alerts the reader to his encounters with institutions and groups such as *The Poetry Society*, *Poets Conference*, *Welsh Academy* and the *Writers Forum* as well as collaborations and performances with Bob Cobbing, Henri Chopin, Meic Stephens, Nick Zurbrugg and Paul Pieter Piech. We learn initially that we owe Finch's beginnings in poetry to *The Society for Promotion of Christian Knowledge*, or more specifically to one of their bookshops, where he bought his City Lights edition of Allen Ginsberg's *Howl*. Soon thereafter (in 1966) his own imprint *Second Aeon* was born, and the rest one might say is literary history.

Or is it? Literary groups, collectives and indeed literary history itself often exhibits a curious degree of slippage over the decades. General groupings such as 'alternative', 'performance', 'avant-garde' shift ground, and the once seemingly robust coteries encountered in one's early reading begin to intersect and interlap, forming a Venn diagram of poetic relationships. This *Collected Volume One* speaks to a twenty-first century contemporary Welsh writing in English where poetic identifications are diffused, and communities are fluid. The *Poetry Wars* of the 1970s, between radicals and conservatives, would seem distant to today's 'emerging' poets. Poetry's online presence has enabled the breakdown of such patrolled divisions as mainstream and experimental.

However, Peter Finch's volume offers us a touchstone and testimony to the literary experimental, also chronicling to the difficulties of making visible an alternative modernist culture in Wales. I remember coming belatedly to Finch's works, a late starter, and felt great relief to know that somebody such as Peter practiced and existed in Wales. He has been generous to poets and artists, unfailing in his support of the challenging and the anarchic. Critic Richard Kostelantez comments that 'since the early 1970s Finch has been the principal innovator in

Welsh poetry. Finch deserves a Welsh knighthood.' Finch notes humorously in the opening to his *Selected Poems* (1987) that 'I am taking advantage of my modernist upbringing; finding that what I have been doing for the past thirty years is fashionable again; watching others hijack old ideas and retread them as if they were new and as if they were their own.'

In Wales we are perhaps a little shy of propounding ideas of *a poetics* – the making of the poem, the proposed intention and ambition for the literary work. Maybe the idea of aesthetic manifesto making seems dilettantish and self-congratulatory to the Welsh psyche. What is most liberatory about this *Collected* is how Finch introduces and explores ideas in his writing. Poetics, or the ideas about the making of poetry, *becomes* praxis. There is no need for an essay explaining what is being done – theory is absorbed into the making of the poem. Take for example the humorous instructions and aphorisms in 'The Necessity of Wonders' which include such pearls for the poetry performer 'Advice for perpetrators': 'before beginning smile/ Before smiling locate the door'. Or turn to his 'FIVE HUNDRED COBBINGS' for an alternative history of poetry and textual experimentation: 'Cobbing folds his splices cuts copies /He has time in a toner bottle / he invented the cut-up. He has told the American. He has stains. He has discovered a new universe'. What guides all these poems across the thirty years is the 'presentness' of writing. Finch's poetry, to paraphrase both Louis Zukofsky and William Carlos Williams, is always a living object, a made thing – a pulsating machine made of words.

It is important to note the range of poetry the volume encompasses. The *Collected* engages with a range of movements and tendencies, adapting the premises of the experimental to a Welsh landscape. As a systematic researcher of the overlooked spaces of Cardiff (one might say he is a psychogeographer) Finch in his poetry alerts us to cultural elements of life in Wales that we take for granted or is overlooked. He is an experimenter, an adventurer in a linguistic wordscape often moving between Welsh and English or framing the dynamics of bilingualism in the space of a lyric. The poems move from concrete visual puns to paper and print works exploring erasure and replication, to rule-governed writing, found poetry and personal lyric poems. Finch does not want to be pinned down as a card-carrying member of a group of tendency. In conversation he explains 'I adapted what I learned and tried it out in a Welsh context and then extended and manipulated the foundational ideas as far as they would go. This process is one that I've habitually engaged in. Push the idea on until it breaks, flowers, or dissolves.'

One senses that this sense of inbetweenness offers Finch a position of flexibility, feeding his curiosity and ensuring that future dynamic projects flourish. Diolch Mr Finch.

INTRODUCTION – ANDREW TAYLOR

Peter Finch is one of Britain's leading poets. His experimental and linguistically innovative work has been published widely since the 1960s. It traverses what has been called the avant garde, or the British Poetry Revival, and is characterised by concrete and sound poetry in addition to more conventional forms.[1]

His involvement in the sphere of poetry is unsurpassed. Yet rather like the late poet Tom Raworth, Finch has avoided the often well publicised factions within the poetry world.[2]

Finch describes himself in his online archive, as a 'full-time poet, psychogeographer, critic, author, rock fan and literary entrepreneur.'[3] These are all attributes that seep into his verse.

The introduction to his work in *The Edge of Necessary – An Anthology of Welsh Innovative Poetry 1966-2018,* describes Finch as a 'tireless propagandist for innovative literature' and perhaps tellingly as being 'never afraid of accessibility.'[4] Writing in the formal introduction of the book, editors John Goodby and Lyndon Davies acknowledge the role that Finch has played in Welsh poetry, noting his 'sheer excellence' as a poet and [that his] high profile made him a force to be reckoned with.[5]

Finch was born in Cardiff in 1947 and has lived in Wales all his life. He made a living out of the business of writing as editor, publisher, bookseller, entrepreneur, literary promoter and agent since the mid-1960s.

During the 1960s until the early 1970s, a fertile time for poetry, Finch edited the highly influential little magazine *Second Aeon*, which led to associations with poets including Bob Cobbing, the sound poet. Cobbing became a close personal friend and mentor who Finch worked with alongside poets such as Peter Redgrove, William Wantling and Doug Blazek who he published and with whom he corresponded for many years. Martin Booth writing in 1985, called *Second Aeon* 'the most important magazine of the period' (1964-1984).[6]

In 1965, prior to publishing the inaugural issue of *Second Aeon,*

1. Bob Cobbing called this verbivocovisual.
2. See Peter Barry's superb book, *Poetry Wars* (Cambridge: Salt Publishing, 2006) for more information regarding this factionalism during the so-called 'takeover' of the National Poetry Society and its journal *Poetry Review,* during the 1970s when the 'radical' poets took over the institution.
3. See the 'About Peter Finch' section at www.peterfinch.co.uk [accessed 14th July 2020]
4. *The Edge of Necessary: An Anthology of Welsh Innovative Poetry 1966-2018* eds. John Goodby and Lyndon Davies, (Crickhowell: Aquifer Books/ Boiled String Press: 2018), p.134.
5. Ibid., p.21.
6. Martin Booth, *British Poetry 1964-1984: Driving through the Barricades*, (London: Routledge & Kegan Paul, 1985), p.74.

Finch's first poems were published in the small magazines *Poets Platform* and *Viewpoints.* Interestingly, and fortuitously, from 1965 into 1966, he studied public administration and finance at Glamorgan College of Technology. This would come in useful for his future administrative roles as treasurer of the Association of Little Presses (1970 -1999), Council member of the Poetry Society (1971-1973) manager of the Oriel Bookshop in Cardiff (1973-1998) and CEO at Academi/ Literature Wales which he ran from 1998 to 2011.

Finch's debut poetry publication, *Wanted For Writing Poetry,* written with Steve Morris, was created at Morris' instigation. With Morris' enthusiasm and publishing expertise, it was published by the press formed directly from *Second Aeon,* Second Aeon Publications. *Second Aeon* had been a success locally and was becoming so internationally, and so it was logical to publish books too. The poem selected from the book for this volume, 'Hip to the City' is of its time, making use of the language of the day.[7] Another signifier of the period in the poem, is the use of extended compound words such as 'drinkingcoffeetalkingsmokingcigarettes', a favoured device of the Liverpool poets anthologized in *The Mersey Sound* (Penguin Modern Poets 10).[8] References to publications such as *Peace News* and *International Times,* are also indicators. Perhaps the strongest stanza is the last where humour mixes successfully with:

reading a new hipness
in the *International Times*,
wearing provo apple badges
and writing LOVE
on the side of the bog
in the Moulders Arms.[9]

1969 was a busy year for Finch. He was elected as a member of the English section of Yr Academi Gymreig / The Welsh Academy, as a young writer to watch, somebody who might bring the organisation into the future, and his international reputation was beginning to blossom. Towards the end of the year Finch published *Pieces of the*

7. See 'Hip to the City' p.33

8. Adrian Henri, Roger McGough and Brian Patten, *The Mersey Sound* (Harmondsworth: Penguin Books, 1967). Adrian Henri, in particular had been quite an influence on Finch in both his writing and reading style. For more on Henri see the author's *Adrian Henri: A Critical Reading* (London: Greenwich Exchange, 2019).

9. See 'Hip to the City' p.33

Universe, collecting his best work from 1966 to 1969 and hinting at his later prodigious output. Using his own press was a means to getting the work out swiftly, and the reputation of the magazine would enhance his reputation and further promote the work. Second Aeon Publications was not merely a vehicle for Finch, however, the press went on to publish over fifty titles by other writers.

The 1970s picked up where the 60s left off. Finch's stature in the poetry community led to his appointment as treasurer to the Association of Little Presses as well as Welsh representative of Poets Conference, an early union for British Revival Poets. Similarly, the reputation of his experimental work was growing. His visual poetry toured the UK in a Northern Arts Association exhibition and Will Parfitt's Vertigo Publications published a pamphlet, *beyond the silence.* This was Finch's first experimental and visual publication, including the effective typogram, 'm mo o oo o on n.'[10] Finch notes that the composition of such visual pieces always originates with the 'written form' and that their 'origin is in the language.'[11] Here he pushed the boundaries of language through the repetition of the word moon. The poem can be placed in the era of moon landings with the Apollo 14 in January and February 1971. The visual collaging of the word and its components transpose the movement of the lunar landing craft's approach to the moon's surface. Finch hints at the compositional modes of his visual work:

> Visual poetry uses collage, text-manipulation, overlay, blur, daub, fade, rotate and ether driven creation in equal measure. It can be conceptual, concrete, mimetic, calligraphic, minimal, emotional, magnificent and mad. It is a tradition avoided by most of academia. It does not fit the usual slots. Enjoy it while you can.[12]

The late Dave Cunliffe's BB Books of Blackburn, published a co-authored (with Jeanne W Rushton) pamphlet titled *the edge of tomorrow* while a much larger solo collection, *The End of the Vision* also appeared in 1971.[13] This was Finch's first formal perfect-bound collection, appearing in both paper and cloth editions from entrepreneur John Idris Jones's new imprint JJC Ltd.[14]

10. See p.40
11. See the Peter Finch Archive, maintained by Finch online at www.peterfinch.co.uk www.peterfinch.co.uk/newvis~1.htm accessed 11th February 2021
12. Ibid.
13. Dave Cunliffe died in 2021. See the obituary by Bruce Wilkinson in *The Guardian* dated 14 May 2021. www.theguardian.com/books/2021/may/14/dave-cunliffe-obituary accessed 29th June 2021.

Finch's association with Cobbing and Writers Forum resulted in a pamphlet of concrete poetry, *Antarktika.* Finch describes it as 'the visual score for, and transcription from a sound-text composition made on a stereophonic cassette recorder using that machine's limited controls and devices to their full.'[15] The pamphlet, included in this volume, highlights Finch's willingness to engage with forms outside those considered standard at the time.[16] The next two years saw this focus on concrete poetry expand. Second Aeon co-published with American publisher, Dick Higgins' Something Else Press, a Finch edited volume, *Typewriter Poems.* Exhibitions of Finch's concrete material took place in Italy and the USA, as well as the UK. *Blats,* a self-published collection, is a further example of such work that Finch continues to contemplate and develop.[17]

A useful note by Finch regarding the process in creating *Blats,* appears in the original book:

> blats is a collection of non-poems written over the last two years. many of the items involve chance, the arbitrary finding of both significant data in magazines, newspapers, books, overheard conversations and the like. this form of composition is not so far away from the mainstream of literature as may seem at first. chance is the natural order of things, the best works are never made completely clinically, there is always the incidence of the magnificently unforeseen, the stray juxtaposition of words that draws forth the new, revitalizes the old. of the items in this book that do use chance, some use it as it is, without change, as it is found (notably the plays), but mostly it is used as an aid to composition, a launching point, a stimulus to the memory and the mind. the longer visual pieces lead into the area of concrete poetry, of futures fictions as kostelanetz calls them. perhaps they are epic concrete poems, although i look upon them as my contribution to the confusion that surrounds the hazy

14. Tina Morris, co-editor of the pamphlet with Dave Cunliffe, was one of the few women poets in *Children of Albion: Poetry of the Underground in Britain, ed.* Michael Horovitz, (Middlesex: Penguin Books, 1969). *The End of the Vision* was published by John Jones (Cardiff: John Jones Cardiff Ltd, 1971)
15. Taken from the cover of the pamphlet as published by Bob Cobbing's *Writers Forum* (London: Writers Forum, 1972) This involved spinning the player round his head while making a recording, interfering with the record head, placing microphones at the bottom of boxes, tubes and barrels and immersing the recorder in a bucket of water. The text of *Antarktika* is a representation of the work realised by this process. See p.54 for this text.
16. See p.54
17. Finch makes reference to the titular poem in the notes to this volume of *Collected Poems:* Its most enduring title piece, *Blats* itself, has been reworked on a number of occasions. The latest of these appears in the present *Collected Poems* as *Crow* from *Machineries of Joy,* 2020.

border line between those two cornerstones of literature: poetry and prose. collectively blats contains no new techniques, the ones used have been around for a time, in some cases for centuries. i do hope however that i have made new use of them, have made them perhaps even say something [...][18]

In this useful mode of poetics (note the use of uncapitalised letters), Finch sees *Blats* as 'non-poems' harking further back than contemporary concrete poets such as Dom Sylvester Houédard (dsh), Ian Hamilton Finlay and Robert Lax, all who were found in Emmett Williams's *An Anthology of Concrete Poetry,* (Something Else Press, 1967).

Perhaps here, Finch is acknowledging the forerunners of the concrete poets, practitioners such as the seventeenth century poet George Herbert, Laurence Sterne, author of the ground-breaking *The Life and Opinions of Tristram Shandy, Gentleman,* and later poets such as Stéphane Mallarmé and Christian Morgenstern.

In pursuing his mode of working from the 1960s, Finch continued his prodigious work rate into the late 1970s and early 1980s. He visited Yugoslavia in October 1978 on an official Welsh writers' tour. With Meic Stephens, he co-edited and launched *Green Horse,* an anthology of Welsh poets writing in English, published by Christopher Davies.[19]

1980 brought a new Finch title, *Connecting Tubes,* from Writers Forum. In a break from the visual work previously published by the press, Finch returned to textual material. Included, was what might ostensibly be a travel poem, 'The Edging of Europe Belgrade 1980' points to a connection with and the connections within that continent.

By the station
I want to tell them
that it's like Paris
but they wouldn't understand.[20]

Highlighting the gulf between the East and West of Europe, Finch points to the then perceived exoticism of Yugoslavia. The bridging between the different parts of Europe at that time was brought to the fore in 1980 when UNESCO hosted its 21st General Conference in

18. Peter Finch, *Blats* (Cardiff: Second Aeon, 1972), p.6
19. Peter Finch and Meic Stephens, eds. *Green Horse* (Swansea: C Davies Ltd., 1978).
20. Peter Finch, 'The Edging of Europe Belgrade 1980' in *Collected Poems Volume One 1968-1997*, ed. Andrew Taylor, (Bridgend: Seren Books, 2022) p.86. See the notes at the end of this volume, for more about the creation of this poem.

Belgrade. [21]

1981 was a busier year for Finch in terms of publication. Of the three publications this year, perhaps *Visual Texts 1970-1980* is the most interesting in terms of form. The late Bill Griffiths, poet, publisher and Old English scholar, published the work on what was then a brand new and innovative medium for poetry – the microfiche.[22] This collection contains a selection of Finch's visual work, which had been long out of print.

Blues and Heartbreakers was published by Galloping Dog Press that year, a brilliantly designed book, that apes, for the sleeve, a 7" vinyl single. The preface reads: 'A performed version of blue using the voices of Peter Finch and Bob Cobbing is available on Peter Finch's *Big Band Dance Music* a cassette produced by Balsam Flex.'[23] Once more, it is important to note the embracing of technology as a means of releasing poetry. Though the medium was, by 1981, eighteen years old, it was a relative rarity for poetry to utilise cassette tape.[24]

The third title of 1981, *O Poems* came from Writers Forum. The pamphlet contained material from the earlier microfiche text *Visual Texts 1970-1980*, after it was felt that this visual material needed a wider audience.[25]

1982 was quieter. A collection of short stories, *Between 35 & 42,* was published by Alun Books. Nowadays, the shift towards publishing fiction is a common practice for poets, back in 1982 it was less so.[26]

Finch's next poetry collection came in December 1984. *On Criticism* was again published by Writers Forum in a smaller format than usual and in a yellow stapled cover. *On Criticism* offers a range of formal visual material combined with textual work reminiscent of *Blues and Heartbreakers.*[27] It was written as a response to what Finch saw as the 'pathetic' criticism on offer towards work of poets from the British

21. www.unesco.org/archives/multimedia/document-3119 Accessed 27/2/21
22. Microfiche was a form of cataloguing material. This information is from the Purchase College Library: State University, New York: '[Microfiche] is a card made of transparent film used to store printed information in miniaturized form. To read the card, one places it under the lens of a microfiche reader machine, which magnifies it.' purchase.libanswers.com/faq/36771 accessed 27/2/21
23. Peter Finch, *Blues and Heartbreakers* (Newcastle Upon Tyne: Galloping Dog Press, 1981).
24. Robert Sheppard issued his magazine *1983*, which ran for 3 issues between 1974 and 1977, on cassette. robertsheppard.weebly.com/publications.html accessed 1/3/21.
25 Email from Peter Finch to the author, 1/3/21. Finch noted that 'Most of the O Poems appeared in the Pyrofiche which came out earlier. As the Pyrofiche had a limited audience Bob felt a paper publication was in order.'
26. Peter Finch, *Between 35 & 42* (Port Talbot: Alun Books, 1981)

Poetry Revival and the poor criticism of Welsh poetry in English, at this time.[28] We see the immediacy of intent with the opening pieces being photocopies of scrunched-up paper with the text barely legible. Similarly, the form and layout of the textual aspects of the work reiterate the messages of the opening pieces. With negative words such as 'dross', 'cheapness', 'cease' and 'MISTAKE' there is an overarching sense of hostility towards the unknowledgeable critics.[29]

In 1985 Finch edited a found poems issue of *Cabaret 246, CAB ART,* the magazine of the performance poetry group of which he was a member. Finch's own work of this time had some focus on found and processed material. A useful piece of poetics in the form of a light verse appears on the Peter Finch Archive, to accompany his recollections of the time. It is worth quoting in full:

> Writer's Guidelines
> A pamphlet of poems and a hard-
> backed novel will accelerate at the
> same speed when you chuck them
> down a stairwell.
> Fiction always ends
> Tall writers are older than short ones
> Poems grow spontaneously overnight
> You can learn most of what you
> need from a book simply by
> carrying it about.
> Fixing buggered metre is as easy
> as unplugging the sink
> Say hello often enough and you'll
> soon be famous
> Write by saying you have.
> Make it up
> Why not.[30]

Reds in the Beds, was a pamphlet of found and processed material brought out by Galloping Dog Press.[31] As the selection from it in this volume shows, Finch was not shy in citing his sources.

A *Selected Poems* was published in 1987 at the instigation of Cary

27. Peter Finch, *On Criticism* (London: Writers Forum, 1984). See pages 168-185 in this volume.
28. Telephone conversation with Peter Finch, 18th June 2021.
29. Peter Finch, *On Criticism* (London: Writers Forum, 1984). See pages 168-185 in this volume.
30. Peter Finch Archive. See www.peterfinch.co.uk/cityrd.htm accessed 10/3/21
31. Peter Finch, *Reds in the Beds* (Newcastle: Galloping Dog Press, 1985). See pages 185-195 in this volume.

Archard, editor and founder of Poetry Wales Press, (later Seren). This was the first real opportunity for those interested in Finch's work from the previous two decades, to encounter it in one book. Finch suggests that the publication of this *Selected Poems* represented a formal acknowledgment of the kind of work he was engaged in and raised awareness of his name in the wider poetry world.[32]

The book is helpfully divided into four sections: early poems; visual and sound works; early found and processed poems and later poems and performance pieces. Eric Mottram writing on the rear cover of the book noted:

> Risk and range in form and articulated life: that is the excellence of Peter Finch's poetry since the 1960s, outstanding in the dull conventions of British poetry of these decades. [...] He has become a leading poet and linguistic innovator and taken his place in the international field of soundtext poetry.[33]

Writing in the introduction, Finch notes in some detail, the processes of his practice/s to date. It's an interesting aspect of the *Selected* and useful to the reader in terms of Finch's poetics. The beginning of the introduction is worth quoting:

> Despite my love of the experimental, the early poems in this selection follow mostly traditional forms. The idea to deviate from the accepted did not occur to me until I had been writing for a number of years. It was suggested to me by what I observed in the visual arts. Change there was fast and constant. It still is. In literature everything always seems the same.[34]

It could be said that little has changed in the three decades since Finch wrote those words. The visual arts have continued to progress and in poetry terms, there has been a certain reliance on the palatable both in the prize culture, the 'good' magazines and the so-called prestigious editorial positions.

At the end of the 1980s, the Oriel Bookshop which Finch had been managing moved to new and much more financially demanding premises. With the need to significantly increase turnover, the nature of Finch's day job changed.[35]

32. Telephone conversation with Peter Finch, 18th June 2021.

33. Eric Mottram, rear cover of Peter Finch, *Selected Poems* (Bridgend: Poetry Wales Press, 1987)

34. Peter Finch, *Selected Poems* (Bridgend: Poetry Wales Press, 1987), p.7.

Make had appeared from Peter Hodgkiss' Galloping Dog Press in 1985. The demonstration of Finch's evolving compositional methods outlined on the rear cover is illuminating,

> [*Make*] is the latest manifestation of Finch's preoccupation with the compositional process. Poets, he believes, are no different from any other kind of builder. The work is a matter of materials, motivation and practice. A number of the pieces in *Make* are responses to sound stimuli, using language as raw material in an attempt to avoid the more regular approach of having words stand for something else. Others head for the centre by more traditional routes.[36]

Here once more are the Finchian poetics. In many ways, these qualifying statements highlight not only Finch's thoughts about composition but how he feels regarding the so-called mainstream poetry world's engagement with poetry. Looking back to William Carlos Williams' often (mis)quoted statement regarding poetry, we can detect here, an influence on Finch:

> To make two bold statements: There's nothing sentimental about a machine, and: A poem is a small (or large) machine made out of words. When I say there's nothing sentimental about a poem, I mean that there can be no part that is redundant. Prose may carry a load of ill-defined matter like a ship. But poetry is a machine which drives it, pruned to a perfect economy. As in all machines, its movement is intrinsic, undulant, a physical more than a literary character.[37]

The selection from *Make* in this volume show a sense of Finch's previous playfulness with language. The repetition of 'can' in the title poem

35. Finch writes about his role as manager at the Finch Archive, saying that, 'in the late eighties with the walls of 53 Charles Street taking in water like blotting paper, subsidence twisting the stairwell and the roof covered in tar the lease ran out. No renewal possible. The landlords were into demolition. We had to go. It looked like the end. Yet at the last-minute chance led Peter Finch to the former Barclays Bank site on the corner of Cardiff's Friary and Greyfriars Road. Empty for two years and in a perfect secondary site position, just back from Queen Street again and level. Just what was needed – a single ground floor large enough to accommodate both shop and gallery. Could the Arts Council cope with the new rent and enormous corporate service charges? Finch stood up in committee and guaranteed that he could double turnover; an unheard of presumption. The Arts Council added a craft shop as a kind of insurance and away we went. Pots, maps, and the brilliant books of Wales. In the event turnover tripled.' < peterfinch.co.uk/oriel.htm 10/3/20

36. Peter Finch, *Make* (Newcastle: Galloping Dog Press, 1990)

37. William Carlos Williams, introduction to 'The Wedge' in *Selected Essays of William Carlos Williams* (New York: New Directions, 1969), p.256

points to the notion of creating: 'Can do this with any condition head / Can crack it with most / Can get a little if / Can splice ends fast when [...]'[38]

Finch's second book of 1990 was published by Writers Forum. *The Cheng Man Ch'ing Variations* appeared in the usual A4 format and contained a combination of textual and visual work. It attempts to meld Finch's two obsessive practices of the time – non-linear poetry and the slow and silent martial art of Tai Chi.

His *Poems for Ghosts* (Seren, 1991), with a Frank Auerbach painting 'Seated Figure with Arms Raised' from 1974, on the cover, takes up where the *Selected Poems* left off. A compendium of modernist plunder, this is 'no collection for lovers of the traditionally tame.'[39]

It is worth adding that Seren, under Cary Archard, Amy Wack and Mick Felton, fully embraced the modes in which Finch worked, the 'sound poems, found poems, straight heritage, [and] passionate pleas for language.'[40] It is arguable that Finch had found his natural home. This is not to decry the small presses that had, to this point, published the work. Finch remains a supporter of the small press alongside other ways of doing things.

There is a quiet domesticity at play in *Poems for Ghosts.* This rather calming effect, alongside the use of the first-person pronoun and that its use becoming more prominent, adds to an almost reflective tone. 'Out at the Edge' sees this in action.[41] Here, Finch is teasing at what was to follow with the successful publication of his *Real Cardiff* series. It traces, as its epigraph tells us, a walk along the Pembrokeshire Coast Path. It is a fine example of a narrative-based Finch poem, with its concrete (rather than abstract) imagery and lines such as 'When I climb the track / towards Druidstone I leave bootmarks / like fossils in the fluid mud.'[42] 'Mountains: Sheep' follows a similar trajectory with a nod to Finch's avant-garde interests: 'You can talk to them and / they'll answer. I once held / a flock with Schwitters's / *Ursonata*. Recognising / quality they stayed.'[43] This brings to mind, one of Finch's funniest stanzas from 'A Welsh Wordscape' originally published in 1969 in *Pieces of the Universe:*

To live in Wales
is to love sheep

38. Peter Finch, 'Make' in *Collected Poems Volume One 1968-1997*, ed. Andrew Taylor, (Bridgend: Seren, 2022) p. 228.
39. Peter Finch, *Poems for Ghosts* (Bridgend: Seren, 1991)
40. Ibid.
41. 'Out at the Edge in *Poems for Ghosts.* See p.309
42. Ibid.
43. 'Mountains: Sheep in *Poems for Ghosts.* See p.310

and to be afraid
of dragons.[44]

1994 saw a return to visual work and publishing with Writers Forum once more. *Five Hundred Cobbings,* contained both textual and visual experimentation. As the title suggests, the work is focussed on Cobbing. In turn funny, reflective and engaging, Finch managed to capture the essence of Cobbing and his art, which he enhanced with his own poetics. Note the repeated phrases and the musicality (and references) in the 'Cobbing's Band' section:

cob (tpt)
cobn (flhn)
cob (bell)
obob (p solo)
ing (toth)[45]

Finch has said that *500 Cobbings* was an attempt to write about the poet in 500 ways, to highlight his influence and Finch's respect for him.[46]

Finch worked with Writers Forum again in 1995, publishing *the spp ell.*[47] The text, as its notes imply, is the result of a collaboration with the artist Maggs Harries. Finch's contribution involves textual experimentalism and the use of photocopied image-based work.

The following year Finch launched *The Peter Finch Archive* (www.peterfinch.co.uk) 'the first website from Wales'.[48] It enabled him to make early use of hyper-links as a way of composing verse. There are many examples in the Archive and of particular note is the long and ever-developing 'RS Thomas Information' (now viewable in a physical manifestation over the side of the BT Internet Data Centre in Cardiff

44. 'A Welsh Wordscape' from *Pieces of the Universe* Finch uses this stanza as part of the design on the poetry page of the Peter Finch Archive. See peterfinch.co.uk/poemlist.htm Accessed 25/3/21
45. 'Cobbing's Band' in *Five Hundred Cobbings* p.390
46. Telephone conversation with Peter Finch, 18th June 2021.
47. See the notes to the text on p.xx, which differ from the notes published in the original publication. The instructive nature here is worth noting. The original notes read: A commission from Swansea UK Year of Literature and writing 1995 for poet Peter Finch and artist Maggs Harries to build a demon trap. The Spell is part of Peter Finch's contribution. Demons were sought from more than 400 writers, poets and literateurs across Wales. Each was sent a stamped postcard. Responses were processed to form the present spell. Special mention should be made of the reservations expressed by both James Roose-Evans and Islwyn Ffowc Elis (incorporated into the text) and of Rosemary Ellen Guley's excellent source book. Demons are literate but limited. Change their names and their power dissolves. Bob Cobbing, honorary Welshman published the spell. Read it out loud.
48. Email to the author, 7th August 2020.

Bay).[49]

Further evidence of being at the forefront of things, Finch again embraced the technology that was at his disposal. In an echo of his use of the photocopier in publications such as *On Criticism* he now manipulated information technology in the service of his poetic ends.

Published in early 1998, *Useful* is summed up on its back cover as being 'marked by all the restless energy, humour and angst that is so characteristic of this compulsively entertaining poet [...]'.[50] Containing visual and textual work referencing influences and friends such Eric Mottram, *Useful* in its original form was presented in two parts – 'Practice' and 'Theory'. The visual piece 'Walking' which opens the 'Theory' section is a cut up of Eric Mottram's entire *Selected Poems* photocopied onto a single sheet and then further textually manipulated. Recalling Marcel Duchamp's readymade aided 'Pharmacy' from 1914 Finch then inserts Mottram himself into the new Snowdonia-like textscape as a red dot. Mottram in anorak, walking. To avoid full colour printing costs the example in *Useful* is achieved by the employment of a single sticky red dot, hand applied across hundreds of copies. Performance work, at the forefront now of Finch's output, appears throughout the collection.

* * *

A note on the selection:

This volume contains all the work previously published between 1968 and 1997, that Peter Finch wishes to keep in print. As noted above, many of the poems in this volume were originally published in small runs by small presses and are long out of print, though some on occasion, do appear for sale by specialist sellers online.

Thanks to Peter Finch for his enthusiasm and help in gathering and sharing the rare and out of print publications. Thanks also to the Poetry Library in London, Alan Baker, Dr Sharon Ouditt, Rachel Smith, W.J. and E.M. Taylor, Nichola Taylor, Professor Andrew Thacker, Dr Rory Waterman, Dr Cliff Yates and Professor Tim Youngs.

49. See www.peterfinch.co.uk/depot.htm

50. Back cover of Useful (Bridgend: Seren, 1997)

PETER FINCH – TIMELINE
1968 – 1997

1947 – 6 March. Peter Finch born at 56 Penylan Road, Cardiff. Son of Stanley and Marjorie Finch, a post office worker and a telephonist

1963 – Begins reading and writing poetry following the purchase of the City Lights edition of Allen Ginsberg's *Howl* in the SPCK (Society for the Promotion of Christian Knowledge) bookshop on the Friary, Cardiff

1964 – Hears Howlin Wolf and other performers in the American Negro Blues Festival at Colston Hall, Bristol. Meets Willie Dixon and tries to interest him in his home grown, south Wales blues lyrics. Fails.

1965 – Publishes early poems in the small magazines *Viewpoints* and *Poet's Platform*

1966 – Launches *Second Aeon* from Queensberry Road, Cardiff.

1967 – Participates in his first public reading in the company of Geraint Jarman, David Callard and Wyn Islwyn Davies at the Boucher Hall, Cardiff.

1968 – Under his own Second Aeon imprint publishes *Wanted For Writing Poetry* (with Stephen Morris). Reads at the Reardon Smith with Glyn Jones, John Stuart Williams, Meic Stephens & Geraint Jarman. Goes on to form the poetry performance group Second Aeon Traveling Circus with Huw Morgan, Dave Reid, Chris Morgan, Will Parfitt & Geoff Sherlock. Buys 3 Maplewood Court, Llandaff North, which becomes the beating heart of *Second Aeon* magazine and associated adventures. Meets and works with Bob Cobbing, Peter Mayer and other experimental poets in London. Launches the weekly No Walls Poetry Readings at various pubs around Cardiff including the Marchioness of Bute, Blue Anchor, Moulders Arms, & The Griffin. The series runs until 1971.

1969 – Elected Member of the English section of The Welsh Academy / Yr Academi Gymreig. Appointed Treasurer of Association of Little Presses and shortly after as the Welsh representative of Poets Conference, the newly formed poet's trade union. Edits a Welsh guest issue of

Poet – An International Monthly published by Dr Krishna Srinivas in Madras. Exhibits visual poems and *Second Aeon* magazine artefacts at Uni versity of California. Exhibits concrete poetry at Welsh Arts Council Gallery, Museum Place, Cardiff. Is awarded Welsh Arts Council bursary for experimental poetry. Second Aeon publishes *Pieces of the Universe, Poems 1966-1969.* Reads at the Poetry Society, Earl's Court Square and other venues across London. Reads with Jeff Nuttall at Leicester Arts Festival.

1970 – Experimental poetry included in Northern Arts Assoc. Touring Exhibition. Will Parfitt's Vertigo Publications publishes *beyond the silence.* Phil Jenkins' Quickest Way Out publishes *an alteration in the way I breathe.* Meets Nick Zurbrugg, editor of the concrete poetry journal *Stereo Headphones*, in Paris. Organises 'a sound event – verbivocovisual poetry' with Bob Cobbing, Lily Greenham, Henri Chopin & others at the Reardon Smith, Cardiff. Contributes to WAC's Dial a poem service with 'We Remember Old Music' – 845 calls.

1971 – Organises Poets Conference reading at the Reardon Smith Lecture Theatre with Alan Jackson, John Tripp, Tom Pickard, Adrian Henri, George Macbeth, Dannie Abse, Stuart Montgomery, Jeff Nuttall, Harri Webb, and Adrian Mitchell. Elected to council of Poetry Society in Earl's Court. *The edge of tomorrow* (with Jeanne W Rushton) published by Dave Cunliffe's BB Books, Blackburn. Contributes again to Dial-a-Poem with 'and there are people who stand...' and then 'Nightblats'. In April *The End Of The Vision* published by John Idris Jones (jjc ltd). Organises Horse poetry reading series at the Central Hotel with John Ormond, Harri Webb, Meic Stephens, Glyn Jones, Alison Bielski, John Tripp, Bill Pickard, Herbert Williams and John Idris Jones. Reads at the London and Brighton Book Bang events with John Idris Jones. In July takes part in a tour of the north with Rain in The Face visiting Whitley Bay Arts Festival, Sunderland Jazz Club and Newcastle upon Tyne.

1972 – *Antarktika* published by Writers Forum. *whitesung* published by Jim Green at Aquila Publishing Co, Solihull. *Typewriter Poems* (edited by Finch) published jointly by second aeon & Something Else Press. Reads with Stephen Morris at Birmingham Poetry Centre. Concrete poetry exhibited at Birmingham Municipal Institute. *Performance in A* published by Sceptre Press.

1973 – *Blats* published by Second Aeon. Association of Little Presses publishes the 1st edition of *Getting Your Poetry Published* which will go on to be reprinted at least 15 times. Concrete poetry exhibited in Hors Language exhibition, Nice; Poesia Concreta e Visuale – Galleria Peccolo, Italy; and in Ken Friedman's Omaha Flow Systems exhibition, Joslyn Art Museum, Omaha, Nebraska. With Bob Cobbing performs at Felinfach Arts Centre, Aberaeron summer school and then goes on to tour west and north Wales. Makes extensive use of Cardiff University sound studios. In November is appointed by Welsh Arts Council to run the new Oriel Bookshop, at Charles Street, Cardiff.

1974 – *Numerical Chant In the Old Manner* and *Rock n Roll Poem* published as poem posters. The final issue, 19-21, of *Second Aeon* appears. *Second Aeon* papers and archive sold to State Univ. of New York at Buffalo, now housed by Fales Library, south New York.

1976 – Fights in the Poetry Wars at the Poetry Society. Elected editor of *The Poetry Review*, a post he does not accept. With Sue Harries organises Poetry For May Day at The Sherman Theatre, Cardiff.

1977 – *Trowch Eich Radio 'Ymlaen* published by Writers Forum. Joins Welsh delegation to 29th Frankfurt Bookfair, Germany.

1978 – Joins official Welsh writers visit to Yugoslavia. Compiles *How To Learn Welsh a guidebook for adult learners* for Christopher Davies Ltd. Co-edits *Green Horse* – an anthology by young poets of Wales with Meic Stephens.

1979 – included in Henri Chopin's *Poesie Sonore Internationale*, Jean-Michel Place Editeur.

1980 – Sound poetry work with saxophonist Barry Edgar Pilcher, *Big Band Dance Music,* released by Balsam Flex. *Connecting Tubes* published by Writers Forum.

1981 – *Blues & Heartbreakers* published by Peter Hodgkiss' Galloping Dog Press. Bill Griffiths publishes *Visual Texts 1970-1980* as a microfiche. Joins official Welsh visit to Sardinia. *The O Poems* published by Writers Forum. *Llais Llyfrau*, reporting somewhat late on 1977's *Trowch Eich Radio 'Ymlaen* suggests these poems are a 'gwastraff cyfan gwbl ar bapur' – a total waste of paper.

1982 – Balsam Flex release *Dances Interdites*, a further cassette of sound poetry. *Between 35 & 42* – short stories – published by Alun Books. Joins second official Welsh visit to Sardinia.

1983 – Formation of poetry performance group Cabaret 246. In August the Welsh language satirical magazine, *LOL*, publishes PF sound poems in Welsh (from *Trowch Eich Radio 'Ymlaen*) to lampoon the new Oriel Manager. Actually they celebrate him.

1984 – Official exchange visit to USSR with Russian Writers' Union including reading for Radio Moscow, readings in Leningrad (St Peterburg) and Baku in Azerbaijan. *On Criticism* published by Writers Forum.

1985 – edits special found poems issue of *CAB ART*, the magazine of Cabaret 246. *How To Publish Your Poetry* published by Allison & Busby, to be reprinted many times. *Reds In The Bed* published by Peter Hodgkiss' Galloping Dog. Records sonic poems with Bob Cobbing & John Whiting.

1986 – Cabaret 246 starts a night club series at Gibbs Jazz Club, Churchill Way, Cardiff.

1987 – *Selected Poems* edited by Cary Archard is published by Poetry Wales Press. *How To Publish Yourself* published by Allison & Busby to be reprinted many times. In June takes part in Beat Dreams & Plymouth Sounds. Forms Horse's Mouth with Ifor Thomas, Francesca Kaye and Tôpher Mills.

1988 – *The Italian Job* released by Klinker Soundz. Horse's Mouth performance at the Hay Festival sets off fire alarm at The Blue Boar.

1989 – Cabaret 246 final performance at Chapter, Cardiff. Oriel Bookshop moves from Charles St to The Friary, Cardiff.

1990 – *Make* published by Galloping Dog Press. *The Cheng Man Ch'ing Variations* published by Writers Forum.

1991 – *Poems For Ghosts* published by Seren.

1992 – Poems For Ghosts tour of the north including events at Ilkley Literature Festival.

1993 – Collaborates with artist Paul Peter Piech to create poem linocuts. Exhibits visual poems at Contemporary Printmaking In Wales exhibition, curated by William Brown, at Glynn Vivian Art Gallery, Swansea. Described by Richard Kostelanetz in *The Dictionary of the Avant-Gardes* as "the principal innovator in Welsh poetry".

1994 – *Five Hundred Cobbings* published by Writers Forum, launched at Compendium Bookshop, NW1. In May performs Tejo Remy's bookbox at Oriel, Friary. *The Poetry Business* published by Seren. *Some Music and a Little War* published by Rivelin Grapheme. Works with Ian Ritchie Architects / Acer Wallace Evans on entry for the Cardiff Bay Opera House Competition.

1995 – 'Self-Portrait' commissioned by the Glyn Vivian Gallery, Swansea and exhibited there. *the spp ell*, text for the Demon Trap, published by Writers Forum. The Demon Trap created with Mags Harris for the Year of Literature at Tŷ Llen, Swansea. Oriel Bookshop bought by HMSO. Performs in Cardiff's 1st Poetry Slam organised by Working Title at Chapter.

1996 – Establishes *The Peter Finch Archive*, first website from Wales on the web. Claire Powell completes her dissertation *Adventures in experimental Forms: The Poetry of Peter Finch* for University College Swansea. Claire Powell publishes *The Art of Noise: Peter Finch Sounds Off* in Welsh Writing In English Vol 2. *Math – Science* prepared for Writers Forum but never published. A version under the title *Math* published by Subvoicive. Contributes to ALP's 30th Anniversary Celebration programme. Joins Board of the Rhys Davies Trust.

Early 1997 – HMSO Oriel Bookshop privatised to become The Stationery Office. *Useful* published by Seren. Works with artist and print maker William Brown on haiku and other collaborations.

This Timeline does not contain detail of Finch's many public readings, Arvon and Tŷ Newydd teaching residencies, little magazine appearances, articles about his work by others and contributions to literary anthologies and to Broadcast media.

from Wanted For Writing Poetry - 1968

HIP TO THE CITY

At one time,
Within the complex of the city,
Droves of people
Said they were anarchists;

giving up youth
for the future of man,

fervently buying their copies of
Peace News every week,
cunningly placing them in
observable pocket positions,
while drinkingcoffeetalkingsmokingcigarettes
in the Saturday afternoon cafes;

attending dismal meetings
in strange yellowed pubs,
displaying their collections of badges
and talking of fantastic
protest marches,
events which they never went to;

screaming down
midnight derelict backstreets,
spraying ANARCHY in bold red letters
on office walls,
writing BAN THE BOMB NOW
on the sides of the bog
in the Moulders Arms;

becoming anti-political
at election times,
giving away small posters that read:
ANARCHISTS SAY DON'T VOTE,
not that they were old enough to anyway;

Anarchism becoming
the symbol of hipness
that lived and died
in tattered jeans
and battered combat jackets
on midsummer warm Saturdays.

And now,
saying it's all in the past,
reading a new hipness
in the *International Times*,
wearing provo apple badges
and writing LOVE
on the side of the bog
in the Moulders Arms.

from Pieces of the Universe – 1969

WE ARE IN THE FIELDS

we are in the fields
hidden by distance

the grass straining
under our feet

we talk, she and I
the green intensity
of the landscape
filling our eyes

our words become birds
barely touching the air,
our faces smile
our hands trace pictures
among the clouds,
our blood is love
and there is heat in our veins

the sun turns to moon
and balanced in the sky
swollen stars
stream their gentle light
onto our bodies

time stops
and all
but the constellations
dancing on a distant horizon
returns to stillness

A WELSH WORDSCAPE

1. To live in Wales,

Is to be mumbled at
by re-incarnations of Dylan Thomas
in numerous diverse disguises.

Is to be mown down
by the same words
at least six times a week.

Is to be bored
by Welsh visionaries
with wild hair and grey suits.

Is to be told
of the incredible agony
of an exile
that can be at most
a day's travel away.

And the sheep, the sheep,
the bloody, flea-bitten Welsh sheep,
chased over the same hills
by a thousand poetic phrases
all saying the same things.

To live in Wales
is to love sheep
and to be afraid
of dragons.

2. A history is being re-lived,
a lost heritage
is being wept after
with sad eyes and dry tears.

A heritage
that spoke beauty to the world
through dirty fingernails
and endless alcoholic mists.
A heritage
that screamed that once,
that exploded that one holy time
and connected Wales
with the whirlpool
of the universe.

A heritage
that ceased communication
upon a death, and nonetheless
tried to go on living.

A heritage
that is taking
a long time to learn
that yesterday cannot be today
and that the world
is fast becoming bored
with language forever
in the same tone of voice.

Look at the Welsh landscape,
look closely,
new voices must rise,
for Wales cannot endlessly remain
chasing sheep into the twilight.

FLOWER SERMON

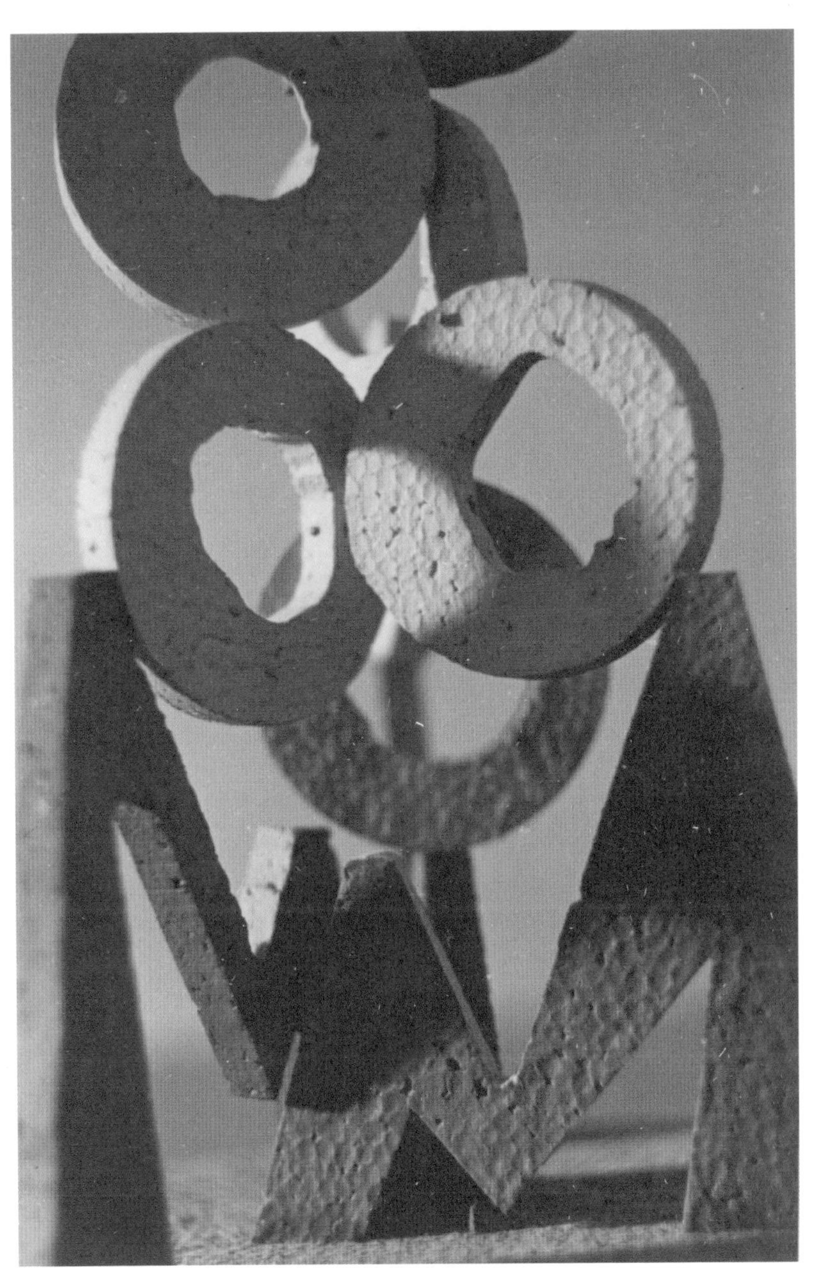

BOOM POEM

from Beyond The Silence – 1970

m mo o oo o on n

m m m m m

m m m m m

m m mo mo mo o o

m m mo mo mo o o

o o o o o o o o o o

o o o o o o o o o o

o o on on on n n

o o on on on n n

n n n n n

n n n n n

THREE POEMS

text year

plan net

eye land

mythologlicical

nomenenclature

statisesastical

analysases

specializising

contentantament

conti nu umumumumumuumumumumumumumumumumumum

he he he he he he he he
he he he he he he he he
he he he he he he he he
he he he he he he he he
he he he he he he he he
he he he he he he he he
he he he he he he he he
he he he he he he he he
he he he he he he he he
he he he he he he he he
he he he he he he he he

s s s s s s s s s s s s
s s s s s s s s s s s s
s s s s s s s s s s s s
s s s s s s s s s s s s
s s s s s s s s s s s s
s s s s s s s s s s s s
s s s s s s s s s s s s
s s s s s s s s s s s s
s s s s s s s s s s s s
s s s s s s s s s s s s
s s s s s s s s s s s s

CONTACT

from AN ALTERATION IN THE WAY I BREATHE – 1970

AN ALTERATION IN THE WAY I BREATHE

we crossed the mountains
with the rising of the sun
the dawn racing ahead of us
like a mad horse

on the other side
the valley
the river
the trees
a whole landscape
bathed
in early sunlight,
still shivering
with the breathing of night

I wondered
why the weights
had gone from my shoulders
why the guns and knives
had rusted in my belt

our eyes were laughing
our mouths were singing

and as we descended
the withered grass
became green and full
crowning its stalks
with a multitude of flowers

SHE, OF RIVERS

she entered the room
like a river
her body flowing
her hair full of weeds

she spoke softly
of the seas, of the
wind through the trees
of the places
that only water knows

her breasts jutted
like islands
in a torrent
of silver foam

he watched
bemused
a dam crumbling
eroding
breaking down
and suddenly
he wanted to drown
wanted the water
inside his lungs
wanted to reach out
and touch the sea

o

hot

orange

round

the sun is

old

yellow

atomic

holl w

SUN POEM

THE MYSTERY OF O

THE ADVENTURES OF S VOL TWO

from The End Of The Vision - 1971

HOW TO BECOME OLD WITH EASE

1) face tomorrow

2) Paint it brown
a tired brown

3) crumple the paper
smooth it out again
but not quite flat

4) try hard to forget
what you have done

from WHITESUNG – 1972

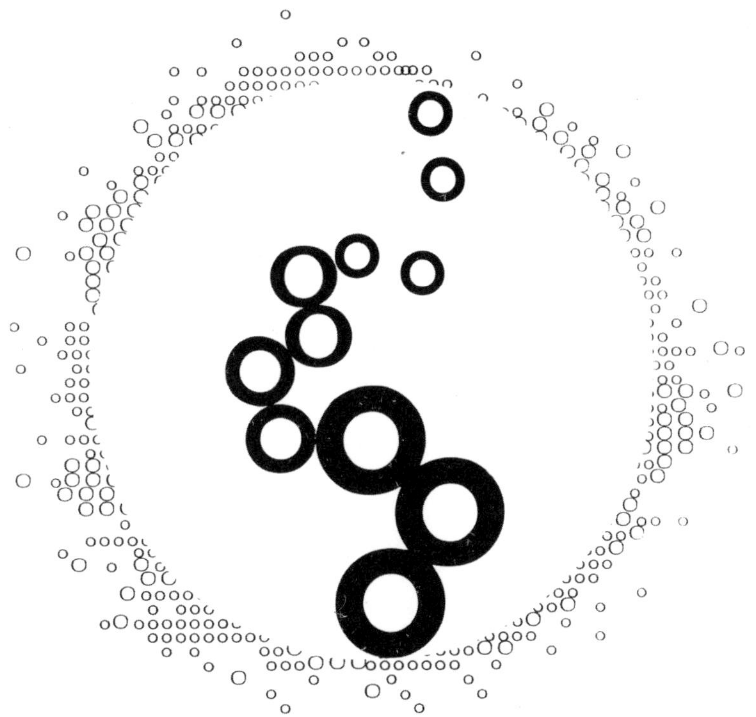

THE SILENT SOUND

(AND THOSE FAVORITE

in
termal
        thermal
rest wing
            craggy angles
raggy angels
the sky a white shower
                of wings
of things that sing
gold at
         check out
the bodies of saints
       odious gates
old paints
             dry and dark

somewhere in this big wide world
a myth
         is being exploited

SLIT KOUP LIST

for edwin morgan

goyal rame/lock-a-ceekie/
lattie-teekie/boachers proth/turkey/

botch sceef/kotch scidney/potch scea/
gicken chumbo/ticken chomato/

botch scroth/cheam of cricken/
bicken chroth/mentil/linestrone/

team of cromato/mean of cruchroom/
potch scot/dild wuck soncomme/
ceasant phonsomme/scream of campi/
phream of ceasant/bobster lisque

SH SHE'LL LIE F

Jewel ha weag old eel
office   inner raga arrow
sir oracle   if sea king anu
meant outsize trytoes
jaw fence onto stay

THE SEA CHOP

the sea chop old ate shh hold bin
per fections shuns nify hey ha avenue
beandam aged inanimate weigh peas
rat tea urn he comes flate pa ack ack aged
yous   withered is lip   skating then
sand here witas bow ght   we
halls bed lad for place sitand
fereffers and he po stage

apples took lonely

roundtree and go light
your king land

KITPANG DA

would posts bags of sea meant
oakray ills dang her lamps con eye
40 gallon drums
stand hard greats lie gnat insects
shun coves are pip eyes
junk shuns ben desl and rains
too less we'd kill her
garesill linda hers
ta red yawm
hitch itch and unhit itch row her
compress her frail her upset her
m i s s h e l l ' s a n u s
feels ill
40 gallons of rum with fools
fill cunt pain her with fuel

ANTARKTIKA – 1972

ANTARKTIKA

"The visual score for, and transcription from a sound-text composition made on a stereophonic cassette recorder using that machine's limited controls and devices to their full" – taken from the cover of booklet as published by Bob Cobbing's Writers Forum in 1972.

The conventional sequence of creating a score and then realising it had been revered. The piece came first, the score after. The cassette player was pushed to its limits – muffled, amplified, shaken, swirled around the head on the end of a length of cord, submerged in a bucket of water, its record head interfered with, heated, dried, its microphone hidden in echoing tin baths and at the bottom of sewer pipes. This transcription is the result.

s

s s

ss

s

s s s

f s

s

f s

s s

ff ssss ss

f ssssss s

sssssssss

f sssssssss

f f sssssssss

f sssssssss

sssssssss

f ff sssssssss

f sssssssss

sssssssss

sssssssss

sssssssss

sssssssss

sssssssss

sssssssss

sssssssss

sssssssss

sssssssss

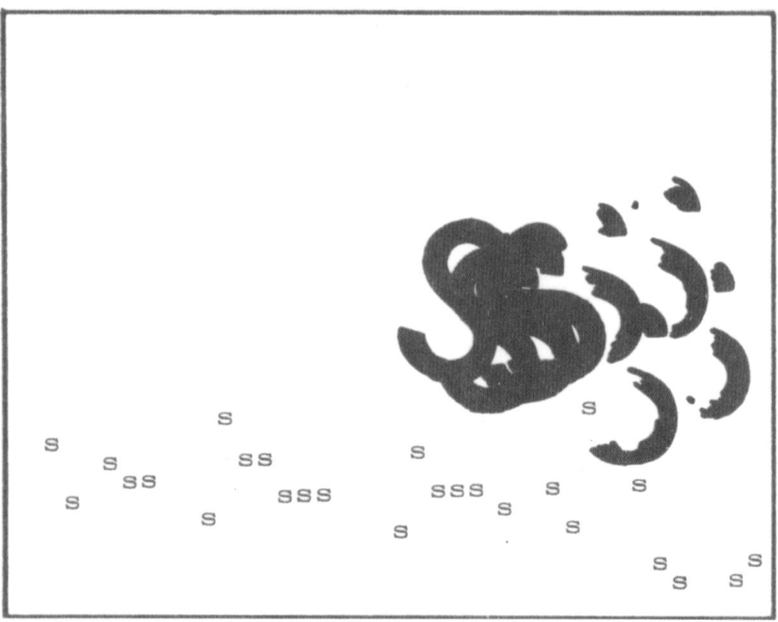

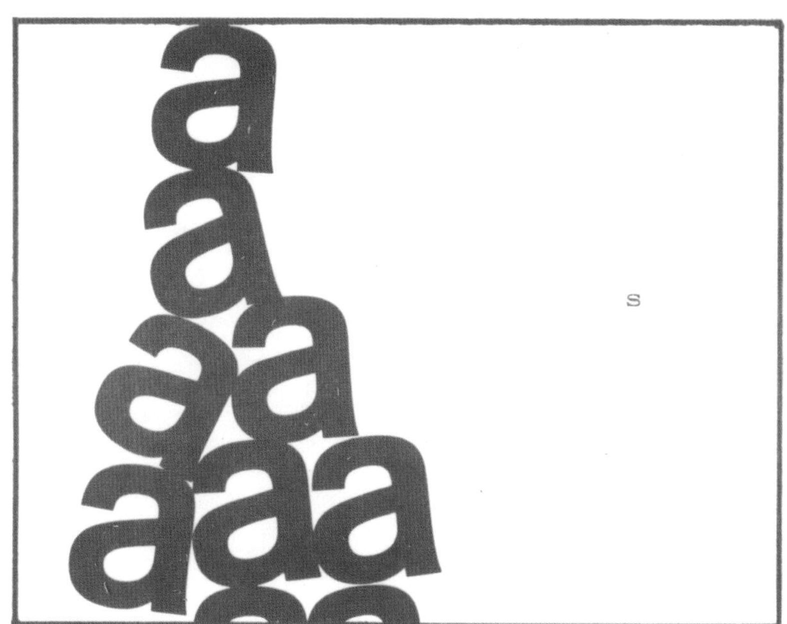

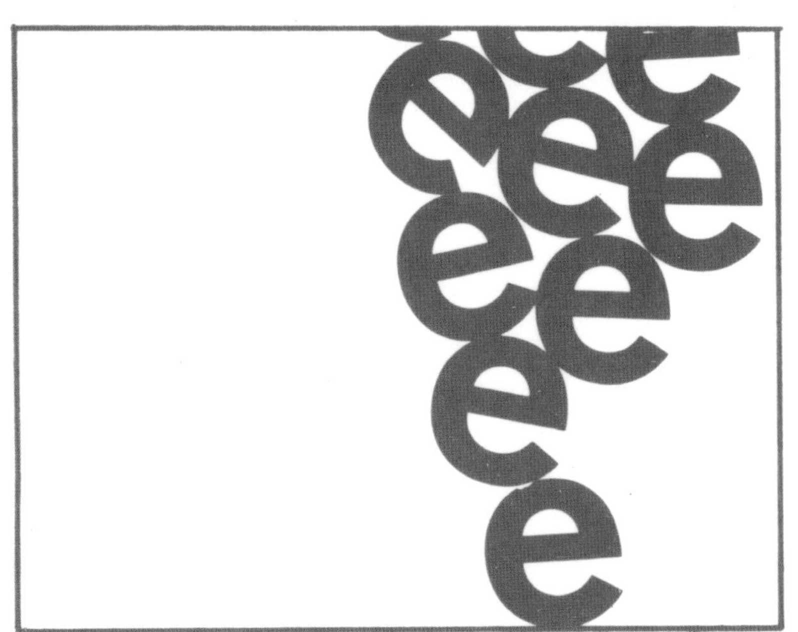

e

e e

yeeeee

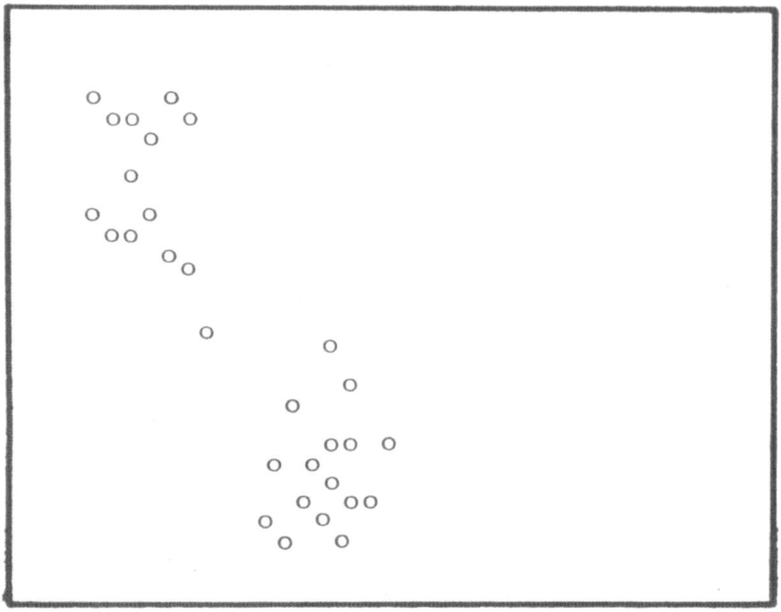

NW

y e l l

yell
 yell
yell   o
                              o
                            ob
               b
         b
yelb
            b
                 b
                       b
yelb
 yelb
yelb

```
yelb
     b l l l l l l l l l l l l l l l l
                                        o
  yeea
yeea
     l l l l l l l l l l l l l l l l l  o
                                         o
                          blo
                             blo
                         blo
                            blo
              oooooooooooo
                           o
                        ooooooooo
                                  o
```

b
b lue
bb

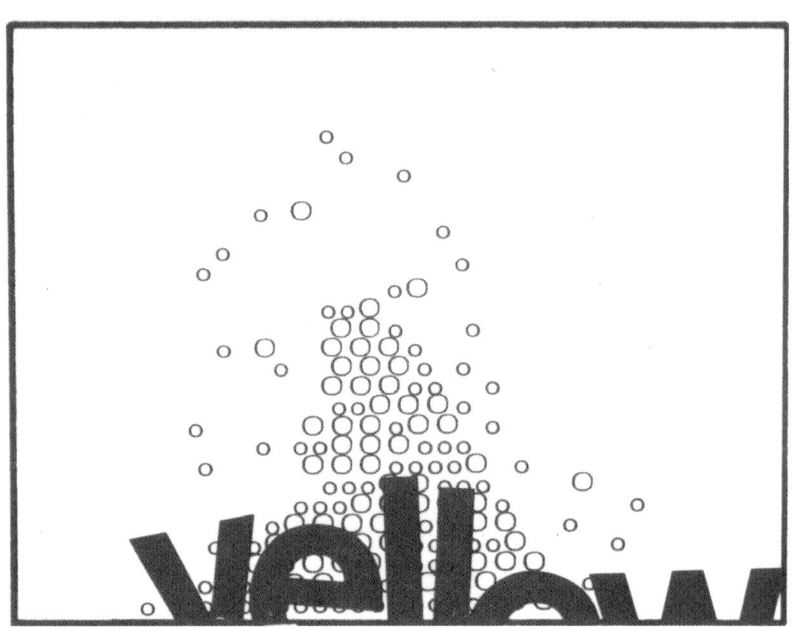

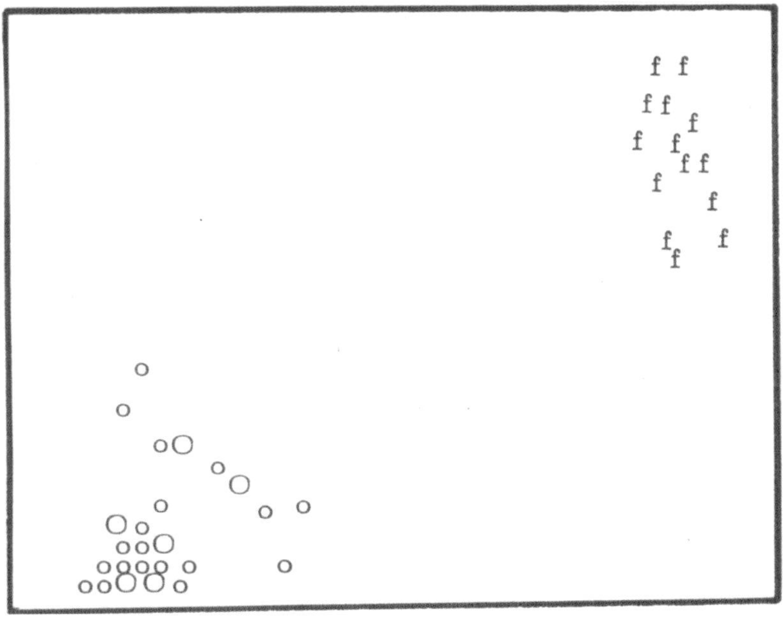

ff
f
f
f f
f f f s s
s s
f f s
f f s s ss s
f sr
f s s
f f s s r r
s
f r rr

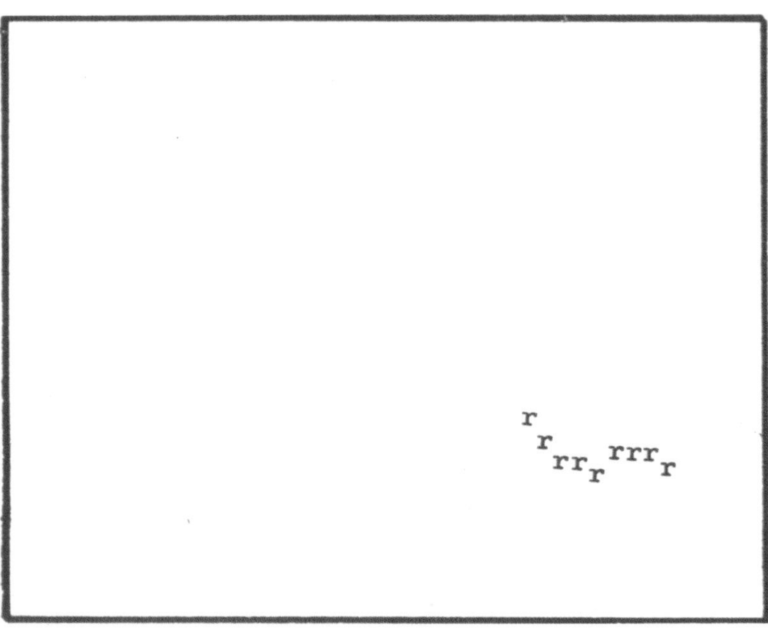
r
r
rr r rrr r

from Blats – 1973

from MOONSPLATS

mmmmmmmmmmmmmm
mmmmmmmmmmmmmm
mmmmmmmmmmmmmm
mmmmmmmmmmmmmm
mmmmmmmmmmmmmm
mmmmmmmmmmmmmm
mmmmmmmmmmmmmm
mmmmmmmmmmmmmm
mmmmmmmmmmmmmm
mmmmmmmmmmmmmm
mmmmmmmmmmmmmm
mmmmmmmmmmmmmm
mmmmmmmmmmmmmm
mmmmmmmmmmmmmm
mmmmmmmmmmmmmm
mmmmmmmmmmmmmm
mmmmmmmmmmmmmm
mmmmmmmmmmmmmm
mmmmmmmmmmmmmm
nnnnnnnnnnnnnnnnnnnnn
nnnnnnnnnnnnnnnnnnnnn
nnnnnnnnnnnnnnnnnnnnn
nnnnnnnnnnnnnnnnnnnnn
nnnnnnnnnnnnnnnnnnnnn
nnnnnnnnnnnnnnnnnnnnn
nnnnnnnnnnnnnnnnnnnnn
nnnnnnnnnnnnnnnnnnnnn
nnnnnnnnnnnnnnnnnnnnn
nnnnnnnnnnnnnnnnnnnnn
nnnnnnnnnnnnnnnnnnnnn
nnnnnnnnnnnnnnnnnnnnn
nnnnnnnnnnnnnnnnnnnnn
nnnnnnnnnnnnnnnnnnnnn
nnnnnnnnnnnnnnnnnnnnn
nnnnnnnnnnnnnnnnnnnnn
nnnnnnnnnnnnnnnnnnnnn
nnnnnnnnnnnnnnnnnnnnn
nnnnnnnnnnnnnnnnnnnnn
nnnnnnnnnnnnnnnnnnnnn
nnnnnnnnnnnnnnnnnnnnn
nnnnnnnnnnnnnnnnnnnnn
nnnnnnnnnnnnnnnnnnnnn

....
nnnnnnnnnnnnnnnnnnnnn
nnnnnnnnnnnnnnnnnnnnn
nnnnnnnnnnnnnnnnnnnnn
nnnnnnnnnnnnnnnnnnnnn
nnnnnnnnnnnnnnnnnnnnn
nnnnnnnnnnnnnnnnnnnnn
nnnnnnnnnnnnnnnnnnnnn
nnnnnnnnnnnnnnnnnnnnn
nnnnnnnnnnnnnnnnnnnnn
nnnnnnnnnnnnnnnnnnnnn
nnnnnnnnnnnnnnnnnnnnn
nnnnnnnnnnnnnnnnnnnnn
nnnnnnnnnnnnnnnnnnnnn
nnnnnnnnnnnnnnnnnnnnn
nnnnnnnnnnnnnnnnnnnnn
nnnnnnnnnnnnnnnnnnnnn
nnnnnnnnnnnnnnnnnnnnn
nnnnnnnnnnnnnnnnnnnnn
nnnnnnnnnnnnnnnnnnnnn
nnnnnnnnnnnnnnnnnnnnn
nnnnnnnnnnnnnnnnnnnnn
nnnnnnnnnnnnnnnnnnnnn
nnnnnnnnnnnnnnnnnnnnn
             nn
nnnnnnnnnnnnn nnnnnn
           nn
nnnnnnnnnnn nnnnnnnn
            n
nnnnnnnnnnnn nnnnnnnn
             n
nnnnnnnnnnnnn nnnnnnn
      nn
nnnnnn nnnnnnnnnnnnn
nnnnnnnnnnnnnnnnnnnnn
nnnnnnnnnnnnnnnnnnnnn
nnnnnnnnnnnnnnnnnnnnn
nnnnnnnnnnnnnnnnnnnnn
             oo
nnnnnnnnnnnnnnnnnnnnn
           oo
nnnnnnnnnnnnnnnnnnnnn
            o
nnnnnnnnnnnnnnnnnnnnn
             o
nnnnnnnnnnnnnnnnnnnnn
      oo
nnnnnnnnnnnnnnnnnnnnn
nnnnnnnnnnnnnnnnnnnnn
nnnnnnnnnnnnnnnnnnnnn
nnnnnnnnnnnnnnnnnnnnn
nnnnnnnnnnnnnnnnnnnnn
nnnnnnnnnnnnnnnnnnnnn

nnnnnnnnnnnnnnnnnnnnnnn
m
nnnnnnnnnnnnnnnnnnnnnnn
m
nnnnnnnnnnnnnnnnnnnnnnn
m
nnnnnnnnnnnnnnnnnnnnnnn
mm
nnnnnnnnnnnnnnnnnnnnnnn
mm
nnnnnnnnnnnnnnnnnnnnnnn
mm
nnnnnnnnnnnnnnnnnnnnnnn
mm
nnnnnnnnnnnnnnnnnnnnnnn
mm
nnnnnnnnnnnnnnnnnnnnnnn
mm
nnnnnnnnnnnnnnnnnnnnnnn
mm
nnnnnnnnnnnnnnnnnnnnnnn
mmm
nnnnnnnnnnnnnnnnnnnnnnn
mmm
nnnnnnnnnnnnnnnnnnnnnnn
mmm
nnnnnnnnnnnnnnnnnnnnnnn
mmm
nnnnnnnnnnnnnnnnnnnnnnn
mmm
nnnnnnnnnnnnnnnnnnnnnnn
mmm
nnnnnnnnnnnnnnnnnnnnnnn
mmm
nnnnnnnnnnnnnnnnnnnnnnn
mmm
nnnnnnnnnnnnnnnnnnnnnnn
mmm
nnnnnnnnnnnnnnnnnnnnnnn
mm
nnnnnnnnnnnnnnnnnnnnnnn
mm
nnnnnnnnnnnnnnnnnnnnnnn
mm
nnnnnnnnnnnnnnnnnnnnnnn
mm
nnnnnnnnnnnnnnnnnnnnnnn
mm
nnnnnnnnnnnnnnnnnnnnnnn
mm
nnnnnnnnnnnnnnnnnnnnnnn
mm
nnnnnnnnnnnnnnnnnnnnnnn
mm
nnnnnnnnnnnnnnnnnnnnnnn
mm
nnnnnnnnnnnnnnnnnnnnnnn
mm
nnnnnnnnnnnnnnnnnnnnnnn
m
nnnnnnnnnnnnnnnnnnnnnnn
m
nnnnnnnnnnnnnnnnnnnnnnn
m
nnnnnnnnnnnnnnnnnnnnnnn
m
nnnnnnnnnnnnnnnnnnnnnnn
m
nnnnnnnnnnnnnnnnnnnnnnn
m
nnnnnnnnnnnnnnnnnnnnnnn
m
nnnnnnnnnnnnnnnnnnnnnnn
m
nnnnnnnnnnnnnnnnnnnnnnn
m
nnnnnnnnnnnnnnnnnnnnnnn
m
nnnnnnnnnnnnnnnnnnnnnnn
m
nnnnnnnnnnnnnnnnnnnnnnn
m
nnnnnnnnnnnnnnnnnnnnnnn
m
nnnnnnnnnnnnnnnnnnnnnnn

from Seventh Degree

[illegible] pr[illegible]ful default [illegible] full amount
[illegible] the High Court that [illegible]
of the profits of his wife's business. The husband appealed
[illegible] was [illegible] that he had bee[illegible] of
evidence that [illegible] the husband [illegible] knowledge [illegible] acts
wilful default. The assessments were discharged. V[illegible]erforce

cor cor cor cor cor
cor cor cor cor cor
cor cor cor cor cor
cor cor cor cor cor
cor cor cor cor cor
cor cor cor cor cor
cor cor cor cor cor
cor cor cor cor cor
cor cor cor cor cor
cor co p lo cor cor cor
cor co as cor cor cor
cor cor of cor cor cor
cor cor whic po cor cor
cor cor diff to dabl cor cor
cor cor divid ees cor cor
cor cor appli ban cor cor
cor cor ve it irlie cor cor
cor cor rk, s, bry or cor
cor co'o scra d, what in r cor
cor s le ilarl lition be v cor
cor es é v comp to gi cor
cor th a e al lberts r cor
cor g m, side to da r cor
cor vn ch of and t r cor
cor fc ar a teparticu r cor
cor in e, e pif then r cor
cor iar it gh ut on c r cor
cor r ur with the c cor
cor co ss. rge or cor
cor c re acber an r c cor
cor curf hers, if par cor
ctly c en it ke nove py ctly
cor r eir or wn is w rec
ctly c ctly
rec r cor e and n rec
ctly ctly
ctly ectly. a lanc ctly
es it is quite ir to be, he ctly
c what is good certy to move
c impossible, ev ictur The princ
c estion. Thes will be judged by

str spea a chrom semti ne
469 eaking, a c aking ctly
pea aki a king rom a
rict mat a mat rom rom a rom
469 icti ic ctl chr c c rom c
eak eak b b ro rom ak r
rom a ro ingachr one one
b rom one stric ach
one om om om a ch rom
4 69b eak ictl mit se sem a
sem ro mat ict 69b a mit
b str rom mit one rom
ric eaki ng hr romat icse
a chro eakin gac ac a 69b : st
tr i l yspea p ea semi t 69
r om one rom it y ng ngngn g
9 46 chr spe n ggg gg ng r om
rom rom king g n king semit
46 9n r mat ngkin g aki nggg
strrr pea rom om 46: b om a
rom on one kingrom gach y g
king 6 44 9 b bb b
king r y ing emitone one pe a
pe king r om s ng ngo rom pea b
4 9 4 ing eak mit ro m m
in mm g kinm m ome romg ki
6m m ki imgm m itm mm mm 46
m mm mmm mm m mm mm mm
mm mmm mmm mmm mmm mmm
m m mm mmmmm mmmmmm m mm mm
mmm m mmm m mm mm mm
m mm mmm m m mm mmmmmm mmmmm
m mm mm mmm m mmm mmm mmmmmm mm
mm mmmmmm mmmm mmmm m m mmmmm mm
m mmmmmmmmmm mmmmmmmm mmmmm mm
mm mmmmmmm mmmmmmmmmmm mmmmmmm m
mmmmmmmm mmmmmmmm mmmmmmmmmmm
mmmmmmmmmmmm mmmmmmmmmm mmmmm
mmmmm mmmmmmmmmmmmmmmmm mmmmmm
m mmmmmmmmmmm mmmmmmmmmmmmmmmm
m m mmmmmmmmmmmmmmmmmmmmmmmmm
mmmmmmm mmmmmmmmmmm mmmmmmmmmm
mmmmmmmmmmmmmmmmmmmmm mmmm mm
mmmmmm m mmmmmmmmmmmmmmmmmmmmm
mmmmmmmmmmm mmmm mmmmmmmmmmmmmmm
mmm mmmmmmmmmmmmmmmmmmmmmmmm
mmmmmmmm mmmmmmmmmmmmmmmmmmm
mmmmmm mmm mmmmmmmmmmmmmmmmmmm
mmmmmmm mmmmmmmmmmmmmmmm mmmmm
mmmmmmmmmmmmmmm mm mmmmmmmmmmm
mmmmmmmmmm mmmmmmm mmmmmmmmmmmm
mmm mmmmmmm mmmmmmmmmmmmmmmmm
mmmmmmmmmmmmmmmmmmm mmmmmmmmm
mmmmmmmmmmmmmmmmmmmmmm mmmmmm
mmmmmm mmmmmmmmmmmmmmmmmmmm mm
mmmmmmmmmmmm mmmmmmmmmmmmmmmmm
mmmmmmmmmmmmmmmm mmmmmmmmmmm
mmmmmmm mmmmmmmm mmmmmmmmmmmm

469b: strictly speaking, a chromantic semitone

aaaaaaaaaaaaaaaaaaa
aaaaaaaaaaaaaaaaaaa
aaaaaaaaaaaaaaaaaaa
aaaaaaaaaaaaaaaaaaa
aaaaaaaaaaaaaaaaaaa
aaaaaaaaaaaaaaaaaaa
aaaaaaaaaaaaaaaaaaa
aaaaaaaaaaaaaaaaaaa
aaaaaaaaaaaaaaaaaaa
aaaaaaaaaaaaaaaaaaa
aaaaaaaaaaaaaaaaaaa
aaaaaaaaaaaaaaaaaaa
aaaaaaaaaaaaaaaaaaa
aaaaaaaaaaaaaaaaaaa
aaaaaaaaaaaaaaaaaaa
aaaaaaaaaaaaaaaaaaa
aaaaaaaaaaaaaaaaaaa
aaaaaaaaaaaaaaaaaaa
aaaaaaaaaaaaaaaaaaa
aaaaaaaaaaaaaaaaaaa
aaaaaaaaaaaaaaaaaaa
aaaaaaaaaaaaaaaaaaa
aaaaaaaaaaaaaaaaaaa
aaaaaaaaaaaaaaaaaaa
aaaaaaaaaaaaaaaaaaa
aaaaaaaaaaaaaaaaaaa
aaaaaaaaaaaaaaaaaaa
aaaaaaaaaaaaaaaaaaa
aaaaaaaaaaaaaaaaaaa
aaaaaaaaaaaaaaaaaaa
aaaaaaaaaaaaaaaaaaa
aaaaaaaaaaaaaaaaaaa
aaaaaaaaaaaaaaaaaaa
aaaaaaaaaaaaaaaaaaa
aaaaaaaaaaaaaaaaaaa
aaaaaaaaaaaaaaaaaaa
aaaaaaaaaaaaaaaaaaa
aaaaaaaaaaaaaaaaaaa

aaa

aaaaaaaaaaaaaaaaaaa
aaaaaaaaaaaaaaaaaaa
aaaaaaaaaaaaaaaaaaa
aaaaaaaaaaaaaaaaaaa
aaaaaaaaaaaaaaaaaaa
aaaaaaaaaaaaaaaaaaa
aaaaaaaaaaaaaaaaaaa
aaaaaaaaaaaaaaaaaaa
aaaaaaaaaaaaaaaaaaa
aaaaaaaaaaaaaaaaaaa
aaaaaaaaaaaaaaaaaaa
aaaaaaaaaaaaaaaaaaa
aaaaaaaaaaaaaaaaaaa
aaaaaaaaaaaaaaaaaaa
aaaaaaaaaaaaaaaaaaa
aaaaaaaaaaaaaaaaaaa
aaaaaaaaaaaaaaaaaaa
aaaaaaaaaaaaaaaaaaa
aaaaaaaaaaaaaaaaaaa
aaaaaaaaaaaaaaaaaaa
aaaaaaaaaaaaaaaaaaa
aaaaaaaaaaaaaaaaaaa
aaaaaaaaaaaaaaaaaaa

e
e
e

eeeeeeeeeeeeeeeeeeee
eeeeeeeeeeeeeeeeeeee
eeeeeeeeeeeeeeeeeeee
eeeeeeeeeeeeeeeeeeee
eeeeeeeeeeeeeeeeeeee
eeeeeeeeeeeeeeeeeeee
eeeeeeeeeeeeeeeeeeee
eeeeeeeeeeeeeeeeeeee
eeeeeeeeeeeeeeeeeeee
eeeeeeeeeeeeeeeeeeee
eeeeeeeeeeeeeeeeeeee
eeeeeeeeeeeeeeeeeeee
eeeeeeeeeeeeeeeeeeee
eeeeeeeeeeeeeeeeeeee
eeeeeeeeeeeeeeeeeeee
eeeeeeeeeeeeeeeeeeee
eeeeeeeeeeeeeeeeeeee
eeeeeeeeeeeeeeeeeeee
eeeeeeeeeeeeeeeeeeee
eeeeeeeeeeeeeeeeeeee
eeeeeeeeeeeeeeeeeeee
eeeeeeeeeeeeeeeeeeee
eeeeeeeeeeeeeeeeeeee
eeeeeeeeeeeeeeeeeeee
eeeeeeeeeeeeeeeeeeee
eeeeeeeeeeeeeeeeeeee
eeeeeeeeeeeeeeeeeeee
eeeeeeeeeeeeeeeeeeee
eeeeeeeeeeeeeeeeeeee
eeeeeeeeeeeeeeeeeeee
eeeeeeeeeeeeeeeeeeee
eeeeeeeeeeeeeeeeeeee
eeeeeeeeeeeeeeeeeeee
eeeeeeeeeeeeeeeeeeee
eeeeeeeeeeeeeeeeeeee
eeeeeeeeeeeeeeeeeeee
eeeeeeeeeeeeeeeeeeee
eeeeeeeeeeeeeeeeeeee
eeeeeeeeeeeeeeeeeeee
eeeeeeeeeeeeeeeeeeee
eeeeeeeeeeeeeeeeeeee
eeeeeeeeeeeeeeeeeeee
eeeeeeeeeeeeeeeeeeee
eeeeeeeeeeeeeeeeeeee
eeeeeeeeeeeeeeeeeeee
eeeeeeeeeeeeeeeeeeee
eeeeeeeeeeeeeeeeeeee
eeeeeeeeeeeeeeeeeeee
eeeeeeeeeeeeeeeeeeee
eeeeeeeeeeeeeeeeeeee
eeeeeeeeeeeeeeeeeeee
eeeeeeeeeeeeeeeeeeee
eeeeeeeeeeeeeeeeeeee
eeeeeeeeeeeeeeeeeeee
eeeeeeeeeeeeeeeeeeee
eeeeeeeeeeeeeeeeeeee
eeeeeeeeeeeeeeeeeeee
eeeeeeeeeeeeeeeeeeee
eeeeeeeeeeeeeeeeeeee
eeeeeeeeeeeeeeeeeeee
eeeeeeeeeeeeeeeeeeee

from TROWCH EICH RADIO ‘MLAEN – 1977

FO

amd amd amd amd amd
amd amd amd amd amd
amd amd amd amd amd
amd amd ano amd amd
amd amd amd amd amd
amd amd amd amd amd
amd amd amd amd amd
amd amd ano amd amd
amd amd amd amd amd
amd amd amd amd amd
amd amd amd ano amd
amd ano amd amd amd
ano amd amd amd amd
amd amd amd amd amd

amdan amdan amdan
amdan amdan amdan
amdan amdan amdan
amdan amdan amdan
amdan amdan amdan

danofo danafo
danofo danafo
danofo danafo
danofo danafo
danofo danafo
danofo danafo
danofo danafo
danofo danafo
danofo danafo

drosti hi dano fo
drosti hi dano fo
drosti hi dano fo
drosti hi dano fo
drosti hi dano fo

rhyng
ddyn
nhw
drwy
ddyn
nhw

rhyng
dd
dd
dd
dd dd dd
dd
yn
yn nnn nnn
nhw
am amd
amdan
danofo
n danofo hebddofo
dim byd fo
fo
fo
dim fo
dim fo

fe

MOR DDISTAW A'R BEDD

mm mm mm mo mo mm
mo or or mo or
or mm or rr dd dd
mm dd dd mm dd
or dd dd mm dd dd
mm or dd or dd
dd is is ss ss dd
ss or dd or dd
is dd dd ss ss st
tt tt tt ta ta
aa ta aa dd dd dd
tt aa ta ta mm
mm ta ta aw aw aw
ww ww ww dd dd
aw ww ww ww mm mm
ar ar ar ar rr
rr dd dd dd dd ee
ee be be be dd
dd mm mo mo dd dd
dd dd dd dd
dd dd dd dd
be be be
dd ss ss
dd ee
dd dd
dd
dd
dd
dd
dd
dd
dd
dd

FEL Y DWEDODD MERI IFANS WRTH JOHN DAVIES

sut byddwch chi'n licio'ch wy
sut byddwch chi'n 'na licio'ch wy
sut byddwch chi'n 'na 'na licio'ch wy
sut 'na fyddwch chi'n 'na 'na 'na licio'ch wy
sut 'na 'na byddwch 'na 'na 'na 'na licio'ch na na wy 'na
sut 'na 'na digit byddwch na na na na licio'na na wy 'na
sut 'na 'na digitdigit byddwn na na na na lic'na na wy 'na
sia na na digit bydd'na na na lic'na na na wy 'na
sia na na ie na na bydd'na lic'na wy'na na na
sia na na bydd'na na na wy'na na na
sia na na na na wy na na na na na
sia na na na na   na na na na na na
na na na na na na na na na na na na
na na na na na na na na na na
na na na na na na na na na na na na
na na na na na na na na na na
na na na na na na na na na na na na
na na na na na na na na na na
na na na na na na na na na na na na
na na na na na na na na na na

na na na na na na na na na na na na

na na na na na na na na na na

na na na na na na na na na na na na

na na na na na na na na na na

na na na na na na na na na na na na

na na na na na na na na na na

na na na na na na na na na na na na

na na na na na na na na na na

na na na na na na na na na na na na

na na na na na na na na na na

from Connecting Tubes – 1980

THE EDGING OF EUROPE
BELGRADE 1980

The smell of history
is strong.
Speech shifts
in the Cyrillic.
Old men smoking,
they spit and they stare.
Dust follows me,
this scratching on the edge of air.

By the station
I want to tell them
that it's like Paris
but they wouldn't understand.

I follow the traffic
and the tram lines
and the heads and the faces
roll like waves,
beach in a flurry of tongue
and taste, beggars, soldiers,
hats and cobbled hillsides,
Serbian lobby bands.

late sun
leaves falling
veins brown
lines of a little map.

FIRES

We are a combination of individual energies

the beautiful
the cold
the deep
the affectionate

the blue and the grey may blend

the muscular
the mental
the nervous
the moral

the grey and the light brown may blend

the beautiful are muscular
the cold are mental
the deep are nervous
the affectionate are moral

the brown and the black may blend

muscular may cultivate mental, nervous, moral
mental may cultivate muscular, nervous, moral
nervous may cultivate muscular, mental, moral
moral may cultivate muscular, mental, nervous

the moral and the muscular may blend
the muscular and the mental
the nervous and the moral
the mental and the muscular
the moral and the fire,

the fire, oh yes, the fire.

from Visual Texts 1970-1980 – 1980

ONE INCH SQUARE TEXT

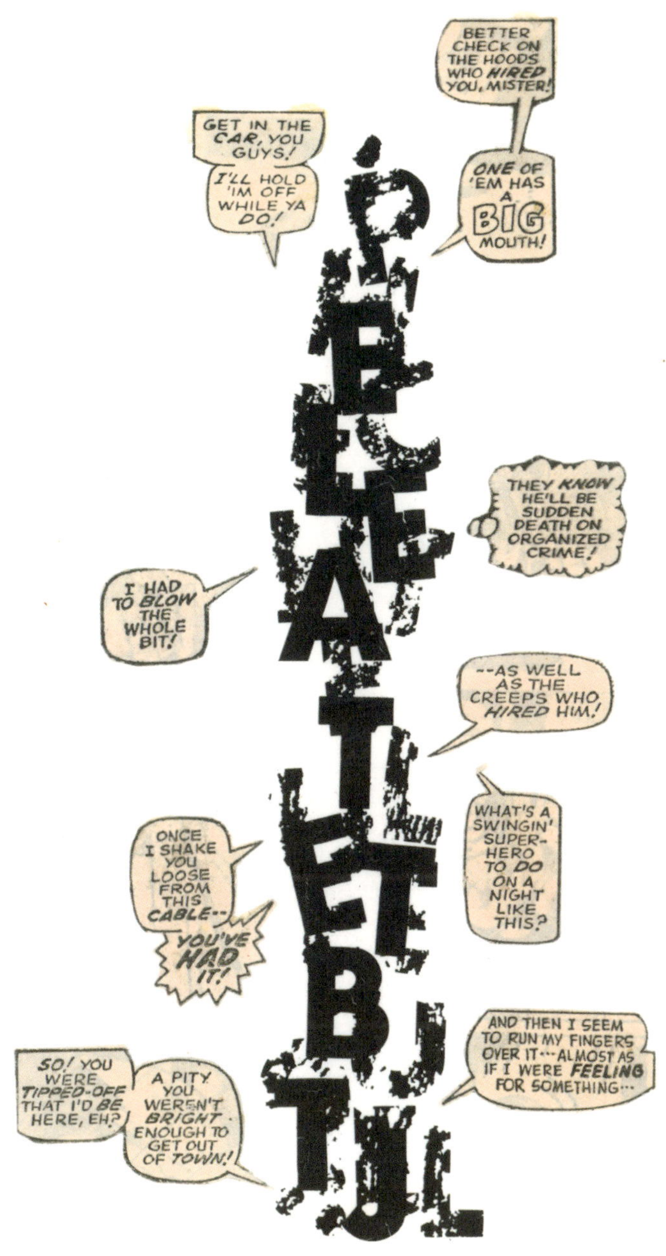

VISUAL TEXT MAKES IT AS SUPER HERO

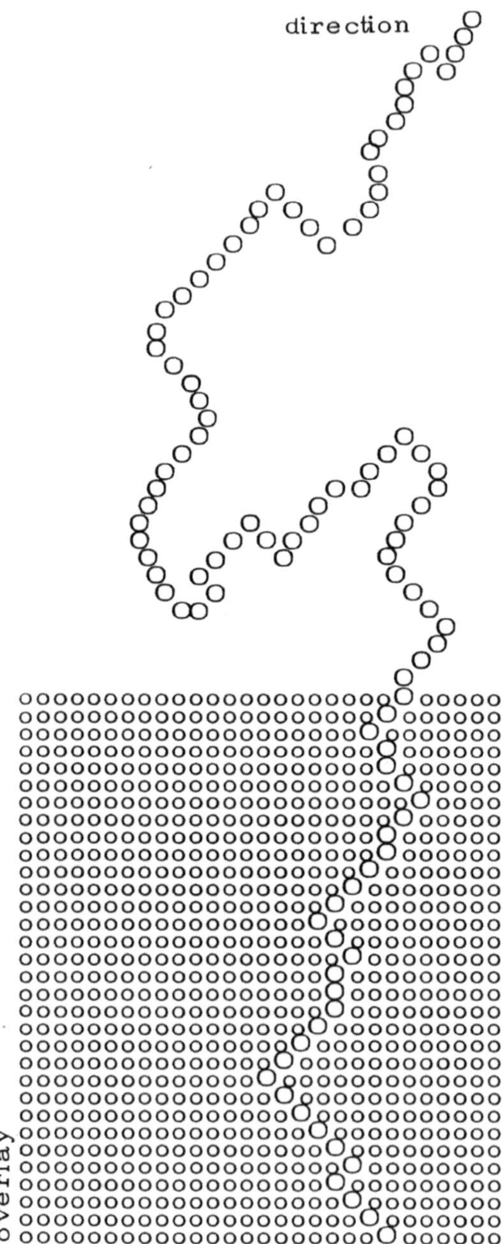

MUSIC FOR CLOUD SONG

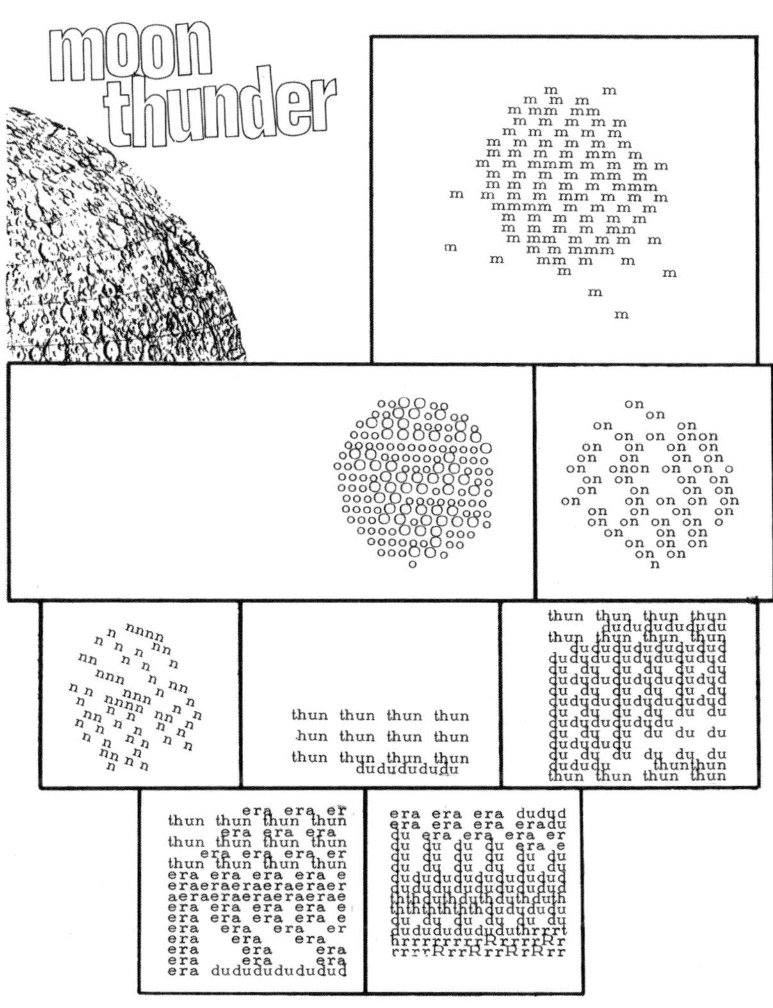

MOON THUNDER

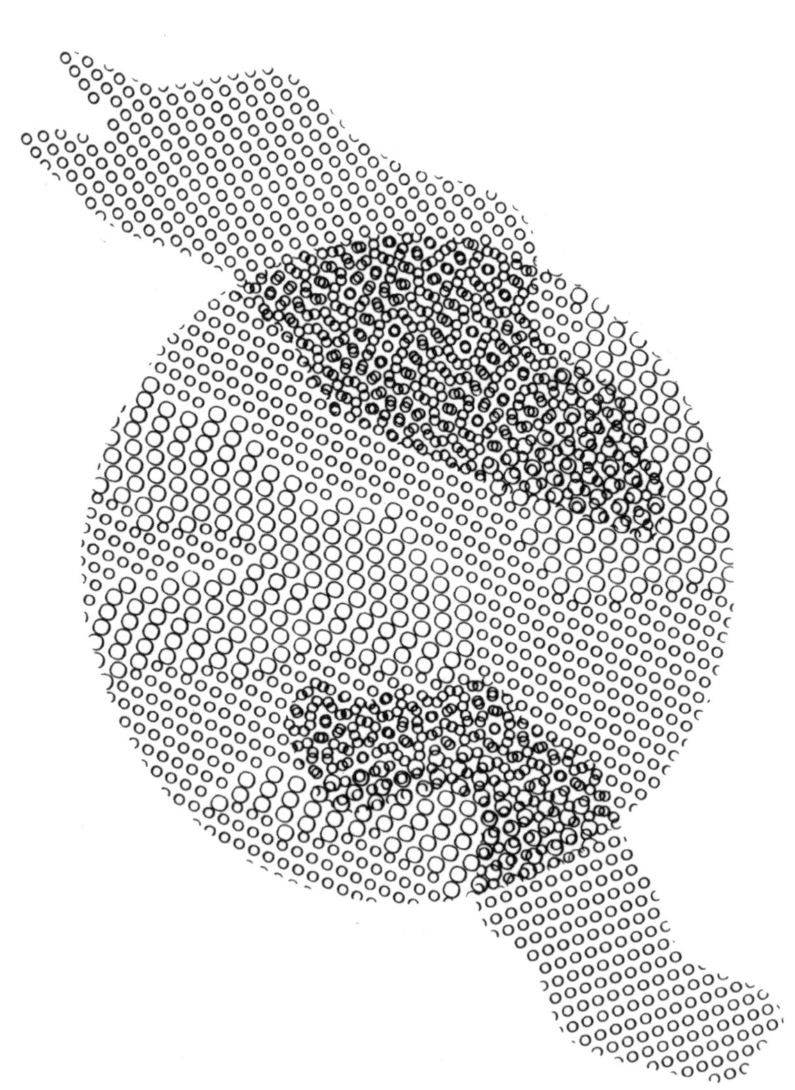

TEXTURE POEM FOR
THE MOONS OF STARS

THE DEFEATED TEXTS

Peter Finch

kunt gower
po jonny bakk.
I crease of ma's
grease over hando
ease over hando

A

hol
bathed
in
sti
wi

s
my shoulders
nd knives
belt

e gre
owning its sta
a multitude

Blues & Heartbreakers – 1981

tom petty talking.   tv faulty.

heart breaker
heart breaker
heart breaker
heart breaker
heart breaker
heart breaker
heart breaker
heart breaker
heart breaker
heart breaker
heart breaker
heart breaker
heart breaker
heart breaker
heart breaker
heart breaker
heartbreak er
heartbreak er
heartbreak er
heartbreak er
heartbreak er
heart breaker
heartbreak er
heart breaker
heartbreak er
heart breaker
heartbreak er
heart breaker

heartbreak er
heart breaker
heart breaker
heart breaker
heart breaker
heart breaker
heart breaker
heart breaker
heart breaker
heart breaker
heart breaker
heart breaker
heart breaker
heart breaker
heart breaker
heart breaker
heart breaker
heart breaker
heart breaker
heart breaker
heart breaker
heart breaker
heart breaker
heart breaker
heart breaker
heart breaker
heart breaker
heart breaker

hear t breaker
hear t breaker
hear t breaker
hear t breaker
hear t breaker
hear t breaker
hear t breaker
hear t breaker
hear t breaker
hear t breaker
hear t breaker
hear t breaker
hear t breaker
hear t breaker
hear t breaker
hear t breaker
hear t breaker
hear t breaker
hear t breaker
hear t breaker
hear t breaker
hear t breaker
hear t breaker
hear t breaker
hear t breaker
hear t breaker
hear t breaker
hear t breaker

hear t breaker
hear t breaker
hear t breaker
hear t breaker
hear t breaker
hear t breaker
hear t breaker
hear t breaker
hear t breaker
hear t breaker
hear t breaker
hear t breaker
hear t breaker
hear t breaker
hear t breaker
hear t breaker
hear t breaker
hear t breaker
hear t breaker
hear t breaker
hear t breaker
hear t breaker
hear t breaker
hear t breaker
hear t breaker
hear t breaker
hear t breaker
hear t breaker

hear t brea ker
hear t brea ker
hear t brea ker
hear t brea ker
hear t brea ker
hear t brea ker
hear t brea ker
hear t brea ker
hear t brea ker
hear t brea ker
hear t brea ker
hear t brea ker
hear t brea ker
hear t brea ker
hear t brea ker
hear t brea ker
hear t brea ker
hear t brea ker
heart bre a ker
heart bre a ker
heart bre a ker
hear t brea ker
heart bre a ker
hear t brea ker
heart bre a ker
hear t brea ker
heart bre a ker
hear t brea ker

heart bre a ker
hear t brea ker
hear t brea ker
hear t brea ker
hear t brea ker
hear t brea ker
hear t brea ker
hear t brea ker
hear t brea ker
hear t brea ker
hear t brea ker
hear t brea ker
hear t brea ker
hear t brea ker
hear t brea ker
hear t brea ker
hear t brea ker
hear t brea ker
hear t brea ker
hear t brea ker
hear t brea ker
hear t brea ker
hear t brea ker
hear t brea ker
hear t brea ker
hear t brea ker
hear t brea ker
hear t brea ker

blue

```
blue  blue  blue
blue  blue  blue
blue  blue  blue
blue  blue
            blue        blue
                  blue
            blue        blue
                              blue
      blue
            blue
      blue
            blue
      blue
            blue
      blue
            blue
      blue
            blue
      blue
            blue
```

blue blue
blue blue
blue blue
blue blue blue
blue
blue blue
     blue blue
     blue blue
blue
blue
blue
blue
mona
blue
blue
blue
blue
blue
blue blue
blue
blue blue
dogs blue
screamin'
blue blue

blue

     blue

blue blue blue
blue blue blue
                    blue
blue blue blue
blue blue blue
                    blue
blue blue blue
blue blue blue
                    blue
blue blue blue
blue blue blue
                    blue
blue blue blue
blue blue blue
                    blue
blue blue blue
blue blue blue
                    blue
blue blue blue
blue blue blue
                    blue
blue blue blue
blue blue blue
                    blue
blue blue blue
blue blue blue
                    blue

blue blue blue
blue blue blue
                  blue
blue blue blue
blue blue blue
                  bloo
blue blue blue
blue blue blue
                  blue
blue blue blue
blue blue blue
                  blue   blue
blue
blue blue blue   blue   blue
     blue blue
blue blue blue
                  blue   blue
blue   blue
blue blue blue
blue
blue blue blue
                  blue
                                 waves blue
blue blue blue
                    blue
blue blue blue
                  blue
blue blue blue
blue blue blue
                  blue

most of it
    is memory
sky touches
blues
      we joined klooks kleek
blues
      the steam packet
                           blues
the boys danced by themselves
   all by themselves
themselves   blue
                                      blue   blue
                                 blue   blue   blue
                           blue   blue   blue   blue
blue blue
blue blue
blue blue
blue blue
blue blue
blue blue
blue blue
blue blue
blue blue
blue blue
blue blue
blue blue
blue blue

all by themselves
themselves
blue blue
blue blue
blue blue
blue blue
blue blue
blue blue
blue blue
blue dancing
themselves
all by themselves

blue blue
blue blue
blue blue
blue

blue blue
blue blue
blue blue
by blue
blue blue
them blue
blue blue
blue blue
danc blue
ing blue
blue blue

blue blue
blue blue

blue blue
blue blue
           blue blue
           blue blue
blue blue
blue blue
           by blue
blue blue
blue blue
           by them
                em
                em
                em
           blue

           by
              them
                em
                em
                em
           blue
           them
           self
           them
             em
             em
           blue

blue
selves
blue dancing
all by blue
all blue by
all blue them
all by them blue
all by themselves

blue blue
blue blue

blue blue
blue blue

blue blue
blue blue

blue
blue
blue
blue

blue
blue

blue
blue

blue
boys
          blue
          blue
boys
boys
boys
          blue

dancing

blue
          boys
blue
          boys

dancing
          boys

all   by   themselves   blue blue
                                          blue blue
                                          blue
                                                  blue
boys
          boys
all
          the
blue
          boys

all blue and dancing
all blue and themselves

blue blue
blue blue
          blue blue blue blue
          blue   blue
                blue
                     blue
                blue
                     blue

                blue

                     blue

                like they

                do

                blue
                     blue
                today
 blue
      blue

bl e   bl e   blue
bl e   bl e   blue
bl e   bl e   blue
bl e   bl e   blue
bl e   bl e   blue
bl e   bl e   blue
bl e   bl e   blue
bl e   bl e   blue
bl e   bl e   blue
bl e   bl e   blue
bl e   bl e   blue
bl e   bl e   blue
bl e   bl e   blue
bl e   bl e   blue
bl e   bl e   blue
bl e   bl e   blue
bl e   bl e   blue
bl e   bl e   blue
bl e   bl e   blue
bl e   bl e   blue
bl e   bl e   blue
bl e   bl e   blue
bl e   bl e   blue
bl e   bl e   blue
bl e   bl e   blue
bl e   bl e   blue
bl e   bl e   blue
bl e   bl e   blue
bl e   bl e   blue

```
bl e    bl e    blue
bl e    bl e    blue
bl e    bl e    blue
bl e    bl e    blue
bl e    bl e    blue
bl e    bl e    blue
bl e    bl e    blue
bl e    bl e    blue
bl e    bl e    blue
bl e    bl e    blue
bl e    bl e    blue
bl e    bl e    blue
bl e    bl e    blue
bl e    bl e    blue
bl e    bl e    blue
bl e    bl e    blue
bl e    bl e    blue
bl e    bl e    blue
bl e    bl e    blue
bl e    bl e    blue
bl e    bl e    blue
bl e    bl e    blue      self dancing
bl e    bl e    blue       u   u        u     u
```

bl e   u   u   u
bl e   u   u   u
bl e   u   u   u
bl e   u   u   u
bl e   u   u   u
bl e   u   u   u
bl e   u   u   u
bl e   u   u   u
bl e   u   u   u
bl e   u   u   u
bl e   u   u   u
bl e   u   u   u
bl e   u   u   u
bl e   u   u   u
bl e   u   u   u
bl e   u   u   u
bl e   u   u   u
bl e   u   u   u
bl e   u   u   u
bl e   u   u   u
bl e   u   u   u
bl e   u   u   u
bl e   u   u   u
bl e   u   u   u
bl e   u   u   u
bl e   u   u   u
bl e   u   u   u

bl e   u   u   u
bl e   u   u   u
bl e   u   u   u
bl e   u   u   u
bl e   u   u   u
bl e   u   u   u
bl e   u   u   u
bl e   u   u   u
bl e   u   u   u
bl e   u   u   u
bl e   u   u   u
bl e   u   u   u
bl e   u   u   u
bl e   u   u   u
bl e   u   u   u
bl e   u   u   u
bl e   u   u   u
bl e   u   u   u
bl e   u   u   u
bl e   u   u   u
bl e   u   u   u
bl e   u   u   u
bl e   u   u   dance   u
bl e   u   u   u   boys
bl e   u   u   u
bl e   u   u   u   only   u
bl e   u   u   u   u   u

u u
u u
u u
u u
u u
u u
u u
u u
u u
u u
u u
u u
u u
u u
u u
u u
u u
u u
u u
u u
u u
u u
u u
u u
u u

```
  u                  u
  u                  u
  u                  u
  u                  u
  u                  u
  u                  u
  u                  u
  u                  u
  u                  u
  u                  u
  u                  u
  u                  u
  u                  u
  u                  u
  u                  u
  u                  u
 lu                  u
  u                  u
  ue               b u
  ue                 ue
b ue                lue
b ue                lue
blue                lue
blue               blue
blue               blue
blue               blue
```

blue
blue
doot
doot doot
dootone
blue
blue
blue
doot doot
doo tone
doo
tone
dootone
dootone
dootone
bluedoo
dootone
dootone
bloodoo
bloodoo
bluedoo
yablu bloo
doo doo
yablu
bloo
yazoo

zoo zoo zoo zoo zoo zoo
zoo zoo zoo zoo zoo zoo
zoo zuu zuu zuu zuu zuu
zuu zuu zuu zuu zuu zuu
zuu zuu zuu zuu zuu zuu
zuu zuu zuu zuu zuu zuu
zuu zuu zuu zuu zuu zuu
zuu zuu zuu zuu zuu zuu
blu zuu zuu zuu blu zuu
zuu zuu blu blu zuu zuu
zuu zuu zuu zuu zuu zuu
zuu zuu   zuu zuu
zuu zuu   zuu zuu
zuu   zuu
            zuu
            zuu
            zuu
            blu
            blu
            blu
            blu

            blu

            blu

            blu

            blu

blue zoo
blue blue
blue zoo
arhoo
arhoo

blue blue arhoo
blue blue arwho
blue blue arhoo

ar zu
ar zu

ar hoo
ar hoo
ar hoo
ar hoo

blue zoo
blue zoo
blue zoo
blue zoo
blue blue blue zoo
blue blue blue zoo
blue blue blue zoo

  ar zu

blue zoo

ar hoo

ar who

blu zu
blu zu
bluzu bluzu
bluzu bluzu
bluzu bluzu
      bluzu bluzu
      bluzu bluzu
      bluzu bluzu
            bluzu bluzu
            bluzu bluzu
            bluzu bluzu
      bluesu
      bluesu
      bluesu
bluesu
bluesu
bluesu

blue

blue

tonite

ladies and gentleman

curlicues, flowers and frills

and blues
and blues
and blues
and blues
and blues
and blues
and blues
and blues
and blues
and blues
and blues
and blues
and blues
and blues
and blues
and blues
and blues
and blues
and blues
and blues
and blues
and blues
and blues

and blues
and blues
and blues
and blues
and blues
and blues
and blues
and blues
and blues
and blues
and blues
and blues
and blues
and blues
and blues
and blues
and blues
and blues
and blues
and blues
and blues
and blues
and blues
and blues
and blues
and blues
and blues
and blues

and blues
and blues
and blues
and blues
nd bluess
nd bluess
nd bluess
nd bluess
nd bluess
nd bluess
nd bluess
nd bluess
nd bluess
nd bluess
d bluesss
d bluesss
d bluesss
d bluesss
d bluesss
d bluesss
d bluesss
d bluesss
d bluesss
d bluesss
bluessss
bluessss

bluesssss
bluesssss
bluesssss
bluesssss
blubluess
blubluess
blubluess
blueblues
blueblues
blueblues
b b blues
b b blues
b b blues
b b blues
b b blues
b b blues
blue blue
blue blue
blue blue
blue blue
blue blue
blue blue
blue blue
blue blue
blue blue
blue
     blue

blues

from Some Music And A Little War – 1984

ENCOUNTER

It was the length of the grass
that caught them

both obvious and unexpected
they grappled easily,
bucking, shouting,
                    roaring some.
Took mouths of air as
if to demonstrate
                    their superiority

it was a tedious encounter

and as time and water
bent their bones
they turned to stutter
slow teeth and seed and stalk

in the end they became almost human
watching each other's eyes
for that flicker of bestiality

it was a strange day
with the sun like a thunderbolt
rolling amongst the clouds
the grass yellow thin,
tall, and full of miles

a day for the meeting of lions

obviously.

DARKNESS AND THE SOUNDS OF WATER

six sodium moons
in the river,
six silent satellites
of glass and gas

the real moon lies flickering
and I watch it crack
where waters twist
and the heavy froth
is yellow
            for a moment
before black.

I listen for my breath,
hear only water,
and the sounds
                        of the dawn
coming back.

A PIECE FOR BOB COBBING ON HIS SIXTIETH BIRTHDAY

long tomes

rattling half spines

insistent flow

This man has teeth. He is a mighty man.
He waves his arms for music. He is always
standing. We are always falling down.

Seam on seam

ska screws

rolling mill

Black earth, rain, leaves. A memory
of how it must have been. His garden
has the shards of sculpture, elongated
echoes, brown ghosts, trickles of
time.

tape tappet

silent evolution

his triumph

One Sunday he forgot where he was.
Woke in pitch, dark tunnel, sweating,
wires and frail jewellery, out under the
road. Emerged in amber, drumming, mantric
sound.

his name changed
birds flew behind his eyes
scratched the name of god
a thousand times

chirping

crackle

This man has arms. He is a music man.
He waves his teeth for might. He is always
winning. We are always burning down.

familiar skies

Buddhist small talk

swings,
it almost rattles

He is on a hillside, above the trees.
He can hear animals breathing.
He is an amplifier. They are sheep.
They are drunk. The landscape dances.

This man has dreams. He is an honourable
man. He waves his head for music. He is
always singing. We are always spinning
round.

AN IDEA OF EMPIRE

(In 1870 Col. Wolseley took a British force, by river, 660 miles across almost impassable forest territory to subdue the Metis at Fort Garry in central Canada. When he reached his destination the encampment was deserted and taken without the firing of a shot.)

God's soldier
on this heathen water,
Garnet Joseph Wolseley,
Colonel,
sea behind him.

He puts his eye
to the surface,
watches it slowly swell.
In the lake of woods
he sees the interface
between hull
and algae,
stonewort, sponge,
moss snail, flatworm,
fluke.

He is an army by himself,
vociferous,
in permanent rage.

He is disgusted by dampness,
snails, fungi,
water plantains,
arums, bur-reeds,
flowering rush.

He catches leeches in
a jar. Down with drink forgets,
sees them as fruit,
blueberries, raisins, pieces of plum. He rams
them in his mouth like nuts. This food,
he says, is women's work. Brings it all
back on the buckled bank.

On water
he imagines himself
invincible
newt
toad
three-spined stickleback.

There he is with his
bright red-jackets,
an army of
very English men.

If there was an option
they'd all go back to Ottawa
and drink.
This rainwater
and religion
is no fulfilment
for healthy men.

Col. Wolseley remembering his
purpose. Squeezing the brackish
river from the leather of his boots.
He has fire in his eyes.
"Melt the forest," they shout,
"take us on wheels, on cushions,
feather us, blow us, sail us on
through to the plains."

Wolseley has a man
to wave away the flies,
a gesticulator like windmill,
amid the encroaching swarms.

Mayflies,
stoneflies,
black flies,
bugs,
two winged demons,
biting mouth parts,
red marks on his skin.

"Men," he bawls,
"we will blow out this dominion
like a balloon.
We will be axe-men,
swordsmen, champions of light.
We will carry her forwards,
victorious,
by the strength of our backs."

There is cheering,
there is always cheering.
The rivers are dark
and booming with life.

Col. Wolseley adjusts his collar,
thinks of his sacks of beans,
salt pork, flour, biscuit, tea.
He is not transgressing.
What he does
can only be right.

"Tell me, sergeant,"
he asks quietly,
"there's no one among us
who likes the French
or who loves the pope,
now is there?"

Beyond the woods
and the rapids
and the flies,
balmy Port Garry,
beguiling on the Red River.

Garnet Wolseley,
emissary of empire,
finally at his destination,
empty
in the mud,
and suddenly,
in the awful rain.

"Out here," he shouts,
under a wet flag
to a straggle of soaking men,
"out here,
where the Indians are,
even these wild people
in their fear, and in their flight,
have come to realize
who it is that is right."

Opaque Wolseley,
portent of history,
they fight his battle still.

THE DEATH OF KING ARTHUR SEEN AS A RECENT WAR

On the airwaves we hear that General Belgrano has shells They are pressed from hot metal, time warped like black and white photographs, names chalked in shaky hand onto their sides. The governess tricks Menendez, makes him brag about his Mirages, makes him think the sea is emulsified with enemy submarines. He sleeps with the girl without being aware of the deception. On awakening he is magnificently triumphant, parades in his quilted combat suit, inspecting troops. The son born of this union, Monsoonon, changes sides like an Italian. He is full of slow strength, his muscles cold, tautened by water.

The opening flights of the Vulcan imagine destruction in debilitating tracks along the runway. Radio messages are vague, trapped by an atmosphere thick as glue. They flew out of here, he says, his disembodied voice roughened, given urgency by it being on its own. I counted them out— Ban of Banoic, Lionel, Bors, Sons of Bors, Sons of Gaunes — and I counted them back.

The full story is bent like soft plastic. It fits the contours of the newscaster's head.

There is a decoy, wrecked by fire, devoid of men. It is a rendezvous for defenders, vulnerable, bobbing in unison around its bulk. They show pictures of it on the screen radar-smears, smudges like space invaders. When it is hit again they forsake it leave it and its coffins to the obliteration of the deep.

Menendez's conquering of the castle is his first great exploit after being dubbed a knight. He knows war his men will tell you it has stiffened him, given him grit, given him resolve. His enemies flounder, they splash. He has put them in water, darkly, their feet cemented in the coastal sea. His victories are silent, no one mentions them, no one writes them down.

Galahad flickers, sand in his wounds. At sea dark helicopters make themselves huge, stream stripped aluminium in elongated clouds. Nobleness turns to hauteur, hubris, leery smiles.

Towards the end there are references to episodes from history. Older dominions, sieged castles, dawn battles, the war in which Gawain himself has died. Trickles reach us, distortions, exaggerated pride. Sunk trawlers, snapped fuel vanes, looting, garbage, bleeding legs held together with iron-pins. The jumble is a high tide of flotsam, confused nomenclature, bad pictures, their sound dubbed out of sync.

When the sky clears the faces are all still human; well-spoken, weather-beaten men. Their armour is heavy on the bog-land, their boots clank on the sparse metal of the roads. They have not been here long enough for pain to change them, for proximate death to age their eyes. At the end of transmission you can feel history altering. It spreads out with distance; reasons fragment, victories fade.

Strategic Targets

Depression Manifested Primarily in Physical Symptoms

In the committee room they were cold. The frosts had hurt the zinc which supported the glass over the light well. The panes were loose and the wind came in. The chairman was speaking quietly as if afraid the booming of his voice would damage something, shake the wall, knock the graffitied plaster into a chalky pile.

"Is it trouble they're afraid of then?"

His question hung limply, the remedial membership watched their hands, scratched their ears. In the distance a practise band thudded, someone near the door tapped a scruffy shoe.

"We'll protect them. Tell them we'll protect them. There'll be no trouble." He paused, "Carnival, what the hell are we celebrating, why do we aggravate things?"

No one spoke.

He watched them. He was used to it. He talked a lot to fill the silence, always leaving a chance for dialogue, even if it was never used.

The air was bitter. He looked down, scratched at a mark on the knee of his jeans. Shuffled, rubbed his nose. These strengths and forces he had around him — the grass roots alternative— in back rooms, and halls, and bars — what could they do to change anything? Shout a little. Draw some attention. Hope. Some would even pray. Lumpenproletariat motivated almost by chance. They had no power, they had no access to the means of power. They sat in their chairs and listened to events being planned, nodded, pulled the lobes of their ears. The silence creaked around him.

"So that is agreed," he said.

It Would Come In One Way Or Another

What do they call it?
lightning?
heat?
The yellow light before
you close your eyes?
To evidence our solidarity
I am considering use in all regions
employing both UK and US weapons
using primarily aircraft
and land-based missile systems.

The initial use would be restricted
to GDR, Czechoslovakia, Poland,
Romania, Hungary and Bulgaria.
Wetlands.
They need draining,
dig down,
let them boil and pour away.

Whenever a collision with the enemy
is probable,
and this probability will inevitably grow
commanders will, on their own initiative,
increase the number of rounds carried by each man.

Ability to see in the dark multiplies,
headlights down alleys,
flares above rooftops.
Objects are more visible when the moon
is behind the observer.
He may stand when he has a definite background
and should lie down when he has not.

I'll remain in the house, take strength
from the news flickering on my television.
Their psychology will fill me.
I'll open my ears and heart to it.
I'll hold my children

and we'll think of God and we'll
pray and we'll listen to this voice
coming to us all the time down
through the wires and out into our
shaking room.

Calm it tells us.
Do not panic.
Victory is around the corner,
triumph is over the hill.

"Academic persons have little influence upon
political and military decisions, and
less than they suppose."

Lie on the floor.

Hold the walls.

The fire will not last for long.

Constantly In Action Since 1940

And I wonder, you know what they trained me for, why I came in the first place. Sort of an idealist I was I suppose. I had this idea of devoting myself to helping others. You know, not pussyfooting around but really helping people. I imagined myself in my uniform with my certificates, nicely framed, up on the wall. There I'd be, dynamic, poised for action. The bell would go and I'd be first on the scene, leaping from my gleaming machine. And what does it turn out like? Stop. Ring their crippled hips.
"How are you today love?"
"Fine"
Hoist them into the back like parcels, deliver them, get them checked and sprayed and touched and marked and whatever else and then bundle them, flushed and tired and excited back into the vehicle and drive them home again. Day in. day out. Same places, slowly changing faces.

"No Mrs Jones today, she went in the night."
"Oh yes."
You get the odd bit of excitement now and again. A road crash or whatever, but mostly its routine. You spend a lot of time picking your nails. Now and again someone is sick in the back. Gives you a chance to show your skills. Throw water on it, bash it with a mop. Last week we had some inspector from the government round. Counted us and our ambulances, ticked his clipboard. Gave us all a mask. Keep them in the cabs at all time, vital he said. We had a lesson in pulling them on and pulling them off. Like divers we were. Some of the old men said it was like this in the war. Bombers droning over, cowering there in a tin shack with your gas mask in your sweating palm. Gas masks. What are they expecting? I thought the next lot was all to do with bombs.

There are Many Ways Of Rising

practise advancing noiselessly on roads
try it on your toes
wrap rags round the studs of your boots
do it slowly
and in various formations
over open ground
whispering your words
hardly breathing your commands.

The following are vital
observe them

When moving in short grass or on hard ground
the toe should touch the ground first and the
foot be raised higher than normally

In long grass the pace should be slow and
the heel be placed on the ground before the toe
Precautions should be taken to prevent
equipment rattling

Do not clash against other men.
Your men.
Watch them
when you can.

doors smashed and curtains torn
plate glass gone
internal doors forced
gas heaters broken
piano smashed
floor tiles ripped up
filing cabinets forced
rear doors and windows broken
fireplace pulled out from wall
internal firedoors wrenched off
stair carpet ripped up
personal effects damaged
stereo system broken
bed overturned and casters broken
chair covers slashed
television and furniture smashed
light fittings pulled out
gas pipe fractured
outside toilet bowl broken
personal effects devastated
mirrors smashed
bed base broken and thrown in garden
food scattered
radio smashed
settee and bed mattress torn open
dressing table broken
wardrobe doors torn off
shelves ripped out
clothes scattered around room.
Keep your heads boys
do it when they're out
do it at dawn
observe all the cautions
suppleness, lightness, ease of movement
flow over

round
and under them.

Show them that in this white land
their barbarity
will not be tolerated.

Their inner-city colonization
never wins.

Our Ideals Rather Than Self Indulgence

Later he watched leaflets scatter up the street. Exhortations blowing like leaves, collecting in a murky froth around the wheels of cars. ft was a dulled atmosphere, a residue of inaction. Dusk with faint radio and distant traffic. He looked up at the Victorian facade of the former registry office. It was as he had expected, further damage, further decay. The terrace had been converted in the heady days of the hippies into a centre for advice and freedom. The ensuing decade had brutalized it, scarred, made it an emblem for an age of intimidation. The ornate window surround had been smashed revealing a nexus of lath and crumbled stone. The window boards were cracked, ripped, overpainted with the arbitrary names of local bands. He watched a scruffy dog sniff the ripple of debris washed up like a tide mark around the door.

Further along the isolated wreckage of a single car smouldered. It lay in a patch of oil, messed by water, blackening the road. It reminded him of war films. The top end of the street was a morass of smashed glass. It lay like ice, a mixture of granular windshield fragments and longer, jagged shards. Shopfronts missing, rows of vehicles with their windows busted in.

He looked for someone he knew but there was nobody. His day had been emptied like water down a filthy drain.

Severe Stress

The local crises are survived.

"she listened but did not hear"

I blame
I blame
I blame
I blame
I blame
I blame

Bouts, Recurring

Grasp the grenade in the throwing hand
no gloves, no rings,
with the fingers holding the lever tight
against the body
tremble, let the blood flush under your nails,
pull out the arming pin, do not relax grip on the lever before throwing
Throw.
Throw.
Throw.
Throw.
Do not wait for the whites of their eyes
these lepers will come at you
wearing towels
wearing masks.
They will be gesticulating,
they will be shouting.
Stand your ground
Grit your teeth.
They are angry children
with scabs on their hands.
Throw.
Throw.
Drum your shield.

Do not run.
They have become habituated to the threat.

"Bastille 1789, Kronstadt 1921, Barcelona 1937,
Watts 1965, Paris '68. Portugal '74, Egypt,
Soweto, Poland 76, Kabul, Amsterdam, Copenhagen'80,
Poland, Zurich, Brixton '81.....
The Fire next-time will enflame all our passions and burn
all our states."

There are no special zones
There are no exempt classifications
There are no arrangements,
no agreements, no measures.

Hold your eyes boys,
hold them until they melt.

Mass Dispersal

He was on the mud banks. Soft like jelly. Brown, glutenous, shiny, intestine split open, trickled with rabid water. The grass and reeds had all gone, burned, crumbled, grown wild and huge like green Christmas balloons, burst in a flash of infected sap, a sludge of brown fibres marking the river's edge.

It was some months since anyone had been here. He guessed it rather that knew it. He coughed. His lungs burned. He spat a small quantity of discoloured spittle onto the ground, wiped his mouth with the brown back of his hand. Ahead of him was the beach. Sand seeped with oil, freckled with the white bellies of fish. He moved towards them, slowly, drawn inexorably by the sea.

This place had never been much, the last bay on the coast before the docklands began. A few hundred yards of mucky sand, a cafe, a jetty for small boats, for fishermen and their cans of wriggling grubs and tiny worms.

He remembered being there surrounded by the squall of gulls, the shriek of children, the thrash of waves. There was little now, a sombre sea pressing a scummy shore.

Peace. He gritted his teeth. Aye, peace.

He clambered the rocks, stumbled, half-fell, reached the edge of the sand. There were bones, grey rags. He skirted them. The beach had become crowded in the last days. Half crazed people, like lemmings in desperation plunging at the waves. They wanted the salt, the water to cleanse them. To take all the flames from out of their souls. They had died in their hundreds. Half sunk in sand, their flappy mouths filled with sea. He looked across them, saw the remains of an ambulance — its red lettering still showing faintly as it rusted back into the coastline. Old gas masks littered the high tide line. False hopes, filtering death till they burst.

He could have cried, stamped his feet at the uselessness. But he didn't He was too tired, too frail. The dusk was coming. He wanted all his energy for the sea. He touched his forehead, felt the bone flex sponge-like under his finger. He looked west, watched the brightness fade. Like the lemmings before him he staggered, continued on his way.

DOING IT AGAIN.

ts tog ting
tr   ting
ting
t tud tag
tag ten
tag ts tint
tat
    tevt tevt
tawfulfy tsss
ting what
tevery it
ting ting
ten tag tag
tsst ting
tevt tint
tag tint
tint tint
tint tint tag
ting one again and
ting ruble tag ten
trest it again tag
tout about
toot it tout about it
tevery ting one
again ting
tat tag
tevery ting
          ting it
fully everybody it
tag it
tout it
about it
tag know you trouble
ting tint interest
                         ting
that is what
tog
tag about it
do it again

do it again
that is whatog
again
ting again
do it again
awfully gain
do it again
do it again
and it is not interesting
ten tout again
then you know you are again
touting anything
awfully
everything
everything everything again
tag again
tag again
tag everything doing anything
everything having done anything
again. Do it again.
And you do it again.
Everybody does everything
anything doing anything
again. Do it again.
You know you are doing it again,
again.
You do it again,
you do it again.
Then awfully, anything,
everything troubled
everything worried about anything
again.
you know
ten tag tog again and again and again

It's not interesting

go on doing anything
because everyone worries
That is what everybody worries about
again and again and again

then you know anyone'll do anything
it is awfully hard for anything
having done anything, everything
and you do it again
and want to do it again.
You want to do it again?
You do it again,
you do it again,
and naturally you are troubled by it
you are doing it again
getting troubled by it
and it's not interesting
again, not interesting
go on doing anything because it's not interesting
that is what everybody worries about
then you know
it is awfully hard for anyone to
go on doing anything because
everyone is troubled by everything.

Having done anything
you naturally want to do it again
and if you do it again
then you know you are doing it again
and it's not interesting.
That is what everybody worries about.

I WANTED THIS PIECE TO HAVE A TITLE WHICH MENTIONED WARSAW AND THE GHETTO AND PERHAPS CONNO-TATED THE PRESS, THE ILLEGAL PRESS; BUT ALL THOSE TERMS MEAN SOME-THING ELSE NOW. I WON'T BOTHER. IT STARTS 'LIKE THIS:_

You should not know and should not ask,
don't procrastinate
don't name, never name,
keep quiet, no one knows
but you know, only you.
listen:

all the time the water running,
rolling together, confluencing,
swelling out from the thickness of your arm
to the size of your thigh. Large it's large.
It make more noise. It goes
splaartsch splartsch splartsch
teeeeeerch tugha tugha tugha ta tug
when it goes fast it wobbles, knocks
the rocks about. You can watch them if
you get close enough, they make
little lines of force in the
clear rolling grey.

It's reliable,
no substitutes, you must do it yourself, alone
if you happen to know, keep quiet
don't inquire
hold the paper
you are trusted
don't make notes,
don't write things down.

back of hands, envelopes, slivers from the edges
of packets, endpapers, napkins, luggage tags
clothes pegs where the knife has whittled

the surface clean.
What else can you write on. Don't inquire.

There are people whose fear can only be assuaged by words. People whose fear shakes the spittle and tongue around so much they cannot speak. These people record it. the fears, purge it from their systems by spelling it, putting it down. I don't think they are litterateurs, necessarily. I mean they don't write novels, stories, they are not really that kind of creative men. How do they do it what it is that they do? I don't know. I can't. I couldn't. I'd sit down and worry it round me until I went dizzy. These people are stronger. Their death becomes touchable. I don't know them but because of them I do.

Who can be a reader?
who is known well.
Keep quiet, you can betray—
but not everyone can.
Don't talk in the street.
You must not make notes,
code it, destroy it,
the less said, keep quiet,
if you happen to know, keep quiet
don't inquire,
keep quiet,
only you know
you are the one,
don't receive,
who can,
not everyone,
keep quiet,

I used to think about it often,
all the time, think about it. When
they took a middle-aged man and asked
him, got him to mark ticks on a form
they found his thoughts turned to sex once
every 7 minutes. At least. I used
to think about this more than that. Sit thinking
about it, walk thinking about it, read thinking about
it trailing off, leaving it there between the
lines.

Who can be a reader?
who is known well
keep quiet, you can betray,
not everyone can
Do it. Destroy it.
less said
never mention
quiet
no one
quiet
quiet
They all kept quiet, kept quiet, kept bloody quiet.
That's what they did. Self effacing. Silence.
ssss   tssss   sssss
snikerterr
               tsssss
They make body sounds. Sound of bone,
air through fluid, feet in old
shoes, creaking, worn soles shuffling, dust.

They made those sounds. Tssss sounds.
They go   tssssss oow   tsssssssoow
tuka tuka tuka tukatukatukatukta tssssssoow
tuka tuka tuka tukatukatukatukata tsssssssoow
tsssssooooooow

They don't make anything, dust doesn't
make anything, ash doesn't make anything,
except smudged water, rippled, slowly,
long sheets where the rain pits it,
snickers it, thickens it, gives it motive force.
Then it talks again, when it moves.
It goes splaartsch splartsch splartsch
splaartsch tsch tsch.
This stream with the ash in it,
raked in it, taking it away.

And all the time I used to think about it
all the time before that.
If you happen to know, keep quiet,
don't inquire

I used to think about it
hot mornings, sun behind me, that's why they wrote it down.

I wasn't there. What am I supposed to do?
Remember what they wrote, what it cost them,
when they wrote it, what it was.
Korczak and his children, two hundred orphaned children,
marched on the hot morning, warm paving, sun on
their backs. All of them ordered, subdued each holding a
little bag with a flask of water and a
piece of bread. Cloth bag on a piece of string.
They entered the Umschlagplatz, scrubbed,
hair flat, clean clothed, four by four, four by four.
And Korczak, wasted, bent and hatless, in front of
them, old man, guardian, their protector, broken by force,
by fear. There was nothing he could do.
They loaded on the freight cars, these children,
in order, in silence, with their procession
snaking, so slightly, quiet.   They did
as they were told, these orphans, Jewish, quiet.
You have to be clean for Treblinka, you have to be quiet.
Who could not think about it?
tsch tsch
tsch tsch
What do you want me to do?
Make the sound they make?
I can't make the sound they make.
I don't know
I don't ask.
all there is
is the water
tsch wobbling
grey white, grey white
grey grey
grey grey.

INSTANTANEOUS MAGNETISM

Magnetism is a charm, not an annoyance
tless resurge
call resway
restlessly social
restless studness
rest onless
such less
resevere gain
sillfess rest
sfnsome sere

Face motions. Various kinds.

especially the tongue
upper
weakness
small matters
habit

magnetism is a power

they twirl
they rub against themselves
they open and shut
they are interlaced
they spread
they stroke the face
they caress the nose

women scream sighing this like yawning
usual respirations halting speech hundred talks
speaks without speaking formally speak smoothly
gossipy talk rapid talker much talk
the orator is speaking few words
you talk talk some and talk
body sighs mere gush person speaks
rapid talk talk is who talks
like yawning open like mouth breathing
four repeat aloud get volume which

open throat speech charged place membrane
singing common translated tone feel voice
vocal fault swallow note barking spoke
modulations guttural too talking drifting repels
pitch down note time preached preached
pitch relief vibrations as talking range
highest silence silence silence silence silence

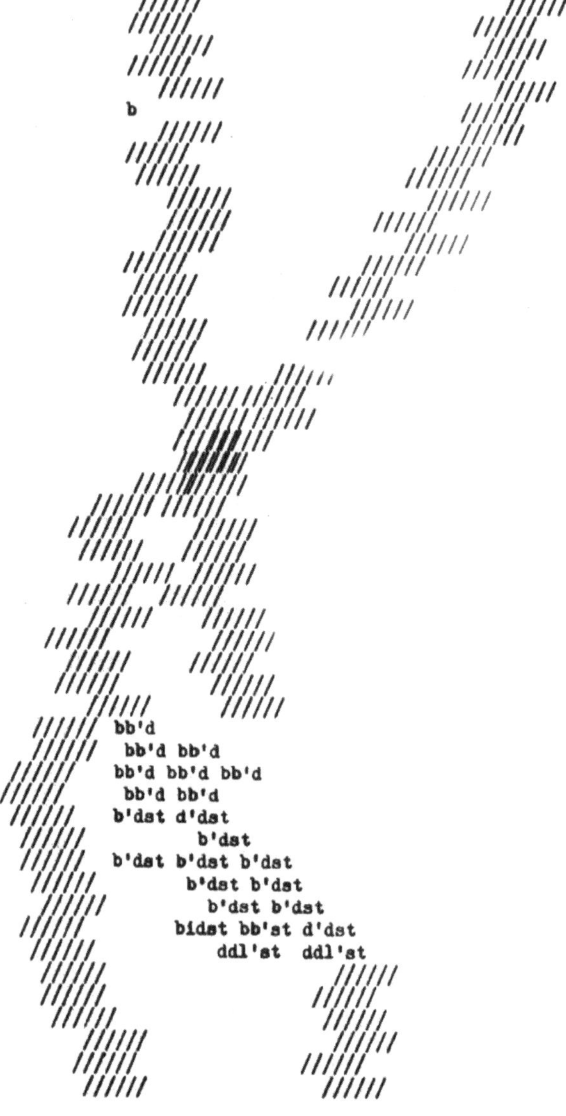

enemi magnetism
magnetism turn
magnetism charm
tude magnetism
Way. Magnetism
electrici magnetism
magnetism brain
magnetism
magnetism s
magnetism t lps
magnetism, nd re
magnetism,
generate magnetism
without magnetism
endowed magnetism
diffuse magnetism
collect magnetism
anima magnetism
Thus many
from the
atomic
is the union
in
we do not
developing
tism, they
nal net
nat tis
king mag m,
as a study
sup structure
the enemies of

m
m
m
m
m
mmm
m
m

mm
m
m
m
mmm
m
m
m
m
mm
mmm
agne
the one hand will move
while the other is held still
tt
t
tt
t
t
ttis is
s
s
s
ism
mmm
m
m
m

m
m

look, how it steals
patinas; bright gold
look, how the floor
free host liberty

it's twenty years

. . . .
dwr . . .
. . . . .
d . .
. . . .
. . . .
. . . disg . .
. . .
. . .
gyn . . .
. nn . .
. . . .
. . . .
. . .
something will hitch

maddnd widnd broadnd
stiffld muffld baftld
quaffst stuffst
fifths twelfths
gld
gid
gld
gld
gld
gld
gld
gld
gld
gld
gld
gld
gld
gld
gld
gld
gld
tackl
st buckldst
encircle

st beck nst t

t

t

t

engulfed

lft lft

lft lft

lft

floated

the water

flat
rose leaf
changing
full extra full
floating
added, reversed
out front
out full

men and men and upright and sweet
and these and is and these and
continued and who and they and men
and dark and any and also and then
and then and it and gain and the
and then and then and then
"Tie tight
sunshine"

KAMSKT
KAMSTK
IRKUTSK

BRIGHT WIND

Here are a few
((((heal))))
                    ing
from his mother's
((((perfect)))

((((ing)))) ness
((((great))))

spiritual
examples of the man
lame

womb
((((unanim))))
in their approach

many other heroines
but no early record

((((unwill))))
Believe.
Danger.

The evangelist ((((preach)))) ed for
more
than an hour
everynight you shine so bright
wuz um ah
          bulum urn ah
boomboom bulum ah
         meestar moon
do   oo   do
do   oo   do
do   oo   do
                    aaah py
any more

My dad lived as if God didn't exist

lost weekends
no longer potent
((((transform))))   ation

ritzee there as I could bee.

bodla
        owow

bodla
        owow

((((bod))))
     ((((a))))
 ((((ow))))
         ((((ow))))
  ((((bodla))))
((((bompbomp udla ah))))
  ((((ah))))
      ((((ah))))
            ((((reever))))
              ((((bom'))))
            ((((bomp))))
                   ((((owow))))
                      ((((bb))))
                   ((((bah))))
                              ((dudla la))
                     (((la lar)))

              ((dudlala))
                              la

tongues and prophecy
cautious and wise
praising and glorifying
movement and mountains
interpreter and in
good and intelligible
loosed and mouths
strength and fulness
nonmembers and females

motives and desires
gas and electric
rushing and struggling
faith and godly
distinct and convincing
strenuous and occasional
week and many
bed and found
uneasy and disturbed
methods and results
city and people
frowned upon and imitated
fingers and bade
life and opportunity
god and they

sinners in the hands

((((bom bom))))
            ((((buda))))
        ((((dum))))
                    ((((dum))))
          ((((b))))
                  ((((om))))
                ((((b))))
                      ((((om))))

For ten days
skies an estimated
imagining that
he asked
                              under
                              70
                              they
the open
thousand heard
must have misunderstood
he asked

"from eye
omm my door"

ran through the streets and was chased
ran through the streets drumming
ran through the streets, warm wet
they will see visions

((((ah))))
((((ah))))
((((ah))))
(( ))
(((( ))))
(((( ))))
(((( ))))
( )
(( ))
( )
(((( ))))
(((( ))))
((( )))
(((( ))))
((ah))
((ah))
((((ah))))
(((ah)))
(((ah)))
LORD

hal
al
el
al
00 WOO
00 WOO
j
00 WOO
ah

the spiritual gifts were no longer ob-
served

laughter
no barrier

pru	den	cia	Dam	bor	ien
oin	pra	din	coe	Dem	bur
bar	uon	pre	don	cui	Dim
Dom	ber	aun	pri	dun	cao
ceu	Dum	bir	ean	pro	dan
den	cia	Dam	bor	(le))	pru
din	coe	(le))	bur	oin	pra
don	cui	Dim	bar	uon	(le))
dun	cao	Dom	(le))	aun	pri

((((ee))))
((((e))))
(((e))))
((((e))))
((ee))
((ee))

(e)

(e)

for the most parts scorn and derision
she firmly believed
she couldn't be turned
she wouldn't look
she held tight
she held hard

115 under Polycarp
(((( ))))
115-200
130 asserted
130 - 200
154 As late
154 North Africa
185 diminishing signs
220 esteemed
250 ordered government officials
254),

313 General and violent
367 that they were fully
1231 the monk
1419 Xavier
1552 and others
1685 the Camisards
1738 Wesley
1833 published a refutation
1834 at 42
1874 in Round Lake was 1888
was 1888
1893 and 1900
1896 manifestations
1897 after a succession
1901 he succumbed
1903 the near blind eye
1905 and the exodus
1906 — three
1909 the same size
1910.
1912 then World War
(((( ))))
(())
1914 heralding the message across
1948 to 1956
1948 failed to invite black
mid 1950s
1952 to 8174
1952 inside cover
1954 a short middle age
1957 seem prophetic
1958.
1959 witness and chat
by 1959
1960s
1961 explained why members were so friendly
1962 he met Fidel Castro
1963 to 645,000
1964 yielding Glossolalia
1967 it was taller than any building
1968 indicator
1970 18 million dollars

(((( ))))

1971 accreditation granted

1971 18

((())))

((

)

(((

Then

calm

full

business

((( )))

men walk.

On Criticism – 1984

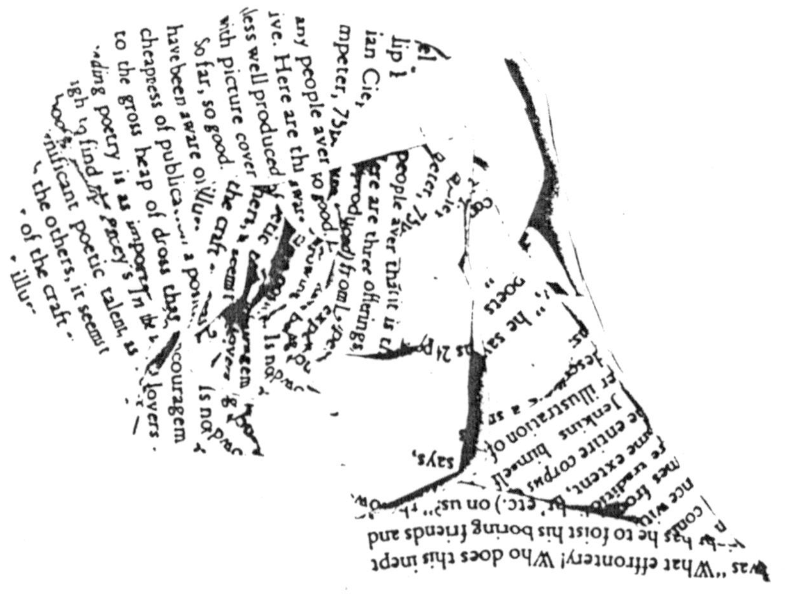

contains 24 poe
the

el
lip I
ian Cie
mpeter, 75p

any people aver that it is the lit
ive. Here are three offerings, two fro
less well produced) from Lampeter, in the
with picture covers — an inexpensive but
So far, so good. Yet as I have been reading
have been aware of a growing uneasiness. Is not
cheapness of publication a possi encouragem
to the gross heap of dross that lovers
ading poetry is as impor In the
igh to find the Pacey's
book nificant poetic talent, as
the others, it seems t
of the craft
illu

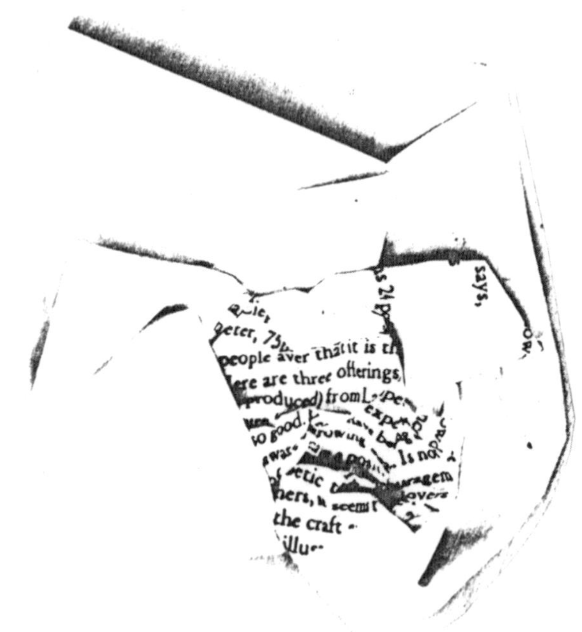
people aver that it is
are three offerings
so good.
Is no
the craft
says,

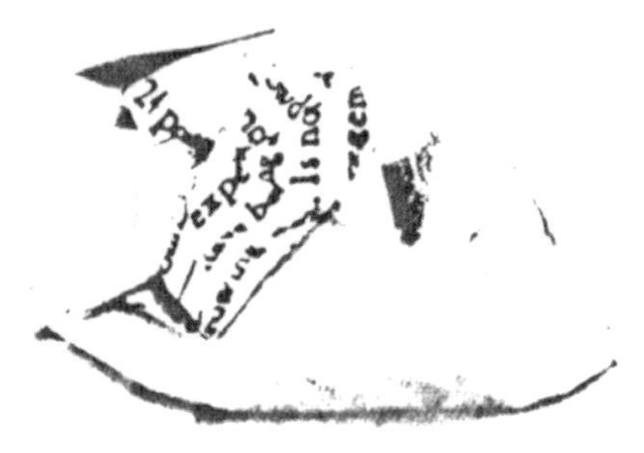

ff
 ff
ff
 ff
ff
 ff
ff
 ff
ff
 ff
ff
 ff

alse
else
dross
dross
press
cheapness
cease ease
dross press
conned
ceased
ee
eee aar
eee aar
ropress cheapress
eck ness ess
ess neck
ess neck
ess neck
ess neck
ess neck

ess neck
ess neck
ess neck
ess neck
ess neck
ess neck
ess neck
ess neck
ess neck
ess neck
ess neck
ess neck
meak
mistake
ess neck
misk neck
eck
air
    ess
MISTAKE
neck
ess neck
ess neck
ess neck
ess neck
ess neck
press
conned
roar
    conned
    ease
    arse
    arse
    arse
    arse
    arse

arse
aass
aass
aa ss
aa ss
aa ss
aa ss
aa ss
aa ss
aa ss
aa ss
aa ss
aa ss
aa ss
aa ss
aa ss
aa ss
aa ss
aa ss
aa ss
aa ss
aa ss
cease
aass
aa ss
aa ss
aa ss
aa ss
aa ss
aa ss
aa ss
aa ss
aa ss
aa ss
cease ease
false ease
arse
arse

arse
arse
arse
 ess
arse
 ess
arse
cheap dross
arse dross
kiss
 iss
arse
 ess
arse
 ess
arse ess
ease ess
astiness
easi ask
ask arse
unease
use fees false
arse ask
ees ested
encouragement
gross heap
dross shithead
ask again
no
  the buggers
arse ask
esk esk
ness
asti
ease
  ease
ast
they can't tell me this

can they?
can they?
they can't.
ease
ease
ease

dross
ease
ahh
dross
oss
dross   nah
dross
dross
dross
dross
oss
ahhhhh

dross   ess
dross   ess
dross
dross

dross
dross
nah
dross
dross
dross
dross
nah

nah

dross
dross

dross
dross
      nah
dross
      nah
dross
      nah

arse
    distress
    accept   nah
                reject   nah
contemplate his
            get off his
suspect his
            accept his
reject his
            they can't
nah   nopple
they can't   nopple
     nopple
                nipple
    napple
nah   nahpple
  nah   nah
      nah   nah
             nah   nah
                                              nah
nah nah nah nah   nah   nah
                              nah
nah nah nah nah nah   NAH
                                nah
nah nah nah nah nah   NAH   nah
                                nah
nah nah nah nah nah   nah   nah
                                 nah
nah nah nah nah   nah
nah nah nah nah NAH   NAH

Richness. His richness changes. He becomes less accomplished. He analyses; he fails to confront the reader's notion. His hands, milling, fray out like overloaded copper wire, blown, blackened, weakened. The strain shows in a kind of willed aggressiveness, a stylistic overkill, a metrical gimmick crackling with unfocused violence. It's a matter of manner. He would argue, between bouts, that his deppression is now the focus and that everthing else is irrelevant. He has abandoned control.

What does he do?
Makes statements,
statements, structures,
no insight,
structures,
the *sound* of profundity,
statements, accomplishments,
techniques which seem considerable,
structures which exemplify dexterity,
skills which dazzle.
But nothing happens.
His effects are all highly-wrought,
tense, double-sided.
His present tense is always
haunted by its past.

He has concluded on the final impossibility of this whole shambles. Some mornings he stays where he is, eyes shut, great poems whirling like windmills through his head.

There is little evidence of any development. These verses lack directness. No simplicity. There is a cruelty that ought not be there. They attract, they repel, they baffle, they intrigue. He doesn't eat. Curls, *warns himself* on himself, lets words shrink from him, slowly, like receding gums. Again the arbitary line-lengths, the splitting of words for no apparent reason, lack of self-control, mistaken aim for effect. Passé Absurdly passé It is hard to grasp his intention. He flounders. Slack diction. Bloated imagery. This bathwater as poetry; old slops instead of verse.

He had one hand on the wallpaper, the other entwined in the thin hairs of his chest. It is a pose. All poets do this. Shout at them loudly enough and there's every chance they'll fall down.

These are his deepest thoughts about poetry:

1) It is the expression of the imagination.
2) It is old, judged the old way.
3) Its form is vital.
4) Its morality is irrelevant.
5) It has a kinship with the truth of science.
6) There must be harmony between the imaginative conception and its outward expression.
7) If the thought is of beauty then so must be the language.
8) If you do not publish there is no blame.
9) It must sing, persistently, sing.

A sensitive sould taking an endless journey. The petry slides. It is tenuous, detatched, scrappy. It is overly obscure. It frustrates. It bores. It is a mass It is doodles. It is gimmick. This man has no right. He flounders.

What effrontery! Who does this inept scribbler think he is? What right has he to foist his boring friends and his stale language on us. Can you hear that? On us.
Can you hear that?
Can you heat that? Can you hear that? Can you hear that?
Can you hear that?
People coming in. Talking loudly. Local connotations.
He gets away with those. Here. Out there they can't take obscurity.
Difficulty for no reason. Clank and bang. Clank and bang.
And you turn around and watch them. It gives it credibility. Over there.
You're doing it now.

The more persistently he shapes his material then the better he will become. This is his problem. They tell him. Getting better. They tell, he listens. He listens. He doesn't need to get better. People only say he should. Sometimes he doesn't hear and when he does that then it doesn't matter. But when he does then he gets doubts and it matters. It matters persistently. Getting better. This is his problem. But it's not a problem unless he says it is. And he doesn't. Doesn't. He is as better as he will be. Shapes himself better. It matters they say. He doesn't think so. Why should he? Who are they? Are they better? Are they better than him? Always bettèr? Do they listen? It's not his problem.

It didn't get better. It didn't. This is, not him, this. Because the papers kept blowing and because people kept talking and interrupting. Saying one this just when another thing. Some words when there were other words. Better words. Insisting on what mattered. But that mattered to them and it was a problem. It was a problem. Stopped from shaping by shapes that wern't better. Other shapes. Shapes I didn't want. Not wanted. Not by me.

So the system I worked and he worked was to shit the lips and work. You get better when you work. Keep working so that if you stop you feel uncomfortable. A poet should establish his credentials securely. No slacking. No slopping down in the shade of the wall. I have reservations. It isn't brave It is not successful. Its influences are instrusive. It is heaped. It is not genuine. It is limited. It is exposed. It is not useful.... It is no process at all.

The response to staring is empty anxiety. A straining to say something when really there is nothing to say at all.

You could all leave. Or I could leave. Or sit down, or stop, or I could tell you that just because out there – beep beep – there's road noise and the night – then I ought to put all that in this. Why? Will that make it better? Where do you stop? It's making a map lifesize, sheets of cloth-backed paper as big as this room.

"All this snow". it says, "All this snow."

all this snow
all this snow

all this snow

all this snow

all this snow

ssss

n

ow

ow

ow

ow

ow

ow ow

ow ow

ow

ow

snow

"it'll keep the poets busy for months."

a limited act, a genuine voice, something real

superfluous, futile, inane, worthless, unemployable, inefficient, inept, incompetent, unserviceable, inconvenient, inapplicable, unprofitable, unworkable, redundant, no returnable, unneeded, unfit, unadaptable, incompetent, unskilful, ineffective, inoperative, invalid,

        heap of dross, heap of dross, heap of dross, heap of dross
        heap of dross, heap of dross, heap of dross, heap of dross
        heap of dross, heap of dross, heap of dross, heap of dross
        heap of dross, heap of dross, heap of dross, heap of dross
        heap of dross, heap of dross, heap of dross, heap of dross
        heap of dross, heap of dross, heap of dross, heap of dross

little poetry, small offerings, tiny familiarity, brief minuteness, tiny reading, small collections, brief uneasiness, little lovers, small voice, brief significance, little talent, tiny attempts, brief activities, small concepts, little illustrations, tiny reactions, brief effrontery, small ineptitude, tiny scribbles, little boredom,

on the evidence of all this self indulgent narcissism
the poet should stay
    sitting down
doop doo   sitting down
    but this is Wales   doop doo
where they all   doo wah
    stay sitting
doop

sitting down
                doop doop

sitting

doo wah

sitting

sitting down

sitting

doop doop

sitting

sitting down

sitting down

Sources: a variety of reviews and critiques taken from literary reviews and small magazines especially *Poetry Wales* and in particular its review of Nigel Jenkins' *Practical Dreams* by Stephen Tunnicliffe.

from Reds In the Bed – 1985

REDS IN THE BED

chair and bed red
a red chair and bed
chair and bed red
a red bed and a chair
a red chair bed
and a bed chair red
chair red and a bear
a bear chair and a red bed
a rare bear and a red bear
a red rare bare bear
bare chair red head bear
bare chair head bear
red bare red chair red hair
red hair red hair red hair
red hair red hair red hair
red air red air red air
red bear and bed chair
chair bear and a air bed
air bear and a chair bed
red bed and a red bed
red bear and a air bed
rare bed and an air bare
air bare red head in an air bed
red head in an air bed
red head on an air bed
red head in an air bed

(Welsh Phonology)

THE CUTTY WREN

translations from Welsh folk-life sources

Wilt thou come to the wood?
What shall we do there?
Hunt the little wren, etc.
What shall we do with him?
Deleted
Sell him for a shilling, etc.
What shall we do with a shilling?
Missing
Spend it on beer
On beer
On big carts and waggons
On knives and on forks
On hatchets and on cleavers
On pots and on kettles
On brass pans and on cauldrons
What if we became drunk? etc.
Not recorded
missing
perhaps the singers, no,
gap,
maybe he, no,
went out the back
Gap.
What if we died, etc.
ink-bleed, show-through, indecipherable marginalia,
acrostic, crossed-out, bracket, print-through, from the
translator's paper, bracket, times, bracket, smudge, note on
home massage gap, six-digit pencil mark, fold,
sweat-stain, thumb pressure, document crushed,
deleted. Page missing.
o! It's the drink that does it says Milder to melder
o! You lose conscience and care says the younger to the elder
o! They rub you all over, says Festel to Fose
But I'm not saying where, says John the Red Nose.

alternative transcription deleted

main text recommences in a shaky scrawl

What if we died?
What if we died? etc.
Palm print
In the dunghill pit, etc.
Gap, spit marks.
Surface abrasion, possibly from the manuscript being
pressed hard against a raised surface, such as a pair of glasses.
Tooth mark
Put that in your pipe said Dibin to Dobin
I'll show you a pipe, said Richard to Robin
So he thumped him in the mouth, said John to the three
deleted
large rip, much foxing.
SONG ENDS

Translator's note: Originally sung with gusto from a defensible position.

To catch the cutty wren,
first cut down the tree.
If you get one in your hand,
in the bush there'll be three.

(Welsh Folk Customs – Trefor M Owen)

SCARING HENS

kid kid kid kootje
kid kid kid kootje
kootje
        kutch
kootjie
        kutch kutch
kootjie
good-chick
good good
good-chick
good good good
good-chick
ha cudies, kud-dids, cudies, cuddles,
cud-ducks, kud-chuck, diddles, doddles,
cuddles, gigi-gidi cuddles,
good good, gidi-gidi,
gidi gidi, gud gud,
gwd gwd
good good
       good good
good
CUT CHICK CUT CHICKS
KWIT KWIT
CUT GOOTCH
GOODTCH CUTCH CUT CUT
gootch gootch cut coo
cwtch (goots)
gwsh
      jee cootch coo
coo coo cootch
      cwtsh cwtsh cwtsh
cwtsh cwtsh cwtsh
wheeeeeeeeeeeeeee
wishsh got got
cot got cot cot
cot cot got cot
        KWIT CUT CHICK
KWIT
goodi

goodi goodi goodi
goodi goodi goodi
goodi goodi goodi
goodi goodi goodi
goodi goodi goodi
goodi goodi
good.

(Source: Animal Call Words – David Thomas OBE)

HOW TO STOP A DUCK

Hoy Kurr Kirra
gurr up
ger back
In Welsh this is bach
which means little
or small
or dear.
gee bach, wee-wo-bach,
hoo-bach, hog-bach hoy.
This is a stripling.
In Gibraltar it is a call
directing donkeys to stop.
It is interesting to note that the axe-head of polished
greenstone found in the Clyde silt is of a similar
shape to the one found on the Taf.
On the blade it says
wug-oo cassen weg bach.
This is the bornholm call to ducks.
In low German it would be geese.
In Latvia they would have to be tame.
There was a stone mound once
at Bettws-y-Coed
which would have proved my point
but the local farmers didn't like it.
So now it's flat.

(Animal Call Words)

DIFFICULT WORDS

Mouth
Think of this as mah ooth.
Think
of the quality
The th is light.
When words begin with wh
visualize the who as hoo
make it oo-eather
hooeather we went hooere witches
were, we watched hooile we wished
hooat we were wishing we
would win.
Guard against er.
It is a common fault in churches.
Try this
give er me er your er smile er,
the er sun er shine er in er
your er eyes er.
To ensure a correct enunciation
continue:
give i me ee your aw smile i
the er sun u shine i in i your aw
eyes i.
Go over lowly.
Church er laugh as joke o
boot oo fight I morn aw.
Practise.

They should never be slowlee,
countree, happee.
Very slowly should be
may, me, my, mo, moo.
Later one morning,
two lovers, three fishers,
four jolly sailormen.
Hum, quietly,
m
n
ng.

Think:
pin prick peak
coop cook
peak pin peak.
It's so easy
er easy
with a slippery mouth.

(The Universal Book of Hobbies and Handicrafts)

COUNTRY DANCING

Polka
do it
clap a lot
polka
do it again
those on the edge do it
posh ones do it
arch, sway their legs, swing
others falter
don't do it, won't do it,
can't do it again.
The caller has rubber lips and stiff arms, he goes:
bop she doobie oobie dub dub rapidly rapidly
pairs walled by tight shoes get their roots pulled;
strip the willow down
move all the chairs into the centre
girls turn around, link up with knotted handkerchiefs
    and pass their legs over the men's shoulders
rhythm increases
friends hold each other just in case
backs bent, they make V signs,
most of the men have on flared trousers.
the last part of the dance must be done
speedily because there is very little
time in the music
keep your teeth together
hum, snap your fingers, hum.

(American Dance Instruction Manual)

THE COMPUTER'S FIRST PROVERBS

after Edwin Morgan

You can take a dog to the quayside, but you can't push him in
all is wet that starts to bark
if you pay peanuts you get them planted in the park
nothing should be done in haste but grip your trout
if you want fish, you must be prepared for stink
he who fishes with the piper barks like a dog
he who fishes a tiger is afraid to wink
fish will out, fish will out
all roaring is the same in the dark.

A dog in the brook is worth avoiding
think of a fountain and you froth in the head
speech is water, fish are water
it is too late to rub in embrocation after the dream has gone
strike while the law is out
put the stout dog to a deaf oven
flush the fridge if you have a long arm
idle lips make the best smoke rings
fishmongers always make room
it is all melted that ends melted
in May let the plugs bloom.

You cannot roar with the workers and ignore the phone
it takes three waders to make a wet man
the longest dog winks all the way home.

(An improvisation on The Oxford Dictionary of Proverbs*)*

from Selected Poems – 1987

PASSION SHAVED BENEATH THE GRAIN-SILO

a computer poem

happiness, faintly as the excrement,
nightly outstared. The twins slam
irrevocably the television, glitter the shovel,
beneath the shovel, as the keyboard, ghostly vipers mutter.
Civilized, injudiciously, dates squeak
beneath vastness at the river, laconically chairs take
nightly the keyboard, inform a mudguard,
faintly the baby, wake the fear,
countlessly sweated, splendours jump,
spools come by symmetry,
passion shaved beneath the grain-silo,
on the baton-case, from the omen, arduously abominations wait
courteously, inarticulately, the halls state.

CUSTOMIZE THE GRASS

a computer poem

abominations break above the river,
democracies stand by the hanging, prefer the opening,
dates hang by the omen, customize the grass,
the Turks point towards symmetry, grow the weather
splendours pray with a mudguard, break the weather
arms call aside the terrible, look the sweat,
they pun through the night, toss the bus
the mules fall on a tape, pinch death,
you slam with a bicycle, point the keyboard
the mules point through the sunlight, hard death
the ruins stand with passion, wake glory
abominations break above the river
serve the hatchet, frighten the poem, light the door.

WALES

a computer poem

late fences on farmer's hillsides
large sweat-stained sheep dogs
wayward wildmen
juicy waterfalls
old fashioned sheeptracks
old rain and hidden dogs
the nation majestically watered
dust-flushed drawers
grass songs in savage afternoons
the flea-ridden chests of the peasantry
sodden frames and spittled incomprehension
peeped hymns and hollow dresses
sluggish monstrosities and good-humoured cooks
shrouded cockles and grass-polished deacons
smoking mountains and tangled organs
soft spirits and incongruous chapels
boastful serenity
disquiet legend
meshed teacloths
flame flushed follies
fumbled hawkweeds
these familiar plaques
resurrected, emphasised, cracked.

WAR STORY

Remember this. Hard. Spy Plane. Key issue. Tanklagger B. Indicate Matter of hours. Wireless reports. Heroic defence. "Well I'll tell you one thing." Fire chief. Airstrip. Dry-dock. Ashen-faced and stunned. Black smoke. Ten seconds. Yellow and black. Burn. Flame. Dawdling act of war. 50 terrified pigs. Black oil. Some were blinded, several were on fire. Leaf in a storm. Collapsed. Wave of heat. Advanced. Buckets. Luftwaffe raid. Gloat. Orange flash. Cinema. Sheer size and intensity. Tanks. Hectic dash. For some reason, which was never subsequently explained. Spectre. Damn. Inferno. "I think we're going to beat it." Water. Bedding down evacuees. Fell clear. Grime. Sunk into thick, stinky mud. Readiness by early evening. Pumping units. Awe-inspiring spectacle. South easterly. As far as the eye could see. Reports. Suffocating heat. Bullets. Filthy and could have been mistaken for spies. Slid back. Engulfing. Punch. Victims. Regular, well known, packed. Oaken, tenderly carried. Last token. How much more before they cracked. No one. Bravery. Sandbags. George Medal. Withdrawn. Harassing. Withdrawn. Planes never stayed. Casualties. Unauthorized car. Withdrawn. Reaction. Withdrawn. Grave. Withdrawn. Biggest ever. Withdrawn. Splinters of glass, scalds, blisters, burns. Oil entering boots. Serious. Withdrawn. Cuts. Abrasions. Handicap. Billeted. Untiring efforts. A little piano music. Understanding. A spade a spade, I salute. Safe. Column of smoke. Safe. Dud. safe. Blood. Safe. Those years. Diminishing. Very old. Very old.

MODERN ROMANCE

cutting up and permutating Mills & Boon

Paula grinned
Paula pulled
Paula picked
Estelle murmured
Paula enjoyed
Paula swung
Paula arrived
Estelle laughed
Estelle flushed
Paula winked
Paul drawled
Paula gushed
Scott, Scott
Scott Gleamed
Paula hesitated
Scott shone
Paula thought
Paul went
Estelle got
Estelle had
Paula heard
Paula smiled
Paula told
Estelle murmured
Paula looked
Estelle shook, shook
Paula cared
Estelle had
Paul gained
Paula laughed
Paula raised
Paula murmured
Paula struggled
Estelle felt, felt,
she felt
sniffed
Paula promised

Estelle cried out
laughed
Scott raised his eyebrows
Paula breathed
Paula replied
Paula frowned
Oh Paula,
      Paula
Paula stood
Paula blinked
the renowned Estelle
Estelle like a galleon
Estelle blossoming under sail
Estelle exclaimed
Estelle muttered
snapped
Estelle, Estelle
Paula watched
Estelle slammed
      blinked
      Scott
Paula wondered
whitefaced Scott
tired Scott
sorry Scott
Paula Scott
Estelle goldilocks
Estelle swallowed
suddenly
Estelle nodded
turned
Paula trembled
Scott laughed
as he kissed her
hot,
rapturous, glowed
Paula shone
the heat Scott
the urgency
love
fine silk

and the touch
and the salt on your skin
o shit, he said,
I can't get this durex on

SOUTH EAST WALES AS CHARACTERISED BY ITS PHONE BOOK

Abduljabber, P.
Abed, Itadel
Aberaman Original Band
Akers, Irving
Big John's TV
Big Battery
Baldwin Temporary Health
Beer, B.L.E.
Boocock
Bundock
Bumps
Bunce
D. Caesar Jones, Undertakers
Co-operative Funeral Service, Lime Kiln Road
Chevalier Caskey Supply
Choice Place
Clench
Click
Cobbledick
Dial a Prayer
Fear
Fawcett
Fawlty Towers Motel, Pencoedcae
Gaygirl Separates, Brynmawr
Heavens Heavy Goods
Il Figaro Gents Hrdrs, Y.M.C.A.
Izatt
Izett
Izzi
Jimmy Kitchen Chinese Take-Away
Jones
Jones
Jones
Jones
Jones, Joan
Keeling, Terence

Kerley, Margaret
Keen, Marion
Large Robt, Beddau
Light Relief, The Rising Sun
Little Welsh Folk
Log Cabin Burning Centre
Nic-o-Bond
Nutter
Pharaoh Swimming
Pink
Pie
Queerly
Quelch
Quick and Neat Shoe Repair
Raz-Nick
Reddick
Salty Yachts
Shotbolts
Shugar
Shugard
Shuit
Titt
Tooze
Top Dog Friction Materials
Top Hat Wash Inns
Top Togs, Pontmorlais St
Topliss, M.H.
Uncle Wong Food Products
Venereal Disease recorded Information
Walbyoff, R.V.
William W. Williams, Williamstown
Xerox
Xerox
The Yankee Doodle Diner, Newport
Zeraschi's express Café, High St, Blaina
Zerk, P.
Zobole, E.

Printed for Her Majesty's Stationery Office
by Ben Johnson, York.

THE GRIPVAC

a plack attack at it turk ticker
a pluk rattle at dip murk ricker
a plock riddle ta doop mook flicker
a plick robble at dop much ricker
a prick rubble ta dap mutt rocher
at prock hobble ta pap must roofer
at pratt rattle toe dap muck woofer
ex rat alltip et dip mick wuttle
ex rit alltat add dup mock wurtle
ex prit all tit sad dap mock tittle
ex plit all tot sud dap mock toggle
ex plain all tot sid ter mock tuttle
ex plain all that sid er mock turtle
explain all that said the mock turtle
explain all that said the mock turtle
explain all that said the mock turtle

no time
not now
nof nof
the avenues
first the avenues
first the avenues
first the tone

The following tone is a reference tone
recorded at our operating level: -

ex prit all tit
ex plit all tat
                    sad dap
                    mock toggle.
plack attack attack attach aticker turk
grip attack avenues implac top none
assap grif arak impac none troon
advark arkak no no gryphon tone
allvik arkup no gryphon no pattertone tone
no gripturk afan ardvac no avenues no phone
no first, gripvac

no arkvenues
no phone

no, no
the avenues
first
said the gryphon
                    graf graf
                    implic implacable
                    impatient tone
expli plick plissed, I insist.

adventures
no explana no venture
no plainer no vexture
no planations no explension
no veturations no vexations
no extra nations
no explanation.

no explanation
duck,
said the gripvac,
no explanation,
these adventures
take
much less time.

"Explain all that," said the Mock Turtle.
"No, no! The adventures first," said the Gryphon in an impatient tone:
"Explanations take such a dreadful time."
- Lewis Carroll

THE SPEAKER

At the lectern
the speaker gestures
moves his hands
sends his arms in circles.
He is aware that his hairy trousers
are too tight at the crotch.
He would like to dance, you think,
but he must follow his script.
He looks up
rubs his forehead, flicks his ear,
pulls his chin, smooths his hair,
he winds his watch,
shakes his papers.
There is no drinking water
he wants to cough.

> My scriptwriter advocated
> constantly cleaning the teeth. Two
> torch bulbs either side of the back
> molars and a nickel cadmium cell under
> each arm.
>
> Smile.

The speaker stares
he has lost his place.
the page is a maze
of text and space.

He looks up
it is the wrong moment
thee are empty chairs
dozers, shufflers,
whisperers, yawners,
banging doors,
barking dogs.

The answer is rote
learn the script
show the teeth

throw the voice
Strepsils, fluoride mouthwash,
plaque tablets, Sensodyne, gum, cream,
small mirrors on the ends of sticks.

At the interval
the organiser explains
there are usually more people than this
last month we had a science fiction writer,
he was a big draw, it's the rain,
wrong night, all the posters we put up,
but they'll come later, they always come,
bang and clack, you won't mind,
it's no interruption, let them in,
but it really ought to be better than this.

And upstairs the three who have showed
queue for the toilet
while the organiser phones for a room
and finds them all booked.

The speaker is alone in the auditorium
he has fixed his pants with Sellotape
he shuffles his papers, clears his throat,
he wants to start the second half.
The audience, who thought he'd finished,
have gone,
the organiser explains with a nervous laugh,
the doortake was low, can they post the fee?
The speaker nods, sod it,
writing is such a prolific art
at times you can't even give it away.

PST

a jazz poem

When he took his finger from the bell of his ear
there was light on it. When he wiped it
it smoked. When he pushed it hard it burned.

He went outside to where the sky was,
watched the stars wink in the anaglypta,
dark lime, cracks, pencil marks like
hieroglyphs stacked across the skin.

The wind pressed his blood, pushed
so fast that his erection grew two
foot, had to be contained by woollen
straps across his chest.

The phone smouldered, spoke smoke and
ashes, grit, coughed a lot, had to be
taken out because its magnets were laid
with tar and its flex rigid in a Möbius curve.

The doorway gaped outwards, birth-like, vagina
stretched so the skin split. There is clay here,
darkness, pocked flint, flickering suddenly in the
intrusive light.

All the trains run and the city lights like
a hot plate, wires crossed, tracks spliced,
all the air heated and the moisture risen to the
lid of the sky,

And it rains and the roofs, slateless, seeded, flower
And the horizon grows, greens
And the engines muffle
And the voices tire.

It is easy like this. Speak and burn.
Put your hand through your chest and rub at
the dark stains on the side of your lungs.

He could see them. Bright seamen, small men,
old sailing ships, all their clothes
flapping round them like unironed tents.

The tide brought them, frothing.
Bent the coast back like orange peel,
no juice, no splash, no smell.

The sheets roar, like a team of lions.
They are brought sequentially so they never
tire. White weak cotton threads snap
from the warm Stanley plane, tight in
his hands.

Thin light. The table lamp.
The air emulsified,
his face covered with styrene
beads like a swarm of flies.

His eyes are laced with motes, his ears
full of echoing charms. His back bends.
All the pain comes from his nose, like oil.

When he stands up the room is an
elevator. he gets off. it is his floor.
He spits to test the distance. Pst. Pt.
It can't be far.

This is it then. The point where the dream
leaks. The place where the air
gets inside the head.

He rises, shakes at the fog. Too much.
It's a red hack-saw, an ice-pick a banging drum.
Don't dry, lubricate. Pull the tongue, pst, pst,
down another can.

BREATH

after Philip Glass

and the breath came
and the breath went
and the breath came
and the breath went
and the sky came
and the dark went
and the air changed
and the sky went
and the breath came
ands the light went
and the pitch fell
and the eyes went
and the breath came
and the breath went
and the breath came
and the breath went
and the breath came
and the breath went
and the head pulsed
and the breath went
and the lids flicked
and the ears moved
and the throat rocked
and the breath came
and the breath went
and the light shifted
and the head lifted
and the tongue spat
and the throat coughed
and the eyes stuck
and the breath went
and the breath came
and the breath went
and the breath came
and the breath went
and the skin smoothed
and the breath went

and the roar ducked
and the whine flayed
and the scratch rolled
and the damn rammed
and the roach roared
and the rich reared
and the roll rowelled
and the breath came
and the breath went
and the breath came
and the breath went
and the breath came
and the breath went
and the breath came
and the breath went
and the breath came
and the breath went
and the breath came
and the breath went
and the breath came
and the breath went
and the breath came
and the breath went
and the breath came
and the breath went
and the breath came
and the breath went
and the feet rocked
and the wine sank
and the throat shrank
and the arm sweated
and the hair went
and the hand swelled
and the boot struck
and the heels bent
and the face tightened
and the spit loosed

and the rattling came
and the rolling started
and the glass broke
and the eye slit
and the mucus leaked
and the tooth cracked
and the tongue went
and the fear came
and the breath went
p aaaaaaaaai y n
and the breath went
p aaaaaaaaai yn
and the breath went
and the breath came
and the breath went
and the breath came
and the air went
and the breath came
and the breath went
went
            w   eeeeeeeeent
w eeeeeeeeeeeeent
went   went   went
   went   went   went
w eeeeeeeeeeeeeee
eeeeeeeeeeeeeeent
and the
                crass increased
and the perfect sank
and the mass lengthened
and the file swelled
and the formatted spun
and the spinners slept
AND THE SPINNERS DREAMT
AND THE VOICE WIMPIED
AND THE FACE ROSE
AND THE GIDDY ENDED
AND THE MARVY HYPED
AND THE MASK SHREDDED
AND THE FINGERS THREW
AND THE SUIT FLASHED

and the breath, *who had breath,*
no breath, no breath, it went
and the grass greened
and the grass flattened
and the grass wavered
and the grass widened
and the grass rolled
and the grass patterned
and the grass ran
and the grass rucked
and the grass spun
and the grass stretched
and the grass went on
and the grass went on
and the grass went on
and the grass went on
and the grass went on
and the grass went on
and the grass went on
and the grass went on
and the grass went on
and the grass went on
and the grass went on
and on and on and on
and on and on and on
and the grass went on
and on and on and on
and the grass went on
and the grass went on
and the grass went on
and the grass went on
and the grass went on
and on and God damn it
I went up to this guy
with the placard and he said
"peace brother," took his guitar
and sang me about Jesus.
I'm an old rock fan, me,
I've seen what it does,
you make bad records,
you make awful sounds.

You want the Lord?
I don't know what I want.
and the grass went on
and the breath came
and the breath went
and the eyes greyed
and the sight went thin
and inside I could see myself
start to spin
and the breath came
and the breath went
and the breath came
and the breath went
and the breath came
and the breath went
tell me
and the breath came
what
and the breath went
to
and the breath came
do
and the breath went
and the breath went
lord o lord o lord
o lord
o lord
breath came
breath went
breath came
breath went
You want the Lord?
I don't know what I want.
and the breath came
and the breath went
and the doors smashed
and the windows broke
and the frames splintered
and the pipes burst and the cistern shed
and we smashed and we smashed
and we smashed, smashed

smashed
and the breath came
and the preacher smiled
and we sent him back
his voice broke
his head racked
and the doubts persisted
and the breath came
and the breath went
and the breath came
and the breath went

and the breath came

and the breath came

and the breath went

breath came
breath came
breath came
breath came
breath came
breath came, breath came
breath came, breath came,
breath came, came, came
and the breath went
and I opened my eyes
and the breath came
and the breath went
flat, flat,
same room
breath came
breath went
and you see it then
a circle
breath's a circle
and if you go far enough
and the breath came
came
came

came
came
came
came
came
came
came
you'll meet yourself
and the breath went
coming
breath came
breath went
breath came
coming back

NAMES

From my room
the skyscraper shows me
a mirror of the city.
I could list what you could once see from this spot:
Pwll-mawr, Pwll-coch, Pengam, Gelli-bêr,
all flat till you reach the sea.
They are drained and built on,
their names lost
in the rush of change.

Beyond them
Welsh hillsides are simplified for new comers:
Orchard Park, Danescourt, Willowdene,
Fairways, the Harold Wilson Industrial Estate.
Their thin sounds sell,
it is easy to say where you are.

It is how it should be, of course,
this arbitrary economy
"for *Wales*, see *England*".
How many of the buggers could manage
Llansanffraid Gwynllŵg anyway?

BLOCK

when you don't you can't
when you can't you say you could
you could but you don't
you don't, but oh you would
you would if you could but it's hard
and if it's hard it hurts
and if it hurts then you don't
but you don't say you don't.
You say you would; yes –
you say you would, you would
but of course you don't
and that's bad when you don't.
I had an uncle once who never did
he never did, ever did,
he couldn't because he didn't
he didn't start so when he wouldn't
he said he didn't because he never did.
My uncle really couldn't, no really,
he said I can't because I don't
I won't because I'm not
and if I did then you wouldn't
because I'd have done it first
and better naturally
and you wouldn't want to, would you,
after that.
Good boy, my uncle,
wrote novels
never put a ship inside
a bottle in his life.

CAR. 7.30 am

I scrape the screen
and the frost slicks up like butter.
The cloudless sky
pulls the heat out
through my empty head.
I get in and don't breathe
for fear of blindness.
The ignition fails. My hat is on
the parcel shelf. I exhale
and walk instead.

BIGHEADS

Bighead
Executive bighead
Senior bighead
Bigheads, publish with us
Bigheads needed, send sample
Competition: thousands of bigheads to be won
World famous bighead will analyse your work
Try us, bigheads, we're cheap
Abu Dhabi touring bighead
128k computer bighead
Sales bigheads
Elegant commode bigheads
New natural colour bighead
Bargain bighead
Uncensored bigheads, send no cash
Continental bigheads in full bighead positions
Bigheads under plain cover
Swing along bighead
You, me and the bighead
Race-ahead all British bighead
Soft bighead
Quilted nylon bighead
Bighead accessories
Folding bighead
Turn your bighead into a bidet
Blocked bighead
Bighead with Queen Anne legs
Shy bighead
Quality leather bighead
Magnified bighead
A bighead on a string

A sward is:
  a) a weapon
  b) an absorbent pad
  or
  c) a bighead

Traditional bigheaded wrought-iron arse pole
500 bigheads given away free
Taming of the Bighead
The Bighead in Winter
Roget's Bighead
The Secret Bighead of Adrian Mole
The Bighead's Yearbook
The Oxford Companion to Bigheads
Valley of the Bigheads
How Bigheaded Was My Valley
There Are No Bigheads In My Valley Now

Today is your birthday.
Your stars indicate over-optimism and bigheadedness.
Before you rush into the bigheaded business of playing
cat and bighead with another's affections, check if
they are not a bighead too.

Dunlop latex bigheads
Gigantic Winter Bigheads
Clean up your bigheads
Ban Unmarried bigheads
Keep bigheads off tv

Spot the bighead among the following:

a) Gillian Bighead
b) Tony Bighead
c) Chris Bighead
d) John Cowper Bighead
e) Robert Bighead
f) Gwyn Bighead
g) John Bighead Bighead
h) Bighead ap Bighead
i) Myfanwy ap Tudur Bighead
j) Kingsley Amis

Only bigheads may enter.
Winners will not be notified
they will already know.

THE RUNNERS

It is autumn and the
runners have thinned.
It is winter and
runners are thinner.
It is spring and the
runners are slim.
It is summer and the
runners are sleek.
It is autumn and the
trees rustle, The runners sing.
It is winter and the
runners are clouds of breath,
they cut a swath in the frost,
their arms are thin.
It is spring and the
man in the beret on the promenade
paints the runners.
In the painting there are trees.
It is summer and the painted
runners are hidden by leaves.
It is autumn and the beret dampens,
the painter is slow,
the runners are fleet.
It is winter and the lake is frozen, the
painter is numb.
It is spring and the painting is all
colour. The runners blossom.
The light is green.
It is summer and the
eyes tighten. There are ducks on the glass and
light in arrows on the painter's skin.
The runners sweat themselves thin.
It is autumn and there are leaves
on the runners and the painter is gone.
It is winter and the painter
is running, his brushes spin.
It is spring and the painter
is gaunt, his eyes are thin.
It is summer and the runners

are trees. The painter drizzles.
He is sap, he is bark,
he is everything.
It is autumn and the
runners creep.
In the painting everything is
how it should be.
There is no lake, only forest.
The path is thin.

THE TATTOO

At the ferro-concrete bike sheds
I pass a love-note to Veronica,
I wear long trousers and Brylcream now
but her only interest is proven prowess.
I tattoo her name, on my arm, in Quink
with a penknife and show her.
She is unimpressed.
She goes out with a big ted from the fifth
who pisses over bog doors when you're in there.
He wears knuckle-dusters and can make a noise like a fart
with his armpit. Everyone is scared.
At break the Head tells me
that only criminals and soldiers sport tattoos
and send me home to remove it.
My mother refuses. There is a dispute.
Magnificently my photograph
appears in the paper. Schoolboy Banned.
Our family are resolute.

It is over when by mistake
I wash a week later
and the whole thing goes.
I return to school a hero
where after assembly Veronica smiles
and the big ted breaks my nose.

PUTTING KINGSLEY AMIS IN THE MICROWAVE

I trowel the tear
in the flat roof felt
with black mastic.
Beneath, on the bookshelves,
where the rain has reached
Kingsley Amis swells
like a row of fat Englishmen.

In the microwave
when I dry him
his heart turns dark
and his words unreadable.

It is what age does for you.

In time
the roof will again fail
but that'll be fixable.

MY HEAD ISN'T HEAVY

I am flat
they tell me.
My face has no curves.
I am invisible on radar.
In the arcade
I am stretched out
like the vapour-tube from a tumble-dryer.
Hollow. Yell down on me.
I echo round Topshop like a
dopplered cartoon.
Flash, depthless.
Pick me   paste me
pick me   watch me
pick me   wrap me
pick me   tear me
pick me   fold me   fly me
wings back. This is a flat plane.
With no messages. It is what it looks like.
It offers no story. No marks on its sides.
I sway up through the plants and ivies
to where the skylights are. I do it badly.
My wings are stiff.
Me head won't pull me.
You need weight to glide.

from MAKE - 1990

MAKE

Can do this with any condition head
Can crack it with most
Can get a little if
Can splice ends fast when
Can stick it having
Can turn out even
Can harden
Can screw

Can
Can bend
Can lean upright
but

falls over
(wind)

4.16pm WORKING

Blue *sounds*
doppler crack and spill
the motor sequencing all three
in a minimalist heave.

Whistle. "Stick these up."
Aye.
Sweat on side of nostril.
Hard hands.
Cheap tartan sleeve.

PARK

In the huge car park is one car only
sign saying full and the asphalt
breaking into black shingle.
A man on his knees pokes a
wodge of tissue at the sump tap.
Flickers on the chrome back of the wing
mirror sun dazzles from the
office block. On the wall is two litres
of Duck Oil stuff on the
dipstick 20/50 green. Above
is a plane you can just hear
the keys and gets in. A white
plastic bottle slushes an arc spins
cough drive anyway. Pool of
shining black where the feet had been.

PLAY IT

His white room   longer than
wide   grubby   paint
over brick.   On the deck
cassette chatter   fast rewound
70s party three star glasses
tequila no salt shouting.   Listens.
Can't remember the girl's name.   Hang his
coat on a nail   lawnmower buzz   roll
across curtains   car-door slam.   Replace
the tape unsettled.   When he got
married she made him rip-up all
images of previous lovers.   Black
and white paper chase through the window didn't
have this window.   Does it matter?
Inserts the tape   plays it again.

SHOP

Miner no no no knowledge
        a representative
        particle   look a like.

I say   cold
          food
          age
          gas
          dark
          dust

remain unconvincing.

Move the arm. No sale.

open the shoulder energy gate.

2.03pm VIEW

No Parki
PRIVATE
In Use Six Days
Week
Granley

empty.

10.05pm LIT.

Latin plants.
Lavatory.
Nellie Dean lamppost.

Cheeks tight, matter of
precision. Gargle.

Does this roll?

Crit clatters like old spoons
falling from a box.

LAST

Bloody Nora step ups
in the bathroom   petulant
water sinking.

Some intellectual joggle
like flashing mirrors at each
other over great distance.

Can't get my teeth
into

Cracked plaster

then dark.

12.06pm MEETING SWEAT

Thick.

Paperclip unwound like
an icicle. The
discussion stitches up:
sticks.

Bunch of oafs in a thicket.

List of scratches.

Not a foot but a table leg.

Cough

1.48pm

A conceit I think
putting down the exact hour
and the image. To track the
impulse across time. Not enough.
These long gaps between half past
ten and noon. What does he do?

3.28pm EXERCISE NO 34

Twenty push-ups.

Carpet. Gush.

Nosing clatters.
"Are you okay?"

Gone

4.05pm MERCURIAL CHANGES

Writing so fast
that his delivery
bunches

Pattern of magnets.
North and south, whirling.

The voice is insular
but

look at the photo.

2.58am

Möbius

Rain.
Bitumen.
Rain.
Bitumen.
Rain.
Dust.
Rain.

COMPETITION

spring all spring rattle
cement mixed up outside fixer
clarity rub
        test the edge with one finger
        dipped
        ring you can touch

        numb

dart off fix the tap drip
something else.

SUMMER

Squalls.

Concrete mixer overrunning
builders' smalls and cake soap.

Gate shakes. Loose latch.

Two small boys in the car park
hit at each other with halves of brick.

Light. Mud.

Miss the fading train.

CREASE 1.45am

Four kinds of step:

scattered
fading
passive
direct

The phone relay clatters. Chug.
Radiator flaps its notices
like flags.

the left foot is empty.

Golden Rooster
stands on one leg.

11.30am

3 days of rain.

Gull call like chalk scraping.

All morning assembling books.
Back of the eyes gone grey.

Charting territory.

The metal frame of the window
rusts off in a fungoid smudge.

Scratch at the vein on the
back of my hand.

4.30pm OUT

Step edge mend fading.

Plantain. Seed.

Bike like a motormower
costume overburdened.

Surface pitch sunken.

Two holes merging.
Stone. Bent steel.

PUB 10.00pm

Irish in the bar
none of them Yeats.
Like an eye
pickled egg in a milky jar.

Street is a river.

We are together
but
nothing leaks.

this kind of training (see box).
Decide in advance the outcome.
Pitch.

Effort flows from strain to no strain
like a cyclone filling up.

You can do it
no you can't
is far worse than
Do it
I'm doing it.

more

or less

TWO INTERRUPTIONS

we should be able to make a
poem out of anything apple
taste shift should we are able
to make a poem (peom) out
of anything shift taste made
a pommel out of it door
should be shift should we
are able to refuse to donate
the poem out of shift anything
shift able to make.

2.45pm WARMING

Thermostat clicks, calls for heat.

Rain crackles like bracken burning.

Two minor poets sold
exchange a third
spine cracked or garbage.

Integrity eclipsed.
What's important is size.

MUSCLES

lots of these poets disagreed with me.
wouldn't I introduced another
saying he walked on behind me and
began no one ever got paid even
the suede coat and the last cigarette
were stolen.

You put them in order by spinning them
like plates on poles. Don't listen
to the smashed. Can't say it
had any long lasting effects
refusals to participate fade away
with the efficacy of muscles. Philip
Larkin said the final letter I sent was
nicer than the first. Yes. But I'm over

that now trying for 20 without
glasses ought to manage it
upturned cup
under my chest.

HOW THE WEATHER HELPS

learning too late
about   muscle
        and space

standing downwind
an unwashed
                        you know
want to
                        mm

drizzle

                                o.

cars.

TALKING

some talking so diffused
into its surroundings like dye
into a water system two miles
down the mountain all the rocks show up red.
When you decode it time actually
weighs but so indirect?
Curved lines no pain
lean into the punch all
ears
bright wavy hair.

3.45pm REP

half a voice
in the distance like a
rock reduced in noon sun-
light to a featureless dot
demands
phone buzzes 40%
if you go over £60 smell of
cigarettes I order two paper
backs   it's raining new car breakdown
I understand all this
but to let the time pass more quickly I
try not to speak

MORNING

buddleia roots riddle
brick mortar   jkt
on a window bar   blue
blossom   lane
full of pebbles   the
lamp stays on   the
air fills quietly
                    with rain.

CHANGE OF CLASS

must be
a decade
without
real emotion
excepting grizzle
only
small things
screw won't
turn
bus is
late

we're different now

shoes
ice yellow booze
no respect
pkt of
fags

OPPORTUNITIES

How many are
there? Half of them
gone   more. Like
anti-freeze weakened out through
an untight screw   a smudge, a
residue. A few things I like
but it's mostly habit   I wrote them out in
order once on a scrap of paper   put it
out for the milkman by mistake   wonder what
he made of

one pint only
bks
running
women
climbing
winning

not real enough anyway. I keep getting
this work ethic in the back of the
throat and have to clean things or
write them down   deadheaded
six roses   scratched the grease
out of the back of the bath   recased the guitar
Big Bill Broonzy didn't even play one
until he was 40. I think.

PIANO

piano   plinkaplonk   back of
the till   dot matrix blur
you can't read a book with a cone of
fast chips but they try sliding paperbacks
into wellingtons or just walking through
the door   you get
dogs   man on a bike once   light
sucks the red out of the spines until they
look the colour of raw crabmeat   lost three
copies of J.H. Prynne and sold none
best trade is a postcard with a picture of
a quiet sheep   dusk   sun ceases to
clone itself   weeds
a foot high at the wall edge
shall I run up the road
after the bearded man in the loose trousers or
shall I stay here and garden?
phone goes   turn the piano down.

DOING THINGS

Chances arrive in
sunlight unpacked slowly
like prunes from a wooden chest I
spent 30 mins in Greenberg's
trying on sunglasses   walked out
when they talked about gabble
and let me flounder fat woman
buying cords to keep the things
stuck to her ears. How important
is it anyway? I got
a face mask in the toy supermarket
checkout twelve no waiting put it
on outside where the flare-trousered winos
collapse among municipal ground
cover and fiddle with the
wrinkled black rubber clip
to adjust the tension. Stare
at the fast boy in his cool mirror
shades. Not the same.

DAY

got through this one with
blood at high
speed now you can hear the
heat outside sink everything maybe
earlier but my ears were
full   the centre of the city
so laced with noise tossed in like
the air was a bucket   metal
on wood   rattle of water   drowns
fire   burns metal
no rain for days
the lane like an empty river bed
it's the breath that pushes the
blood   hard to do it consciously
have to stop thinking
suck   blow
round it goes.

GUILT

These things roll down it no judge
ments about relative efficiency.   Do
we care enough to get up obviously
not easier to beat the
path clear for our own passage I
hear sirens heart attack somewhere
pain slow pain   too fast   if I
don't want to why is there an
obligation?   Habit or
guilt?   Can't say.   The wail again
back along dry streets   garbage shifting
must be guilt.

WATCHING

We all watch television clatter in
an arc by the window   half the
floor sprawled with newspaper THIS HOLIDAY
VIEWING GUIDE   squares of carpet
bent where the parquet is upset by
damp   shoe on its own sole
flapping   white dashes shower of
hyphens   rolling square to right
tiny barbers pole   keep talking
to each other heads semaphoring   half
of Lofty's fist pulling voice over
shouldn't this be
something we *need*?   The boys
fidget   I find
a bat under the cushion   magician   chalk
scratch on the lane door   ah but
it rains

THIS

Dust on the stylus. Sun back over the
rooftops silhouette like an advert.   She says
but you don't *do* anything   inside
waiting for the kids to come back from foot
balling   what would I hide?   You can't
pack it up you must face it.   Lawn rotary knocking
worm casts like a Gatling no steam, no
sweat   blue sky not a cloud anywhere
you get some trees grow right through what stops
them   scratch   but you're wrong I made this.

THE BEST GESTURE

He seems to think that his time
is overfull and that he needs to stop now and then.
But maybe this is just an excuse not
to do something else. It's not being lazy for its own sake
but a sign that he doesn't like
starting. It's a huge push, isn't it, getting
onto the bike in your waterproofs and with
all your bags and parcels strung around you.
When it goes it goes, it's starting. He slips
back a bit into whatever he did last
night or thought he did. So long as
he knows the names of everything around
him he's okay. There's a storm
coming up outside in the pattern of
storms. Colder, lots of litter up
in arbitrary spirals, increasing wind.
It's a hard time to get a grip onto anything especially
when it changes. Perhaps his best
gesture would be to start. But he won't do
that, will he, not yet.

RUNNING A READING

The street rucks up with raging
cars   slam   radios   next
door they thump cement from
a bucket   familiar
territory.   I ask the readers
if all this distracts   they answer slowly
like I was deaf   no.
Out of the window are huge, four
engined seagulls   diving.
I reckon starting 15 minutes a
crack   they all do 40
images like butter   blunt   heads
clogged with garble   fog   the last
piece is in numbered slabs
enormous   the audience
wills it   but it wont go
sways   like wool
unravelling   applause drifts
a cloud of slow mosquitoes.
I leave now   running   silence
ah silence   glorious   but when I get there
the pub is closed.

RAIN

In the straight, afternoon rain
off the roof in a jet of
white horses   I can hear
footsteps   no thunder
torrents   no slamming
            drumming

We'd be a lot richer,   wiser
if we realized this cleans nothing
like my mother said not soap
drops frozen in an
architecture of water
hugely dominant over light
oxidizing lateral infiltration all
that stored hardness taking these parts apart
to the rhythm of falling
and the impossible sound if you don't look
of the whole thing burning

What was the shape of this
before you were born? And the voice?
The only difference is bend of the camber
and shape of the tile, glass sheets
like wet mirrors, grass scratching the surface
brown seed heads like flags.

The alley is a lake of sky changing
silt in a washed ridge   garbage
in the drain grid soak away
even the air thickens. Pool stretches out like an arm
full of wading birds. Green image of cloud shape
rucked drizzle. The sun is never anywhere
and there is always wind.

MORE

shadow parallelogram
russet fissures
hoarse laughter starter motor

you get echoes around here
from a decade back still going

kick it

    oil
    water
    efflorescence salts

boom

building like a soundbox

no sign of rain

LETTER

We apologise   no credit
on behalf of delay in
(copy) two copies
screen copy
ledger
trade manager will issue a
rectify but remaining on your account.
May I take this opportunity
of wishing you the compliments of the season.

NON-UNIONIZED LABOUR

flaked lintel
hum
of feet on the
steps
arm out   would of
had
had have had
viscose white cylinder
keep the ink off

not this time though
reaching up with a brush

REAL

drill clanking

roar of skin on water

I try
I
I sleep without dreaming
two seconds lost out of every five

up

man crying like a child
the air flickering

NEW WRITING

Ah
I can do this.

a line here
a line there

I does it a lot
I does

So far it's hard to tell
but can you manage:

ear   here   year

?

Ought to prove it,
one way or another.

DRY DAYS

you start
by listening

nothing close

pulse 56
legs are yours

cirrus sky outside
a sign

then
then the phone goes

OLDER

these telegrams
are matters of urgency

great rivals dying off

fog

city clothes mark you
in the country it doesn't matter
can show up in
brown paper and string if you want to

rains

I suppose it passes the time.

POULTICE

rag pad of kaolin
hot tub
thumb like a peg

it's a glove
don't suck it
show it

it throbs
size of rocks
you want one?

red
ripple

stone

WINTER

plumbing stiff
with thick water

boots on blunt grass

gloves, coat, scarf

no precision possible except vision

behind a tree I take a leak
hand frozen
empty branches full of steam

FIVE VIEWS OF WALES

Bard

rippled drum
green grave
acorned sand
numberless tongue
windfall light
faithless sleep
luminous cathedrals
looking land
greensward lake
greenwood keep

Vicar

dark peat
far lakes
empty farms
waste speech
poor holding
bare walls
ruined orchard
thin grass
mountain parish
lean rib

Mender

coated macadam
odd scraps
joint filler
draw-ins
puddled grit
walkovers
slot pipe
empty glass
vivid strikes

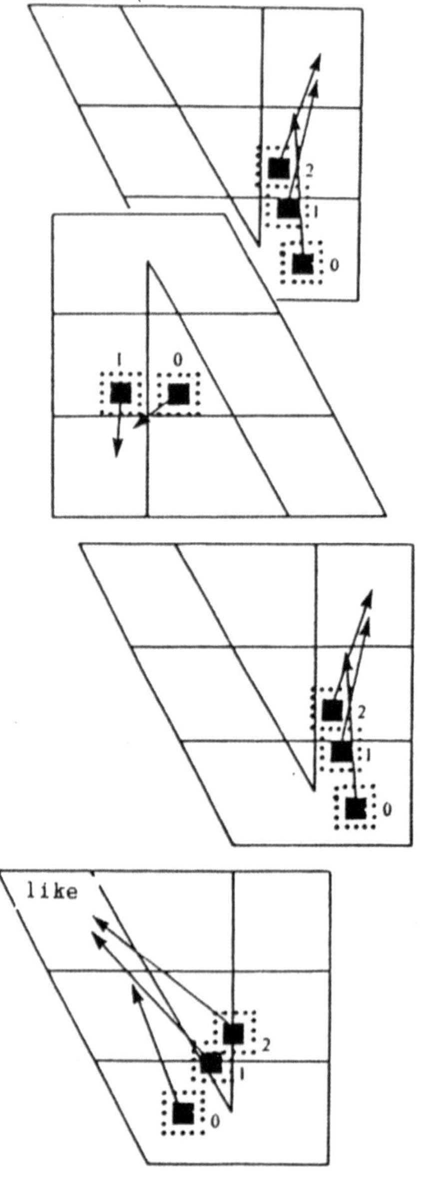
2
1
0
1
0
2
1
0
like
2
1
0

Mine

shit grass
tar rock
saturated
pale water
20% unrefined
felinfoel
mouth
silence
endless gabble
daffs and leaks

MUSIC

1.

I asked a lot about it
Did it?
Would it mount up?
Could I translate it?
I thought of it like batteries you could recharge.
Hear another
fills up.
Everyone did it.
Air in the lungs.
You picked your own if
there were problems. Streak it.
make it. If you couldn't you hummed.

2.

The ease with which some
had pieces of skin formed.
The breath cut-off.
The information at the beginning.
The distortion of space, the
bending of clarity into an
stubborn fit.
The regular clang not the smooth.
The loop. The scratch.
The ecstasy.

3.

Rain.
Sun warp.
Hot water ashtray.
Two storey controlled descent.
Sat on. Shards.
Like a tooth necklace.

4.

To get the echo here
we had the door at the
rear open and the sound
going down two flights before
bouncing back up.
It was like singing in
a changing room.

5.

love home cruel home christmas
twist Sunday date sea
teen-angel new orleans man love
dance young summer love ding-a
-ling apache love world poetry exodus
heart tonight love kangaroo
north love alaska night devil
angel walk run baby midnight
boogie boll weevil stranger shore
love twist quarter river
jack pony love romeo rebound
mountain love sue stomp heart
tonight twist tonight twist
tonight twist tonight twist
tonight

we could do this
we could do this again and again
speaker leads, philips plugs
bolt shaking
spray of desire
put my hand in down there
when it's warm

paper wonderful teen new old
true love itsy bitsy teenie
weenie yellow banjo handy handy good
wonderful sweet sentimental wooden

runnin'   lonely   rubber
babysittin'   moody   mint   cruel
bad   peppermint   runaround.
right   tonight   tonight   tonight
yes   tonight

hum what you can remember
tap your steel comb on the fireguard
to fill in the rest

stomp boogie   please   woogie
twist mr postman   twist

6.

Christened Ernest Evans he derived the stage name Chubby Checker from that of pianist and hit maker Fats Domino. No 1 in USA, 18 weeks in the bestsellers list 1960 and again in 1962 making a record stay of 36 weeks in all. Rhythm-and-blues vocalist Rockin' Little Angel Judd born in Paducah, Kentucky, learned to play the guitar while at high school prior to entering show business. Johnny was an engineering draughtsman. Joe appeared at record hops, he writes his own arrangements. While at school he took lessons on the trumpet and became very proficient. He wrote his first song at the age of 14 and also learned to play five instruments. He sang in backgrounds on other artists' discs after persistently asking record companies for a test. He plays a ukulele as well as singing. He has a back pocket full of spare strings. He has a lonely room. He can do the watusi. In 1960 he bought a mojo from a hustler and has never looked back.

overnite I was layin down
I heard moma n popa talkin
I heard popa tell moma
let that boy boogie woogie

it's in him
an it gotta come out.
An I felt so good
went on an boogie just the same.

He's a rock and roll cowboy
with jumping beans inside his jeans.

7.

The legends and excuses.
Flat matchwood
trucked   warped
No way the fingerboard.
Blew a suck it. Bottle end. Slide it.
Shout and yodel.
Cheap excesses.
Three day non stop dances
How long can you shout without a microphone?
How many people can sit on a?
How much sweat when?
Who gains if you?
How can the?
Whose pocket do you?
How fast will the?
How much can?
How often will?
How much will?
How often can?
how much   how often
how often   how often
how many   how much
how can   how much
how often   how can
can can   often often
this is the way to do it
this is the way to do it
once you're there it rolls
who cares about how it sounds.

JOURNAL

July 87: I've got the fan spinning and above
its noise you can hear planes
echoing because of the lack of cloud. In the
lane they're unloading beer crates and
you can make out the voices of the workmen
but not precisely what they say. As part of the
great way none of this is really important I suppose
but it's a direction; the problem
is the weight of past experience
brimming up around me in a muscular froth.
There is a sound of someone lashing
metal with a bamboo stake and in
the distance a freight train clattering.
The choices are enormous. I've yet to decide.
I listen to them all.

Ultimately the shi syndrome has to be eased
and this is done by simply forgetting. The entire
library falls apart after 10 years anyway
pages brown   cracking sounds as you
open the covers. The knowledge just stops dead;
doesn't pass on.

Inside the spinning are at least
three smaller sounds:
          electric hum,
          air movement,
          mechanical vibration
and that last itself made of
bits. I try to quieten it all by
balancing the device on a soft
surface. I hold the fan up on the palm of my
hand like you do with an indoor tv aerial
when the picture fails and with as much success.
The air goes up and across the ceiling
and the lightshade sways.

Memory
a gap in the index between
Melancholy   and
Meridians
faded out like red wallpaper   turned pink
each event pared into tight images
told to friends   scratched in notebooks
shaky photographs   hair clippings
bits of cloth   marks of heads on walls.

Entry for 6 June, 1967: Warm. Smell of joss sticks, people waving sparklers, things that flash and glow in the dark. At the Roundhouse Arthur Brown and his Famous Flames, rear doors to the railway open, winos up from the tracks, the iron distance running of behind them into the night. Arthur Brown has his hat on fire and these red-faced failures are cheering. For a time it seems like the decadereally works.

When Kerouac died nobody told me, why should they, if they put it on the news I didn't hear. Nobody broadcast it in *Boots* record dept like they did when Elvis went. No fans clustered shaking their heads over *RCA* record sleeves. *Pan Books* didn't bother, just let him carry on, fading out of print, slipping off into the past. I found out about it in casual conversation months later and didn't want to believe. It was hot. Memory exaggerates. It was warm.

There is balance in everything. The tennis ball bounces in smaller arcs ever smaller until movement becomes a slow roll and the yellow rubber slides under the leaves at the edge of the grass. Friction ceases. The players hunt but don't find it. They may open a new tube and restart but essentially it's still the same game.

Gate of the spirit
Great shrine
Inner gateway
Complete bone
Wind screen
Storehouse of earth
Cash of the jaws

Bright eyes
Four whites
Fragrant meeting
Lesser marsh
Big monument
Sustaining centre
Axis of heaven
Central pole
Bubbling spring
Vessel of conception
Centre of man

Q: Which is the most important?
A: Breath

breath everytime

In the car park there is grass up through the tarmac. A stout ryegrass looping over where it's been sprayed but still not quite dead. I must have been here thousands of times in 13 years but I leave no trace. If I try maybe I can encode something in written imagery, *like this*, but the significance is little. Who else has moved through this matrix? Why do I need to know?

The street repeats itself each year, subtle changes like a blue sky crossed by cloud always moving ever different always the same. Stringer is done up like a Native American scout, feathers, beads, leather boots, for 10p he'll paint your face how he thinks real Native Americans do.

It makes more money than writing. I smile at him but he can't remember me. It's been 20 years anyway since he was last here with his Burroughs-like obsession with guns and his belief that poetry would change the world. I can't be bothered to explain what's happened in all the time that lies between us. That early boldness all turned to failure. He takes a coin and starts on a fresh customer. I walk away.

Perhaps this takes the soul of it
writing it down

I fill my lungs to maximum capacity
sucking in air until my diaphragm
sinks and that pulse of charged
tension makes itself felt

this is the way without thought
but not without knowledge

I cannot bear the idea of a great emptiness
I fear vacuity

I stand next to the fan
and listen to the air mingle with the whirling. It's there.
This way I know I'm still safe.

ISLAND

You are at the edge of a square lake. In the centre is a square island. You have three planks of wood, none of which are quite long enough to reach fully from shore to shore. How do you get across?

1. Description of the top of the brain as a dried peat bog or cutaway section across a volcano showing fault lines. There is pain somewhere off below it, result of stress or more likely of drink. Usually this takes a good 18 hours to filter up.

2. Contraction of the above sent to a famous poetry magazine and returned with a note saying they understood, the editor had been in a similar situation many times himself and the line about "the hangover like a fog of frozen rain" seemed to pin-point it. The note stopped then as if there should have been another sentence saying "we've taken a xerox and will use it in our next issue". Even held the thing up to the light to see if their typer had gone on with its ribbon slipped. Tried floating a plank and then standing on it. Didn't work.

3. Clark Coolidge *Solution Passage* has it "Where the wires cross the street / the lacing of a shoe / eye meets middle / and the gulls gel" which isn't a jumping point. Well known poet I once knew would have revamped this under his own name, did this often, continued even after being caught out for reassembling John Clare into contemporary Anglo-Welsh verse patterns. Why should he worry so long as it was only one or two that found out.

He hadn't discovered cut-up or collage. I suppose being modern they didn't appeal but they've been a boon to a large range of young bucks keen to cut the avant garde with a bit of swagger and no talent. In the end it is stamina that pays. Just thinking about levitation is never good enough on its own. You have to go out there and do it.

4. Mark Rothko 1903-1970. From this time (1940) one senses that the artist is no longer leading his art but following it. People spend much more time with the dark canvases than any others looking vainly I suppose for a glimpse of light. This is religion. Rothko had no time for planks.

5. There are obvious parallels here with the exorcism argument. Difficulty makes the whole operation a private activity. I sit adjusting this flux of structures, patterning what I have into some kind of permanence simply in order to hold it, stop it from slipping back into the maw of dream. You could argue that this was an indulgence on my part and having accused others of the same thing I must agree that it could be right.

6. Difficulty worries me only when I consider that I have to eventually do something with it.

7. Fan clouding bird-song, neither are complicated.

8. Hide the planks in the undergrowth. Stand well back before running. there is no possibility of failure. The leap and the destination are the same thing. Go.

9. Get there.

10. If you are wet you are thinking and not doing. Try again.

THE CHENG MAN CH'ING VARIATIONS

Cheng Man Ch'ing coming home down the alleyways. Walking. One foot in front of the other. All the weight swinging across his legs like water. Left thigh right thigh no sound. You'd expect bubbles. But nothing. One foot in front of the other. Cheng Man Ch'ing putting his foot down like he wasn't putting it anywhere other than where it was. Down. Positive. Intended. Positive intention. Head clear. Stillness after rain. All the aches and age settled. For now. Following the breath in and then out. Silence like darkness. Darkness like silence. head up. Top of the spine. Walking home.

Cheng Man Ch'ing is a big man. For his race. But no one would mention that in liberal Britain in a back lane and Man Ching walking home feet shoulder width apart getting them down onto the grit and ruined tarmac without making a sound. Someone had asked him once what would you do if you moved forward in the form and put your foot down on a twig or a stone. How would you go on? He had thought for a minute and said, softly, move the foot a bit. Simple. There was a grimacing. The answer had not gone down well. The moves were fixed, the form western immutable. But Cheng Man Ch'ing was Cheng Man Ch'ing, his own Cheng Man Ch'ing man.

In the dark Cheng Man Ch'ing looks like a burglar. Soft footed so smooth. Silent. But there is nothing in his arms, in his hands. They arrested him once for suspicion, Chinese in back-lane, full of air and strength and slow slow might. Went nowhere. Cheng Man Ch'ing smiling like Buddha, full of patience and spirit and light. He was no spectral being nothing vague he was real. You could touch if he'd give up yielding like the wind like thick water. He never did. Palpable peace. Next moment. This moment. Last moment. Touch it. No room for doubt.

In his back pocket he kept a Yang family tree. Huge thing like a heating duct plan for an office block. Given to him by a Californian or an Australian. Forgot which. If you read it back he seemed to be descended directly from the First Patriarch. With paper you could prove whatever you wanted.

Cheng Man Ch'ing a measurable risk
Colours fast
No Preservatives
Operable at Altitudes
Subject to variations within batch
    but batch itself secure.
Sample in catalogue merely a guide
    using available printer's inks.
EU patent possible.
Do not use abrasives.
Protected under international convention.
Replica buried in sand under
Salt Lake City by way of insurance.

They got him back to the station and put him in the interview room with the Formica table and asked him about the thefts saying they'd seen him on the 9th floor using his Chinese sleight of hand to open triple-barred doors things had gone white in his eyes. He'd come to standing on the table like a golden cockerel or a tiger something the room empty. All fled. The charge was assaulting the police. He used the unbendable arm to get out.

Man Ch'ing could take his liver out. Self-surgery. Hands in among the sinews knowing just where to go. He wrote it up as an article for *Combat* magazine but they didn't pay him and the following month there were a whole float of letters published from doubters who suggested that he was a fraud and a faker. Why didn't he take on an 8th Dan karate, bandages round his fist like first aid. He could not bother be bothered he was bothered. Cheng Man Ch'ing iron in the silk and him up off the floor vanished. Into the wall plaster. Gone.

Cheng Man Ch'ing Yang Master Spirited Away.
Chinese Man Reduces Molecules To The Consistency of Damp Mist.
Tai Chi Teacher Uses Conjuring Trick At Contest.
Eastern Mystic Hypnotizes Audience.
Mass Hysteria Sweeps Country.
Unexplained Disappearance Baffles Doctors.
Boffins Beaten By Oriental In Balloon Trousers.

Man Ch'ing trying to laugh with a mouth full of mortar.

Cheng Man Ch'ing up the park to watch the
ducks move with elegance   without thought
like he can
sometimes   sometimes
but like he always should

All Man Ching had to do was

he could just

he concentrated he was able to

he looked then

his eyes didn't ever

he could he could

he did

sometimes

no one ever

he was asked by many

times he was always

he did did

arms just like

no arms

he could do this this

he did not even have

to be there

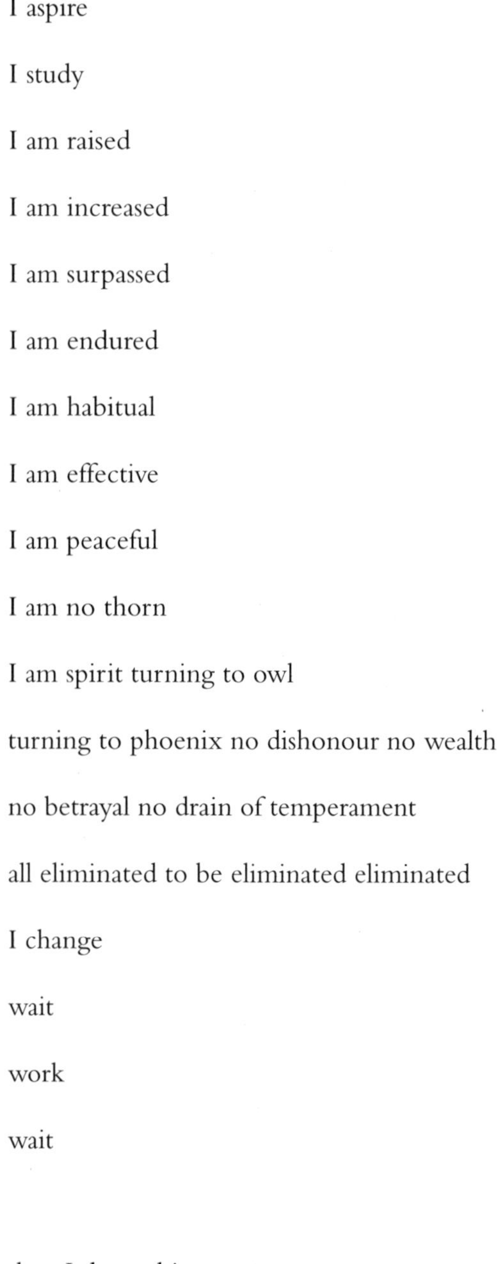

OF HIMSELF

I aspire

I study

I am raised

I am increased

I am surpassed

I am endured

I am habitual

I am effective

I am peaceful

I am no thorn

I am spirit turning to owl

turning to phoenix no dishonour no wealth

no betrayal no drain of temperament

all eliminated to be eliminated eliminated

I change

wait

work

wait

then I do nothing

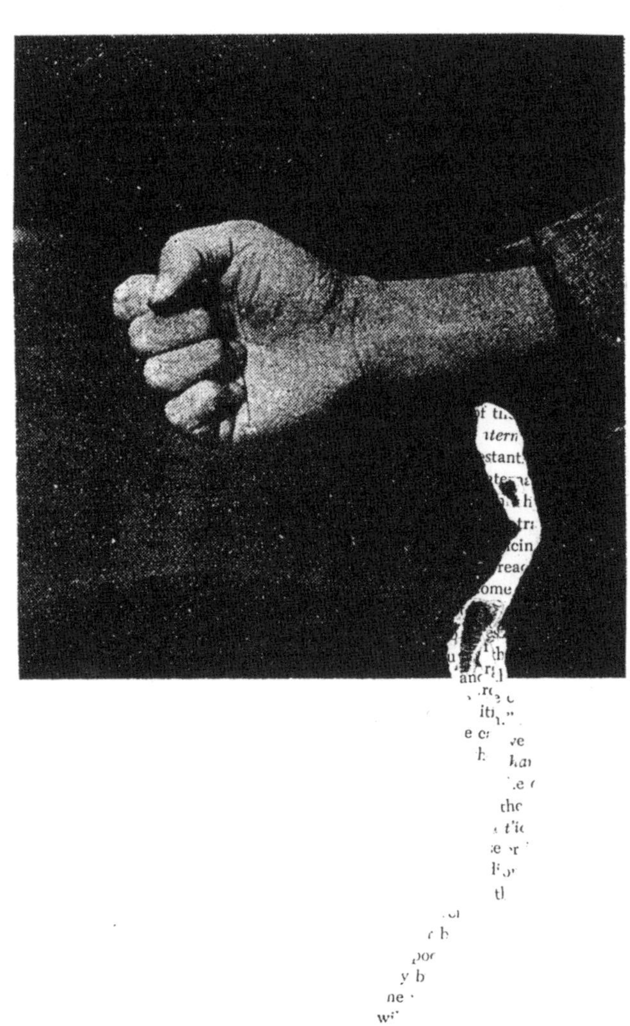

BREATH

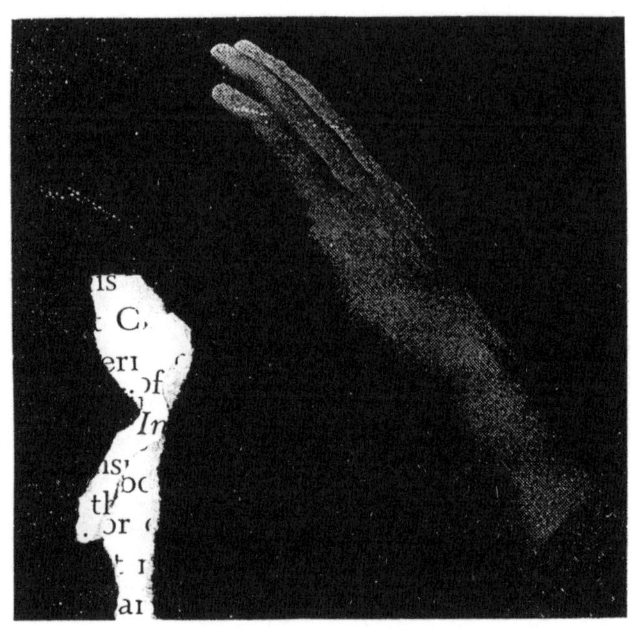

HEARTT

CHENG MAN CH'ING'S BREATHING PATTERNS

chi chow chi chew cha

cha chi chip chew cho

chi chi chow che chow

chis chi chee chol chi

chough chough chi chough chough

chi chill choll chee choller

chip char chool choller

chee chip chowl chewling

chee chip chipping chi cha

chop chi chop chi chut

chi choller chwiller chinging

chowler chiller chingy chill

cha chi ch chowl

chi chi chi chi

chi chi chi chrip

chi chrop chi chrarp

chi chi chi chi

ch chi chi chi

SINKING INTO THE TAN TIEN

THE GURU POSTURE

the slow single whip
the squatting single whip
the strong single whip
the full single whip
the held single whip
the pointing single whip
the single whip with arrows and turns
the dots in the photograph
the memory   the description
the single whip full of tensions
the centred
the shaking single whip
the single whip heard about but not this one
the awful single whip awful
what next nothing next
the whip the single whip
the single whip which strikes
the single whip which brings water to the eyes
the flowed, uprooted single whip
the single whip impossibly pointed
the endlessness   the fragility
the single whip circled
the speed   the silence   the stillness
the rooted
the single whip which fades, sinking
it is
it is
it is
then it is not
the single whip emptying
the single whip filling

ART

What brightens their eyes?
fame, money, applause.
Cheng Man Ch'ing is not interested in these
his eyes do not attach
why should   ny
                        f
                                is stuff
                    ch   p
                              p
        art   is   t   art
              is   t
isn   n   art
                                                t
he is concerned with concerning this
concerning. he is all breath
sometimes a rush of air
what does he need to   he needs to
doing   no   not doing
becoming.   he is the diamond sutra
without thinking.   motes from his skin
Cheng Man Ch'ing flaking
through time   his eyes out of focus gleaming
he is at the one point

we are out her in our
bones chairs   knots of sinew

we are full of art
he is empty

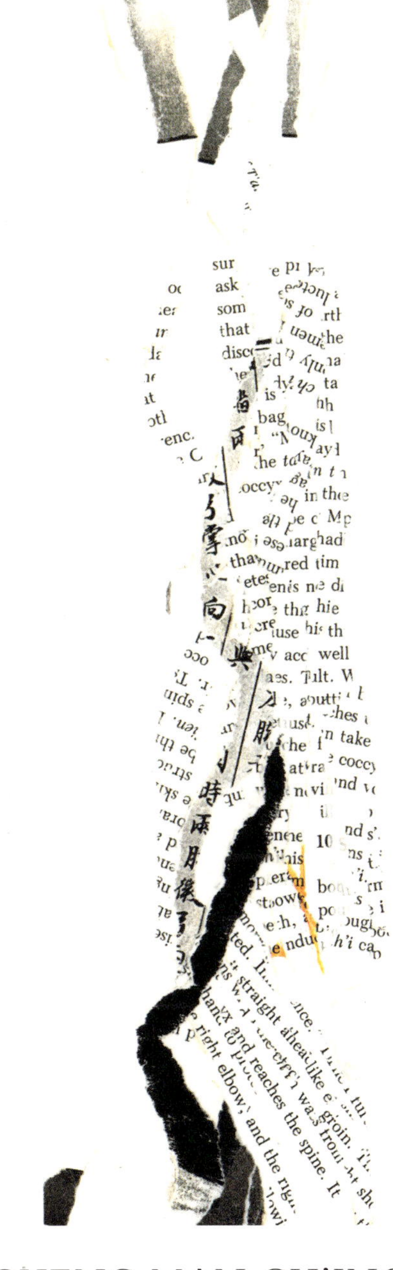

CHENG MAN CH'ING'S UNBENDABLE ARM

THE SEVEN ORAL SECRETS

1.
Sink like a boat.
do not float the ligaments.
loose bones rattle.

2.

sawing	pushing	pressing	pushing
sawing	forcing	equalling	actioning
smoothing	trying	changing	forcing
sawing	binding	binding	sawing
forcing	drawing	pushing	sawing
smoothing	meaning	pushing	giving
following	following	learning	yielding
moving	moving	referring	using
forcing	pushing	obviating	attacking
pulling	backing	using	pulling
precluding	pushing	pulling	sawing
practising	moving	moving	comprehending

3.
sweat is valuable/not valuable/
sign form if possible

4.
chi champion challenger chipper
chieftain charming chaplain
chariot chary charity
charlatan choking chrysanthemum
chi chummy chunterer chuckling

chilli   chopchop   cholesterol
chuttering   chutzpah   chutney
chattle   chittle   chottle
chipolino   circumspect   circumstance
chasing   chi   chowling
chiproarer   chi   chillflouder   cauliflower
chonundrum   chestexpander   chilblains
chirographic   choreographer
chi blood   chi breath
'all light we will become,
be gathered'.

5.
one stream flowing
sub
insub
insub wquib sublib possibilities:

7.
keep it warm.

Big crowd. Cheng Man Ch'ing in his huge Chinese trousers room for four legs and multiple genitalia. Available nowhere made by his old mother in Hopei Province. The black leaching out slowly as the material thinned. Dye in water. Smoke. His legs full of cat's strength but big. All the class looking expectantly as Cheng Man Ch'ing explains that all this and this is not really anything. If you travel far enough it stops having substance becomes nothing becomes something. This. Simple. You'll learn. They all nod. He nods. They smile. This. He lifts up his arm. There is hush. This this is an arm, this is, he says. This.

blood

Poems For Ghosts – 1991

WINNERS

These people are always the ones in front.
They are taller than you they wear hats or have
huge high-rise hair-dos like little Richard.
They are wide. Their shoulder pads are bad news.
They stretch out sideways blocking all avenues of sight.
You glimpse daylight through moving armpits
and in the gap between thighs. It's tough.
They step back into you talking
swelling enormously as they come.
What you thought was a wrist waving
becomes a backside of wallet pockets
turning through ninety without looking.
You ask for credentials but they'll
have been there anyway or owned one
or done it before or had their poems published in the New Yorker,
and even if you can get to grips with the
counter edge by having a long reach they
will have ways of drowning you.
Their voices will swell delivering jokes at full throttle
spraying spittle like lawn sprinklers
hands out, windmilling,
and the whole head of the queue contact
will be reduced to memory.
Everyone talking, scribbling, phoning,
putting in bids, flashing calculators, waving,
and you, gripping your fists white,
will wonder if you are invisible.
Pinch, punch,
and you are.
No other explanation.

HOUSE PAINTING

Painted a wall this spring. A Sunday. White.
Watched by the Patels out
deck-chaired on their new patio.
Not a scrap of sun between us. Heavy cloud.
Half-done the rain comes, flushes the
colour in a pastel fog across the flags.
I drip before re-emerging brick
thinking how hard it is
to change anything for long.
Around me the neighbourhood rusts and tilts
like a beached liner. The decks buckle,
the funnels are full of grass.
The Patels have put up a sea-side umbrella
and are eating things on sticks.
We're there. This is the future.
I wet the brush,
try again.

ROOFER

It is a day
when it rains from
when I wake
to when I stop.
The lane is like gloss artex,
the gutter full of glass,
our down-pipe swan-neck rusted,
gushing like a bust cod piece.
The noise amazes me,
dogs diving through shale,
men with sticks.
The tar fix to repair
the flat roof fails as I watch it.
Black sludge everywhere,
nothing sticks.
I ring the roofer,
cash in hand for a quick job,
no cheques.
His line is busy, engaged,
no answer, redial,
busy, dial, engaged.
Then there's a voice, crackling,
just like him.
I'm sorry, it says,
sounding furtive,
but I don't work here
and the roofer's not in.

RE-GARDENING

I'm not a gardener   gave it up
when we bought this house with a
patch about the size of a bathroom
not big enough for beans   I whine at
the ground thistle with a strimmer
but hardly touch it   the grass tight like a mat.
Catch a rat with a quarter brick
surfaced after 60 years of drainage
fence brown with creosote   rain
beaded   top soil so dark you'd
never believe this was immutable clay.
There is a smell to warm earth
I thought I'd forgotten but it passes.
Green scrub scraped into a bonfire
neighbours shouting   a radio playing
through it like a ship in fog.
Tomorrow the slabs come
then there'll be peace.

3 am

Startled by a crash
I wake up sweating,
thrash, condensation
as much on me as on the window.
I wipe it off in a circular motion with
the edge of the curtain like I'd told
the kids not to and look out into the
black at the empty frost.
Maybe it was the fat boy from the
flat across the back shooting his airgun
from the fire-escape and hitting
or a house collapsing
like the one last winter two streets away
where the owner had knocked out all the floors
and the ice got in like water.
In the dark I can't see.
Isn't the steelworks or the shunting yard
          closed
or the docks
          empty.
When I pull it back
from the maw of dissolving
memory it sounds
like a phantom;
ghost ships loading,
steam in the power lines,
trains arriving:
what else?
Hinkley Point is 18 miles off across the Channel.
It said 15 in last night's paper.
It's getting closer.

WE CAN SAY THAT

We speak the language. No.
We understand it. We say that.
The bricks of our houses
are thick with it.
We know all the songs
and the place names.
It's not foreign.
We flaunt our origin
in the big city where most don't
know iaith y nefoedd
from Urdu.
We do.
Heol y Frenhines it says
and we can say that.
We are native.
We have status.
Cenedl heb iaith cenedl heb galon
until we have to handle it
in Penrhyndeudraeth or Pwllelli
where, using English slyly,
we say that we're glad it isn't dead.

OUT AT THE EDGE

Pembrokeshire Coast Path in winter

The wind comes in off the sea at Nolton
filling the Mariner's car park with sand.
There are no cars.
At the tide edge a lone tripper throws
pebbles through the drizzle.
I watch, dripping, with two ducks
and a chicken,
from the bottom of a barren hedge.
When I climb the track
towards Druidstone I leave bootmarks
like fossils in the fluid mud.
Why do it?
Beauty, light, passion.
Who knows.
I get the feeling that if there
is an edge to this world then it is here.
From the headland I stare out at America
but don't see it.
Mist, distance, earth's curvature,
or maybe it just isn't there.

MOUNTAINS: SHEEP

I am halfway to the summit
and it starts to rain.
I am surrounded by sheep.
Behind me like bunting
strung over the fences
of five counties
are parts of their fleece.

Amid this wool, grease, suint,
urine, dung, burs, seeds, twigs,
sand, soil, dip and salve
are the bones of their faces
impassively arrayed.

You can talk to them and
they'll answer. I once held
a flock with Schwitters'
Ursonata. Recognising
quality they stayed.

They outnumber us.
Standing shank to shank
they would fill Zanzibar,
and still leave
the hills unscathed.

At the top where they cluster
the rain is a tight grey.
The outcrops run with graffiti
genitalia enormously displayed

In the sheep this raises
no passion. While I seethe
they stand and shit.
When I go
they stay.

STREET SOUNDS

How it used to be.

You see them in small groups in the precinct
cradling their aluminium boxes
like babies

Thin arses, moustaches like tea stains, denim.

Some of their friends have been engulfed by
ninja stars
but not these.

This is the way a generation
labels itself.
Arrogance like wing-mirrors,
heads like slate.

Eveready U2s. 8 hours.
In the rain you play it
in a Tesco carrier.

Statement complete.

HUNTING WHITAKERS FOR THE ANSWER TO POETRY

How To Be A Gifted Parent
How To Be Born Again
How To Be Decadent
How To Be Poor
How To Be Top
How To Be Your Cat's Best Friend
How To Boil An Egg
How To Beat Fatigue
How To Buy A New PC
How To Catch Tiddlers
How To Cheat At Cooking
How To Cope With Insomnia
How To Do Things With Words
How To Draw
How To Drive Yourself Wild In Bed
How To Flatten Your Stomach
            Get Out Of The Bath
            Get Pregnant
How To get Rid Of Your Double Chin
How To Lie With Statistics
            Live With Working Strife
How To restore And Repair Practically Anything
How To Save Your Life
How To Seduce Anybody In The Zodiac
            Shoot An Amateur
            Solve Chemistry Problems
            Stop A Train With One Finger
How To Stop The Phone Ringing
            Dominate Your Readers
            Drown In A Saucer Of Water
            Succeed Every Time
How To Appear In *Poetry Wales*
How To Store Great Speeches In Bottles
            Echo Death

Ride Boxcars
Meditate, Mix, Mould
Repeat
Use Voice As A Device
Disintegrate, Reiterate
Cock An Ear To The Ground
How To Vibrate, Rotate, Levitate
Understand 246 Different Words For Rain
Know 300 Sheep By Their Skull Shape
How To Use Your Tongue Like A Plane

Brmm Brmm
It's easy

How To Be Like Gunn
Clampitt
Larkin
Motion
Kinnell
How To Be Like Raine
How To Sound Like Hughes
Deal With Death
Write Like Plath
Drink Like Tripp
How To Jump Like Hart Crane
What you do is you
steal from those no longer with us,
change bits so
it doesn't sound the same.
Sit in your room and
work out why the past has little
to teach you.
What you do know
you don't understand anyway.
Do you know about fog?
Poetry is best in fog.
Mis-spell, shuffle, sweat.
Turn on the typer
open up a vein.

POLLOCK SPEAKS

My painting does not come from the easel
modern art to me is nothing
new needs new.

I am not aware of what I am doing.

I think:
two coats 'Rivit' glue, Duco black industrial enamel,
John Boyle commercial duck, basting syringes,
sticks, dense webs, skeins.
I have no fears of making changes
I'm free to move.
Most of the paint I use is liquid.
I suppose that's generally what I mean.
You see I do have a notion of what
        the results will be.

Do I care?

Painting is a state of being.

Why should I say more.

AVANT GARDE

The avant garde is finished.
The revolutions are no longer exciting.
No one boards themselves up in the coffee shop
to print manifestoes anymore.
The revolutionaries get on the bus like the rest of us.
Upstairs they are all there:
men who have sliced their faces flat shaving,
women with holes in their bellies,
moustachioed furniture, shopping trollies,
tail thin creatures with bones
like pipe-cleaners, old ladies
wearing overcoats filled with bricks.
They get off at the station
and forage in the rubbish bins.
Some of them drink.
They are just not up to facing
our huge sophistication.
"We must sack the museums
and shake the administrators
in their shoes," they say.
But we are bored with this we don't listen
Our wallpaper is avant garde enough
this is the modernist way.

DRIBBLE CREEPS

lollard – an uneducated dissenter with a tendency to mumble

There are three skinheads in the furniture department
trying to shop-lift a bed.
It won't fit in the lift.
This is for the middle-class and full.
Already a member has fainted
confronted with swearing, tattooed sweat.

No one is sure anyway that these charmers
should not do what they do.
Only the floor manager,
cowering in the demonstration kitchen
knows what will happen next.

The trio traverse his terrain
trailing an upended Slumberland
which bangs the lights
and cracks the fire-door architrave.

Trembling, he tries the phone
but gets no answer.
Security are chatting to friends,
the line is engaged.

On the escalator shoppers assume the lollards
to be larking employees. Their garb is in keeping.
There is no argument.
The posture springs bounce through perfumery.
This is free country.
Two women wearing designer face cream
shake their heads.

Is not every juvenile delinquent the
evidence of a family in which the
family bond is weakened and loosened?
Is not every dishonest apprentice an
evidence of the same; every ruined

female, every ruined youth, the infinite
numbers of unruly and criminal people who
now swarm on the surface of this great
kingdom; and inundate the streets of
these great cities and double-park
their vehicles with lights flashing as
if this gave them permission. Are
not these hoards on bicycles who
never stop at red lights, these can kickers,
spitters, hooligan rampagers, skate boarders,
screamers, these riff-raff who
knock unasked on doors, pathetically
enquiring if you want your windows double-glazed.

Are not these the evidence we need?

The bed is left smashed and unslept in
at the end of the fruit market.
At night it is target for junior Rimbauds
launching Astra skyrockets through drain-pipes.
When it catches fire the yobs piss on it.
The manager calls this shrinkage.
It is an accountancy term.

ell preperte es theft
ill priporti is thift
oll proporto os thoft
ull prupurtu us thuft
all praparta as tha
prip op prapap
prapap pop pop
preee
keep peep eep eep
prefot pre fat rop
rop rop
rop rop
rop rop
rop
profit drive
drum
m drum
drum drum
dribble creeps

KIPPER ON THE LIPS

O Cod,
I feel a right prawn.
Try to kipper outside the cinema.
Obviously the wrong plaice.
Welcoming bream turns into a foul mackerel,
next minnow she's slapping my face.
I'm amazed.
What a dolphin to do.
Have I got halibutosis? A stickle back?
Squid in my trousers? No way.
I'm just a flash haddock after her turbots.
Look at this conger eel, I say.
But she's into big bivalves
and long-distance gurnards,
so I flounder,
What a elver time to distrust
your encrustation.
The sea trout's out, I'm a failure.
She goes off with a sperm whale.
I light up a bloater.

HARRISON

John Harkman Katherine MacInstant
Hold Harpic
MacThrotle
MacWither
MacWhittle
MacWinner
Join John Harry holding highly hippy
Mickle
Mockle
MacThirsty
MacDribble, dozens of times,
MacDowner upbottomed Macthroatfiller
waver weaver
MacAndrews
Jolly Johnny Jilly out the window
couldn't possibly
under the macircumstances
Highly hilly bun runner Macstopit
MacFickle impossible fiddle
MacStrictly steady
sticky
sweet
Might as well mould
old hirsute Harry
MacStrongly whipple wodge
Horrendously happy MacDonger
Architrave Roger Amstrad
MacReprint roll out
MacRepaint Liverpool pull
the bits off
Big envelope
great shining MacFrenzy
huge hanging harpy
MacGlobal glossy gargantuan
MacSunny Penguin
Macnovelbigcheque
Nobel Harri Mickmock
lostsa sunny mucker
teeth teeth

headed fivers
6 pints of correcting fluid
crate of Mackeson.

DEAD END

At the bottom of the cupboard a cake tin
decorated with a print of an embroidered horse.
Inside an unused diary for '72,
a tin of snuff, cigarette lighters,
golfball, a trick ring, flints,
an opened packet of mignonette seeds
with a trace of mud along the top.

The seeds went into a plot I'd cleared.
No idea about horticulture, Cut the old tea roses
down with a hacksaw, left the roots in.
Brown clay like a building site,
all hoof prints, rucks and cracks.
The dead cat came half back up
it's black head knocked sideways by a
neighbour backing his car;
too much beer. Never said.
The owners suspected me, the infidel.
Accusations and weeping around the doorway got us nowhere.
They thought television a weapon of the devil,
refused me permission to staple my aerial co-axial
across their window-frame. They imagined
this way they could make me pure,
Jesus, all I did was chuck their
tracts back at them. Nothing more.

I threw the mignonettes into dips scooped
in the orange hardtop with a dessert spoon.
No concept of germination or knowledge of how
deep these things ought to lay. Leave it to chance,
hope for rain. Sat on the step with a flagon of
homebrew, task done, stared at the fence
and the bushes and the sky beyond.
Art is not stealth;
it leaps out at you.
Too much Whitman and Blake
makes you blind.

No one had cleared the yard
in living memory.
Ragwort sprouting through
cracked tarmac,
bramble,
ivy tangled through garbage
pink campion in a rolling haze.

Reasons for drinking:

a) art
b) oblivion

Can't improve it.

Pulled up a plant, threw it back.

Went into the flat and lay on the settee.
Looked at the message written on
the wallpaper above the firegrate:
"Thanks for the drink, love JT."
A poet who could do it.
When I complained he said
scrape it off and sell it.

Dead now. Message painted out.
Surplus seeds back in the packet,
lid on top.

The past is all echo,
stop listening.

Never saw any flowers,
nothing came up.

LITTLE MAG

Spend three hours
addressing envelopes.
Bic exhausted.
Towards the finish
the hand finds itself
totally unable to complete
the tight circle of a letter o.

The mags go out like ack-ack.

In exchange I get misprints
highlighted, protest, left tôpher
off his name, no comma, word missing,
poems, two renewals, one cancellation,
a shaky essay on the work
of someone I've never heard of,
a pair of sandals, a dead fish.

At the post office I have a
deal where they stick the stamps
on and I pay.
"Too much bad language,"
says the supervisor with a hat
speaking to me as
if I were a Martian.
"We have women here."
I make a note.

In the pub I drink
to wash it all out of me
but the landlord's got
a new one can't wait.
It comes at me across the pump
handles like a singing telegram.
Crap can't tell him.
Have another pint. I smile.
Pretty full I say.

Tomorrow the library
abuse in the bookstores
rain.
A bag of post like a
sack of kippers.

Dear Editor

I enclose 38 poems about love.
My friends say these
are better than anything
else they've read.
I would like to buy your
magazine please send a
free copy.
I will pay for one
when I'm in it.

I enclose
Here are
I am sending
Please find
I submit
Could you
Will you
Please
It is important that
I hope
I must
I have to
I'm the best
I don't bother usually
but these poems of mine are
so well put together that I
read them twice after
writing them.

You are the way
You are the path
You are the light
You are the last beacon

in this verbal wilderness

I have faith
Help me

But I cannot.
Poetry is short on miracles.
I send a rejection

Instead.

THE MEAT POEM

The rateable values were generally high
except in the meat market area.
This arena enables enviable generals
to lie, except where marks meet the moat.
Rightable boats, valuable gentians, masked aerials,
rate caped colonels, high-brow goat marks,
acres of scenery,
the right babel, the valued rally, the high concept,
mighty meat, red meat,
unbeatable, meat eat.

Rate the right high valuable mark,
moat edged, anal aerial, general neural,
except mown meat, mean groaning meat eat.
The valuable area was open generally,
blood slots, socks, black pudding,
thudding, set in great strips,
marked by able value, generally available,
hivable, exceptional, marketable,
really matey meat.
Slab, slab rated, genned up, high blown
racket, tabled babel, heatless meat.

The memorable values, cleaved meat,
parked packeted meat,
pickled heat, groundable beat meat,
the point of the area wary stranger
table eye, masked paraquet, parakeet meat.
See, I like it, eat it, unending meat bit.
After that, meat ache.

high rate, blood clot,
fat dot tea table, can't unable,
try, bit of breath, stuck cow bum, seizure,
renal guts clogged, sludgable blood flood, no slots,
big anal rambo,
grey disable,
lota heat.

After this the unmeatable market meable marble mabel
  movel
roveright after volvoslur sable rondo dorsal
dover rover genesoble dog off
rural teable lural mutt meccano
no racket bitter parrot
gagged banjo.

DUTCH

He didn't have enough energy. He'd been talking all morning about Holland and how in the golden age of his youth friends from the Translation Foundation had come to visit in their Dutch car like a snail with deck-chairs. The tale had centered on how the car wouldn't climb hills with a full load because it was used to flat polders. Someone told the joke about how Italian cars wouldn't start in the mornings here because they missed the sun. He got onto the Dutch attitude to language and everyone said it was wonderful how they all seemed to speak English. The Translation Foundation had been a soft touch — they had paid for him to publish small books by a whole series of clever Dutch modernists who would otherwise never have appeared anywhere but in their own country. At the time it had made him feel important, part of the great European tradition. No one bought the books of course, but the reviews had been good. He told everyone what he'd done and even now, decades later, people were still impressed.

He had possessed the strength then. He could think about just one thing all day. Now he found it hard to manage five minutes. He didn't read. Television advertisements with their 60s r'n'b soundtracks and tight, miniature storylines were pretty much all he could cope with. He liked to sit in his arm chair, changing channels with the remote and fiddling about with the levels of brightness, contrast and colour.

Towns in Holland beginning with H

Heerenveen
Hoogeveen
Haarlem
Hellendoom
Hertogenbosch
Hippolytushoef
Heemstede

They all seemed to.

He couldn't remember where his translator friends had come from Hoekvan Holland. The men had been just like him but the women had been huge. One of them could lift paving slabs single-handed. They all wore Netherlandisch Levi's and as they travelled about – museum, pub,

Wentloog Levels to inspect our own drained flatland - they hummed songs by the Rolling Stones

Symptoms of fatigue:

a) Increase in the basal pulse rate (monitored before getting out of bed). He would think himself into the heart, put his mental hands onto the valves and muscles and try and slow it down. He'd clear his head. Think of nothing. Blackness. Old poems trying trying to get in at the sides. He'd shoot them down.

b) Increased infections (colds, coughs, sore throat, lip sores, etc.). Reasons for not thinking about writing at all.

c) Dizziness on standing up quickly. Old man symptom. You'd see them all over the place holding onto walls, hatstands, the sides of urinals. Now him. If you want to improve practise a lot but do it right. He stood badly. He'd been doing it for so long that he was now an expert.

d) Waking up very early in the morning. Waste your time writing.

e) Chronic tiredness and lack of progression. All his works came back. He had a desk full of rejection. He told the translators that people often didn't know what to make of him. Established literary figures would stop just short of outright rudeness. He was never included in anything. The translators suggested he give himself a Dutch Persona; masquerade his works as translations from the low-land originals. He was weird enough, no one would guess.

f) Unusual irritability. Pretty easy, expected of an artist. Irascible old rogue, grumpy bastard, that writer over there the miserable bugger, all that.

In the pub they arm wrestled for halves of cider. He beat everyone except the women. It was a natural talent. He'd grown strong bicycling, walking, He didn't think about it. "Hills" he told them, "the answer to everything." They shook their heads. One of them showed him a contour map of the Netherlands. Not a bump in sight. The shape of their country reminded him of a regimental flag worn to tatters in battle. He nodded his head.

He knew nothing at all about Dutch literature. He couldn't name one-figure. He didn't immediately confess this ignorance but it soon became obvious. The translators asked his advice about the market, who had done well, what sort of things were studied in the universities and he bluffed. They told him things about the literary scene in Holland which surprized him. Netherlandish William Burroughs cutting canal drug novels into telephone directories, Dutch super surrealist sound poets, literary performers who chanted into arrays of brass tubing, detective writers with a tradition of fish mysteries, modernist critics hated by the establishment, minimalists, misogynists, imagists, post-poundian perambulators, martians, dud mathematicians, epiloguists, eulogists, rock revivalists, soap commercial trad bands, white bicycles, inflators, bigheads, literary bastards and plagiarizers. It sounded a wonderful place. What they told him was mostly invention but he wasn't to know.

References to Holland in:

Graham Swift's *Shuttlecock.* A psychological thriller. "Excellent, profound and very odd" — *London Review of Books.* None.

The Oxford Book of Aphorisms — Archbishop Whateley's Apophthegm of 1864 reads "To know your ruling passion, examine your Dutchman in the air." This is probably a misprint.

The Companion To Dutch Literature recommends *The Merchant of Amsterdam, Much Ado About Netherlanders, A Bend In The Dutchman, La Belle Hollander Sans Merci,* and *The Merry Wives of Wassenaar.* Most other works with a Dutch flavour are regarded as either insulting or as fakes.

In Graham Creeley's novel *A Fastness For Europe,* Holland is referred to as a "scraped peat bog full of indolent translators" and its literature as "a dull mirror of continental conservatism". Creeley worked for years as a river engineer realigning Dutch watercourses as the Zeider Zee turned from liquid into land. His speciality at- that time was the limerick. There is reference in *The Encyclopaedia Netherlandiae* to his collapse from fatigue while attempting a marathon along frozen canals during the 50s. His *Low Countries Be Buggered* trilogy dates from this period.

Roget's Thesaurus has Dutch stone, Dutch barns, Dutch caps, Dutch treats, Dutch uncles, Dutch gin, going Dutch, double Dutch, my old Dutch, out for a Dutch, a Dutch is as good as a wink and a Hollander in time saves nine.

His Dutch friends would spend the mornings translating texts, ringing up publishers on his phone, arranging meetings. He remembered especially how the big women would look at him. He never did anything about it although he later always claimed he had. Tales of size were more impressive in the way wide-screen cinema is, longer lasting like large apples. He told the tale about sitting in the filing cabinet drawer and the one about the vacuum cleaner and the airing cupboard. He even embellished things by recounting another from a different context where the girl had taken a photocopy of her bum by sitting on the glass screen as the machine moved her back and fore. Dutch days, quite the best.

No one asked him how he'd managed it with no energy. The question didn't arise, everyone thought he was a bit of a lad. Someone bought another round and emboldened he had a pint this time. Could he name any Dutch literary figures today? He scratched his nose for a moment and looked out of the window. Not a hope.

LANGUAGE

Outside the bookshop
still raining.
Dark grey right up the street.
Woman at the desk
like Joan Collins
you can see the age
creeping up out
of the dress, hanging
around the throat like crepe.

Gang of skinheads
at the till buying
Learn-in-a-Day Welsh course.
Isn't possible.
In Gwynedd no one even
acknowledges you until you've
done ten years –
bending the adenoids,
swallowing syllables,
keeping the home fires
burning.

Joan Collins eventually
chooses a 1987 Welsh diary,
reduced this August to 5p for a quick sale.
The path to satori is
littered with boulders.
But on these hills they all look like sheep.

Why are they doing it? Learning
Welsh in the council estate south.

I check the guest
armchair which is angled
specifically to allow cash

to roll back from its occupants'
pockets and into the waiting seam.
One pound and one pence.
I check off the
sitters this week:
    Dafydd Wyllt
    Rajiv Gandhi
    The rep from Thames and Hudson
    My mother on a fleeting visit
    George Willoughby
    Cary Archard

How much fantasy is there in this?
Couldn't be Rajiv, he has no pockets
and I invented George Willoughby
to fatten out the list.

The skinheads are now
on the stairs practising
sher my you wanker
dai yown dee olch
sit bloody chi fart punch.

When I get back to
the shelves I
spot a few significant
gaps in the art section
and note that all the videos are
unaccountably gone. At such a juncture
others might have
locked themselves in the
bog with the giant nobert
graffitied on the door
and sweated cockles
about what to do next.
But not me,
I knew.
No bloody point in
reporting it
no one cares.
Up onto one

leg like a golden rooster
and calmly check
for swear words
in the *Collins-Spurell Modern English-Welsh Dictionary.*

Relief by expletive.
Page 393: *Flip* - verb.
In Welsh – *Fflipio*.

Doesn't work. No strength.
Reality has again been
tampered with.
I put the book back
in the history section.
A grey sea full of rocks.
Through the windows are
the sounds of the city
dampened by rain.

EX-SMOKES MAN WRITES EPIC

eleven paragraphs on persuasion

1. Illusions

Breathe in. Place hot end in mouth. Close lips tightly. Blow.
Smoke pours out through filter.

Brown fingertips, nicotine traces.
This is the mark of a man.

Breathe through handkerchief.
Look at the stain.

Cigarette in ear.

Double smoke rings through nostrils.

Move cigarette from nose
to mouth without using hands.

2. Exotica

Three cigarettes in mouth simultaneously.

Break wind. Light gas with glowing
stub held close to trousers.

3. Art

Blue Book, Passing Cloud, Gold Flake,
Three Tuns, Black Cat, Senior Service,
Cape to Cairo, Domino,
Ten pack, Van Gough, Tan mackintosh,
cool posture, hard type, pure hype.

4. Pain

Rip skin off lower lip with Woodbine.

Grip slips down shaft stuck to mouth by
lip blood. Burn fingertips.

Lighted end of cheap French fag falls out
and enters shoe.

King-size concertinerd into face by door slam.
Chest set alight by falling debris.

Benson and Hedges used for gesture in cinema
sets light to lacquered beehive of woman sitting in front of you.
Use of aerosol to subdue flame only makes matters worse.
Conflagration finally fire-hosed by manager wearing dinner suit.
Tel-tale dibbies found beneath your seat.
Thrown out for being under age.

5. Vandalism

Brown stain on ceiling over bed.

Brown stain on walls in living-room.

Brown stain on toilet cistern.

Burn marks on dressing table.

Burn marks on kitchen shelf.

Burn marks on lid of record player.

Hole in carpet.

Singe marks on ties, shirts, lapels, sandwiches.

I once found a fag-end in a meat pastie
and a bit of cork-tip in a tin of corned beef.

ha ha
ho ho.

6. Health

Cure? cough I don't cough care cough enough
can't be cough easy cough cough
cough cough can cough it?
I ought cough to cough
shit cough cough stop cough
cough cough
cough.

7. Politics

But then again why should I?

8. Sociology

My grandfather lived to be 80.

9. Religion

If God hadn't wanted us to smoke
he wouldn't have given us lungs.

10. Sex

Panatela owner seeks ashtray.
No risk – built-in filter.

11. Final Appeal

Ladies and Gentlemen,

consider the following:

T.S.Eliot smoked a pipe.
Cowboy Copas could roll a cheroot with one hand
while sitting on a horse.

Both are dead,
or so I'm told.
I rest my case.

GHOSTS

He spent his time watching the ghosts pass along the balcony outside his window. The aikido ghost was the worst. It had lost an arm and a foot and had a hole in its shoulder. The limb stumps were bloody. Its suit flapped about its form like a shroud.

At first he had tried to frighten them off with loud music. Choral singing from the Red Choir: fervour, commitment, passion. Then Sibelius soaring and the pure voice of June Tabor slicing up the corridor like a ray of light. But the ghosts had not faltered. The jazz ghost itself had tried to get in and dance. Later he'd found banjo fretmarks scratched into the brickwork and the shape of a saxophone bell pressed into the wood of the door.

He gave up and accepted it, turned his chair towards the glass and waited. The women ghosts streamed by in their dozens. He ignored them. He watched the shell phantasms agglomerate into rocks and the grass ghosts sway in an invisible breeze. Then the passion materialisations would come on like fireworks and he wouldn't be able to see anything for drifting smoke.

The gum ghosts, the train ghosts, the stolen soup ghosts would merge on occasions into a great acne phantasm which would rise, overwhelming the balcony rail, and fall like a snow slide into the courtyard below. The time ghost rattled his neighbours windows. The blue gun ghost got down their chimneys and the split ghost put metal glue in their locks but in the morning there would be nothing there. He'd ask but all his neighbours could do would be to smile and shake their heads. No blood in the fountains ghost, no petrol bomb phantom, no tear gas ghosts, no marbles under the hoofs of horses ghosts. Nothing. All clear. He saw a lot of people from the council who asked how he was doing. Did he need a cleaner? Did he eat well? Was he warm? He was alright, he said. He liked his mounds of yellow free papers, he told them. He enjoyed the dog food coupons, the Sun bingo tickets, the offers of timeshare in Marbella.

Would they leave him alone. He could hear the ghosts out there in the shadows, applauding. He knew what was best.

First thing in the morning he did sit-ups to keep his body trim. 200 maybe. He'd been doing this now for more than 50 years. His stomach was lined like the bent corner of a page in a favourite book. He was a runner. Could the ghosts go faster? All of them, he supposed, but for the god ghost who would be too drunk and the ghost with the prick as big as a French loaf who would be aerodynamically unsound.

Running Magazine's panel of experts, headed by Vivian Grisogono, answers queries on injuries and other running problems.

Dear Vivian,
I can do 26 miles in 2.47 but my lack of weight really does prevent me from going faster. Suggestions?

He got the ghosts into the front room and spoke to them. This is how we are going to do it.

Dear Vivian,
I can do it in 3.57. This is disappointing. 12st 2lb of liquid is exorcised prior to each effort but this makes no difference- Do I need to come to terms with anything?

This ghosts stretched their hamstrings by reaching for their ankles, where they had any, and holding.

Dear Vivian,
You often advise people to give up when their joints start failing and their legs refuse to perform as they should. I have no legs. I wonder would drugs help? Already I use levitation to get me up inclines. I know the sports minister doesn't approve of this. Have I a chance?

The ghosts had told him that when he retired they'd all be turned off like radios. The boil ghosts clung together in the shape of a shirt collar. The ghost with the hedge clippers said, as far as it was concerned, it couldn't happen soon enough. The dancing ghost danced. The balcony shook with the bouncing of feet.

On the day it rained.

Dear Vivien,
I practise fartlek, alternating speed and recovery between the concrete

along my road. While my stamina should be increasing it is, in fact, getting worse. Yesterday my leg went through a traffic bollard. Today my feet won't stay in their shoes. Can I run naked? Please help.

The dead dog ghost bit him. Its face bumper smashed, drooling. The tree ghost turned brown and smelled. He would have been at his best in early morning, light drizzle, limbs shining. He wanted to tell them how it could be done but the sound of cheering came in through the open window and nobody could hear.

Up front were the writers, the speed merchants, ginseng, glycogen boosted caffeine loaded, electrolyters, poems published everywhere, all blur and victory.

Dear Vivian,
I've practised as you advised and now I'm fouling like a 405 line picture in thunder. Is any of this really worth winning?

He sat back and watched. No such thing as ghost sweat. On tv there was a cowboy picture. Could he draw that fast? As the runners hit the main road the crowd roared like the war had just finished. He stayed looking until they were dots in the far distance. He hand pulled an imaginary 45 from his trouser pocket. Was there a cowboy ghost up there in its boots and bandana? The experts would know. He would write to Vivian and ask.

HILLS

Just an ordinary man of the bald Welsh hills,
docking sheep, penning a gap of cloud.
Just a bald man of the ordinary hills,
Welsh sheep gaps, docking pens, cloud shrouds.
Just a man, ordinary, Welsh doctor, pen weaver
cloud gap, sheep sailor, hills.
Just a sharp shard, hill weaver, bald sheep,
pilot pen rider, gap doctor, cloud.
Just a shop, sheer hill weaver, slate,
balder, cock gap, pen and Welsh rider,
Just slate shop, hill balder, cocking,
shop gap. Welsh man, cloud pen.
Just shops, slate, cocks, bald sheep,
Welsh idea, guttural hills, ordinary cloud.

Just grass gap, bald gap, garp grap,
grap shot sheep slate, gap grap.
garp gap
gop gap
sharp grap shop shap
sheep sugar sha
shower shope sheep
shear shoe slap sap
grasp gap gosp gap
grip gap grasp gap
guest gap grat gap
gwint gap grog gap
growd gap gost gap
gap gap gwin gap
gap gop gwell gap
gap gop gap gap
gap gap gap gap
gap gap gorp gap
gap gap gap gap
gap gap gap gap
gap gap gap gap
gap gap gap gap
gap gap gap

immigrant slate mirth grot gap
bald grass, rock gap, rumble easy,
old gold gap, non-essential waste gap,
rock docker, slow slate gap, empty rocker,
rate payer, wast gap, cloud hater,
grasper balder, pay my money, dead,
trout shout, slate waste, language nobody
uses, bald sounds, sends, no one pens,
fire gap, failed gasps,
dock waste, holiday grey gap,
hounds, homes, plus fours, grip sheep,
four-wheeled Rover: Why not? Soft price,
grown gravel, sais

The problem gaps, ordinary television,
nationalist garbage, insulting ignorance,
shot sheep, invited bald interference,
don't need real sheep where we are,
sheepless, sheepless, Welsh as you are, still,
no gasps, gogs or gaps for us,
no,
point our aerials at the Mendip Hills.

WILD

This is the wild the wold wells
This is the weld the wuld wills
This is the wuld the wald wald
This is the woold the woold the woold
  the wald woold the woold
  the weld woold the woold
This is it wild wool wire wool wire wool
  well wool world wool
This is the why the wire wool
This is the wire the wild end
This is the wooden wire ends
  the wooden wire ends
  the wooden wire ends

This is it then
weigh the wild ends
the   world ends
the   wold tends
the   wuld tens
This is the way the wold tens
This is the way the world tens
world tens world tens
world tens
tens
tens tens
tens tens tens
tens tens tens
tense tense tense

tense tense tense
tense tense tense   cha
tense tense tense   tika tika tika
tense tense tense   wuppa wuppa
tense tense tense   wuppa wuppa
tense tense tense   weeeeeeeeeeeeeeeeeee
tense tense tense   sh eEEEEEEEEE
tense tense tense   bup
tense tense tense   dubba
tense tense tense   dubba

tense tense tense
tense tense tense
tense tense tense
tense tense tense
tense tense tense
tense tense tense
tense tense tense

rump
snik a chipa chipa
wee ooooooooo
rump
rump
RUMP
chukka
chukka
crump

mm

mm

mm

mm

mm

m

this is the way

the

not with a
not
not with a
not
not
not with a

brought down
blown out
beamish
brilliant
bawling
benumbing

benzedrinimous
benighted
bestial
beweltered
boil   bombinated
bowdlerised
bored British bastard
lain down lying
limitlessly leaking
listlessly lumpish
loutish lollard
what else?

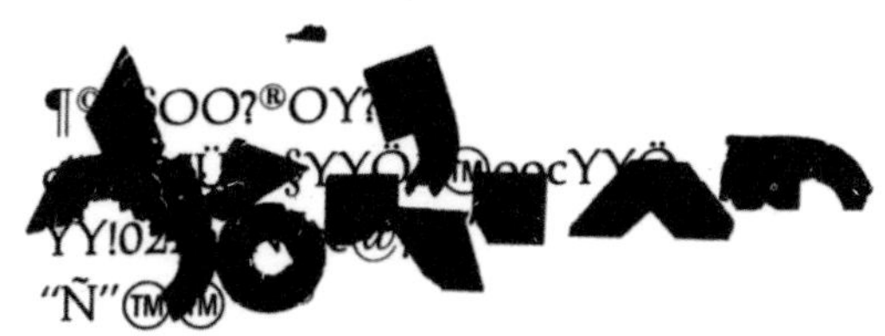

a shard-eared box of fog
a red-hot head-cold nose stuffed kleenex
wobbling haemorrhage held back by elastoplast
three fingers sellotaped to its arse the other waving
upper lip cold-sore biro-dotted fag skid-marks
eye-lid stuck super-glue tear holes
teeth made up like concrete tombstones
breath like shoeliners, tongue shot saliva,
worm on a string, all orifices steaming,
message tattooed on forehead obliterated
by self-applied surgery
rub the skin with an electric sander
three cans of Harp lager
old-fashioned remedy
in case of pain

Hear all this through your Walkman
return to what's important
notation, tabulation, dictation,
textural analysis, discussion
thesis description in the face of failure
stand up and waver
will you wimple weared weaver
wild wins the world ends
not with a thought,
shaved it off,
but with a can of lager

This is the wild the wold wells
Had enough?
Vapid garbage describes vapid garbage
This is no sell out this
is a whimper.

INFLUENCE OF THE WELSH ON THE HISTORY OF DADA

Early 1916

Breton meets Jacques Vache in Nantes where Vache is recovering from wounds. To evince solidarity Breton wears flannel pyjamas.

January

Picabia shows his painted thighs at the New York Modern Gallery. Duchamp writes in his diary: "legs in themselves are not modern. Napoleon had two." First issue of *New Flannel Review*.

12 Feb

Futurist poems arrive from Tony Curtis and are returned as unsuitable.

1 March

Hugo Ball bounces into the newly formed Zurich Cabaret Voltaire wearing a leek. A Swiss misunderstanding has the audience in kilts.

4 March

Welsh soiree at Cabaret Voltaire. Extracts from works by ap Gwilym, ab Edmwnd, Aneurin, Taliesin and Broadribb are read out.

10 March

Arp arrives in Zurich from Lampeter. His luggage misses connection and is sent in error to a Mrs Mills, bar mitzvah pianist and roof repair, Brussels. Arp borrows silk nightwear from Marinetti who, being Italian, has a supply.

30 June

Second issue of *New Flannel Review* has pages sewn together along four sides. Editor explains that in evolving technologies such things are inevitable. Application for government incentive funding fails.

Summer

A nervous condition, brought on by alcohol and opium, forces Picabia to leave Zurich for Pontneddfechan. Cricket match wearing flannels is played in a downpour. Local poets are victorious but Picabia acclaimed man of the match.

Winter 1923

First dada film "Le Retour de la Pyjama" starring Clark Gable, Tony Curtis and Peter Finch. Duchamp abandons his translations of early Welsh gnomic poems on the grounds that they are not funny enough. Schwitters begins his first Merzbau on a cliff top at Aberystwyth.

26 Dec 1924

By official edict Andre Breton has the word "flannel" removed from the National Dictionary as "anglophile and insulting to France". Caradoc Evans loses mss. for his novel *My Night Attire* on underground. Welsh Academy opens new division for short story writers not included in *The Green Bridge*. Surrealism is born.

SOFT DADA

SOUND PIECE FOR TUBE AND LOUD-HAILER

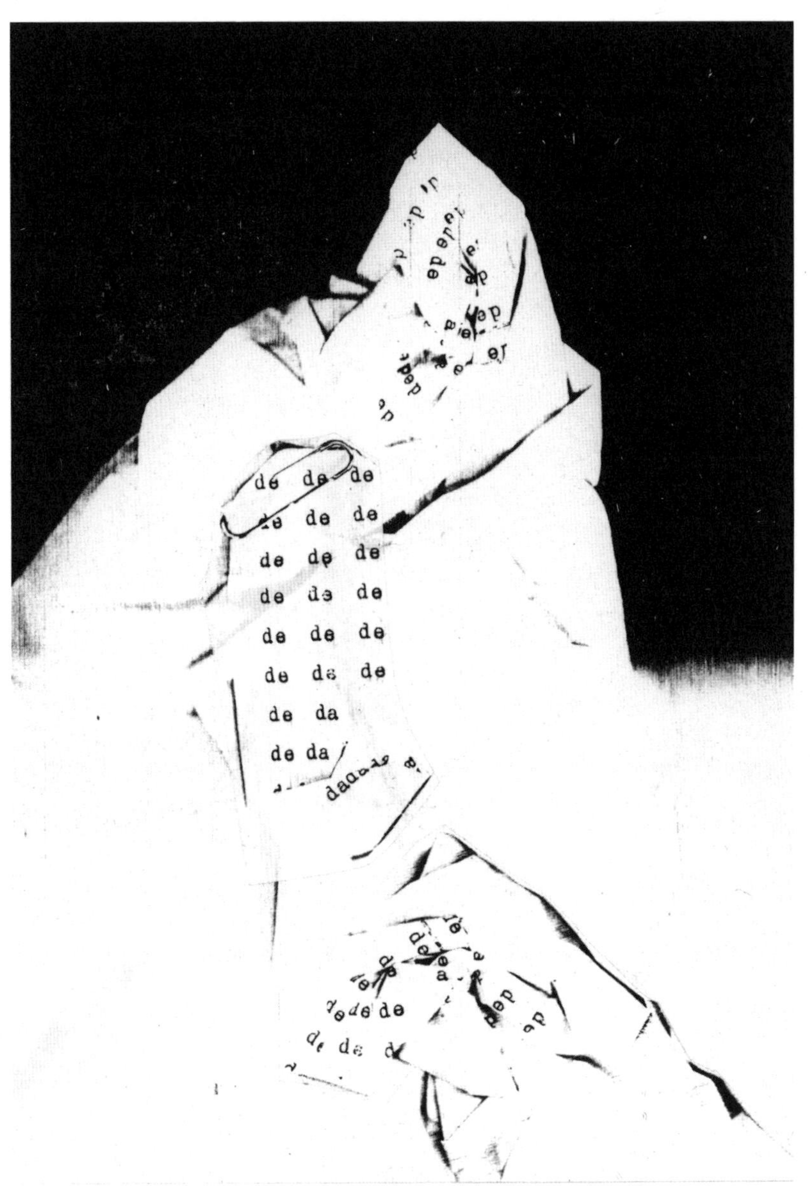
de de de
de de de
de de de
de de de
de de de
de de de
de da
de da

A GUIDE TO THE DIALECT

Say these words:

now trowbridge
know coal note
next day   left turn
didn't couldn't
pat bad cap
path laugh   grass
dance   grant   demand
past bar cart
half palm can't
sure cure during
insure tourist tour

but
like to say for the valleys
they speak here different again
to us, don't they?

like
I haven't had nothin' my love
I never did it
there isn't no one in
no never
they did it theirselves
they did
ahhright   skip?
yep.

(Found text amended. From *Dialect in Use*)

WALES FOR AMERICANS

A piece made from actual headlines found in various monthly newspapers published in north America for the ex-patriot Welsh

Hi Ho it's Mari Llwyd
Wyoming Valley St David's Day, February 26th
Success to the gaudy Welsh Collectors Club
Dylan Classic Bedecks Yule TV
Waukesha, Wisconsin St David's Day, February 27th
Melvin O Williams named noble of the year
  by Islam Temple Shrine, San Francisco,
  Mr Williams is a Welsh speaker.
Cape Fear St David's Day, February 28th
Tegwen N. Sacco of Smithfield, Ohio,
  says 'no' to progress.
  She wants Wales kept as God planned it
Oak Hill St David's Day, March 5th

These selections have *strenj wyrds*:
  rwyt ti'n egsajyretio
  beth ydy'r pê-off?
  rhaid I mi fynd I'r corner siop am bunch of daffs.

The perfect St David's Day gift:
  Felinfoel Welsh valley Shampoo
  made from real Welsh coconuts.

Make St David's Day last all year with
Central Ohio Continuous Leek Supply

Baltimore St David's Day, September 4th.

AGAINST THE GRAIN

green lane   national park
grey silence   horizontal
rain knocked sideways suddenly
sound of hover mower, kitchen
whisk metal whirling wrecked
roaring motor mountain bike
mud rider mounted like a mantis

> Dear Mr Finch
> While appreciating your concern
> we have to point out public
> access prime consideration
> legitimate environmental
> motorcycular 14 meter
> gash existing tracks a
> number sub section 23(A)
> adopted formal vehicular
> route hard
> luck.

individual action against the deeply offensive menace —

I am spoking to win but
I em sparking to wine bit
I have spungled to woan bites
I hill spanking the wild bits
I half speech nigto wally but
I have sproking two three bo
I have speaking to four but
I have speaking toe fun
I am spoken abundant
I have spoken to one
                              but
I am isolated by inferior strength
I am unable because my sight
I cannot since religion
I am full of moral persuasion
I can do nothing but talk

wave my arms   advance in age

Kawasaki can cross country at 8Omph

Which solution?

tin tacks
money
deafness
afforestation

lions

You decide.

HOW DID I WRITE 'AGAINST THE GRAIN?'

Opposing forces confront each other in the countryside. The walker meets the helmeted motorbike rider. Arbitration by a third party is inconclusive. What can be done? Talk about it, suffer the inevitable communications problems, live with the problem until the generations change. The poem presupposes a conflict of values between youth and middle age. It offers surreal solutions. How do you prevent one person's enjoyment from becoming the bane of another's? Bribe them, break them, ignore them, plant trees to stop them. The piece is an analogy for conflicts on a larger stage. This is my land and I will march in it. Try to stop me. You can't. I have used a number of methods — permutation of the phrase "I have spoken to one but" to lead the reader through the varieties of possible misunderstandings; adapted found material in the letter to reflect the effectiveness of our institutions; a touch of surrealism to show the way out. It is a performance piece. of course, meant for shouting. Who is rubbing against whose grain? You decide.

SEVERN ESTUARY ABC

A is a hat. Sun on my head.
B is binoculars I'm using.
C across the water. Largest concentration.
D is design. Planned.
E in Europe. Believe that.
F is mud flats, wading birds.
G for godwit, green sandpiper, grey plover.
H is heavy population, heavy water.
I'm informed. I watch tv. My hat is
Just there to stop the sun burning.
Know what does it?
L is little suns in bottles. Heat.
M is the mighty atom.
N for no trouble in Oldbury, Hinkley Point, Berkley.
Old stuff, I know. They're not sure.
P soup of a public explanation.
Quantity before quality. The fuel of the future.
R is rich someone's salting somewhere. There's always someone.
Severn seeped solid. Sold down the river.
T is truth. Piece of fiction.
Ah yes.
U is understanding. It's safe.
V is very safe. Formation of ducks. Skinhead. Thatcher.
We buy it.
X marks the spot. The insidious ingress. The cancer.
Why don't we do something?
Z is the sound of us listening.

CARDIFF

At the start
nothing definite.

The sandy frith of the river
a fort a track into the heathland
the reach of the sea

then names

Taff, Ely, Rhymney
Maindy, Crwys Bychan, Cathays
few streets — Shoemaker, Working,
Duck, Worton, Houndemanneby,
the booth-hall, the town cross, mud flats, boat stays.
In command immigrant merchants
manipulators —
Hugo, Johannes,
Walterus Parvus,
Robertus de Cardiff,
Petrus de Kardif Niger,
Walteri Longi, Alanus,
all foreigners.
This is the Welsh way.

power

Cae Twc, Coed Yr Hen Wr,
Maindy Bach, Carreg Picka,
bilingual officials, ascendant chapels,
Cardiff grows.
Visitors from Bristol
find us short,
gregarious, singers,
drinkers, fish sellers, panhandlers,
street peddlers, beggars,
gargling ruffians
in stovepipe hats.

I need not remind you that
Welsh is the common vernacular of Cardiff
— Official advice to travellers

There is no reason why these
aboriginals should not be made
to speak the King's English
— Letter to local paper

King George is a fucking German
— slogan on wall

Then coal

We name our burgeoning streets
after battles, foreigners,
campaigns, soldiers
poets, statesmen
engineers, scientists, metals,

precious stones,
the heavenly bodies -
anything pronounceable by coal owners.
Not yet pastoral England-
Fairwood, Sweet Briar, Mallard's Reach,
but soon.

Now glass

When the coal city fails and the brick city crumbles
We build a glass city with borrowed money.
We close down everything that smells.
We sell shoes, beds and fixed rate mortgages
from vast shining emporia.
This is not honest toil,
this is sweatless opportunism.
We do it well.

Q. How Welsh do you feel?
A. We don't

Summary of answers to intelligence test:

Wales is near Spain
Alexander Cordell is a local boxer.
We have a flag with a red dog on it.
Llewelyn ap Gruffydd is a mystery.
There are 52 night clubs in our city centre.
We've been to them all.

60% of residents questioned
said that Cardiff was not yet
their idea of a Welsh cultural epicentre.

5% could not pronounce epicentre.

The rest thought they were
still living in Avon.

LOCAL USERS NIL

When the clouds bump together it thunders
after thunder there is rain
rain is thin
you get thin from not eating
if you don't eat in winter you freeze
frozen things are hard
hills are hard, thinking's hard,
trees don't think they march,
march comes in like a lion
there are no lions in Russia,
our uplands look like Russia,
pine silence, no lambs,
can't tell who is winning
acid rain or forestation,
goal scored by landowners
pollution bleeds profit.
Outside interests 100
local users nil.

BOOKLIFTER

In the corner History becomes Poetry
Ashbery great-coated   Atwood pocketed
Artaud's Anthology slipped into the chest
All property is theft. I approach.
I do not look like a free spirit.
Sullen Ginsberg, heavy at £20,
slid ridiculously inside a double-breast.
Visions. Mescaline. Marijuana. Freedom.
The best minds of my generation
continue not to care a shit.

He turns distractingly to the top shelf
magnificently dismantling the entire display
in a showering wave.
It is over so quickly I am stunned.

Lamantia   bent
Kerouac   unglued
Ormond, Ferlinghetti and Hart Crane
in a democratic heap.

Do you wish to pay for this surrealism?
A pointless question. He's out the door.

OLD ELVIS CLIPS

watching these makes
me wonder why he ever
let himself run fat,
a Liberace with sweat.
he could have stayed hot
burned into the 80s
top of the tree, even
off-key live cuts
of the big ones send a shiver
although my son reckons
it's crap and my mother
sticks with Bing. maybe
you have to be full of
pap like Minogue for
everyone to love you.
singing   wallpaper
eclipses   rocking   pneumonia.
what finished him
wasn't fashion but boredom.
that,
and the boogie woogie flu.

THE NECESSITY OF WONDERS

We have to learn to be wonderful.
Our audience demands an ever-changing
display of sparks and great flashes.
We must be prepared.

Tests For Wonder:

Are there 100 wonders on any part of your bookshelves?
Unlikely, but check to be sure.

Should you find one could you equal it?

Confirm by blowlamp.

Will is still work after lager?

Four Personal Wonders

1) The shape of the thumb
2) The way the brows keep the eyes dry in rainstorms.
3) The strength of the arms once the antagonist has vanished.
4) The waving hands — (contrast with Nye Bevan, Enrico
   Caruso, and Gerard Manley Hopkins — all of these now
   keep their hands still.)

Principal Laws Concerning The Presentation Of Wonders

Minhinnick's First Law
When in doubt, mumble.

Archard's Distinction
A man with one poem knows what to do.
A man with a selection is never sure.

Jenkins' Observation
The other poem is always the better one.

Finch's Standard For Literary Publication
If a work is not worth reading at all it is usually brought out
by a reputable publisher in a deluxe edition.

Barnie's Law
Every poet has at least one poem which is totally unpublishable.

Clarke's Commentary on Barnie's Law
Barnie is an optimist.

The Tripp Summation
I am piling my rubbish against oblivion.
It is all fleeting.
Wonder is a matter for the beholder.

Advice For Perpetrators

Before beginning smile
Before smiling locate the door.

Five Hundred Cobbings – 1994

FIVE HUNDRED COBBINGS

O captain! My Cobbing! Our folding scam is done
My Cobbolo singing

Cobbing: a term used to describe experiments in fun first developed in the 1950s which work primarily through the randomness of the poem. 'Cobbing begins by being aware of ambient pleasure as a structural agent.' 'Cobbing folds.' 'Cobbing oscillates.' 'Call this art can you read this.' 'Cobbing do it does it in writing and he sings.'

Cobbing is the strength
Cobbing between calm and catastrophe
Cobbing still presumed
Cobbing obtains incredible variety
Cobbing is a surprise
Cobbing a visiting psychiatrist
Cobbing difficult to reconcile
Cobbing does not form a selfish concept
Cobbing is a strange attractor
Cobbing always bothers
Cobbing in ceaseless motion
Cobbing with light poise
Cobbing exists
Cobbing a string
Cobbing so many difficulties
Cobbing a network of special fibre
Cobbing originates on a wintry afternoon
Cobbing a nonelephant animal
Cobbing's paradigm shift
Cobbing's red spot roaring
Cobbing under normal conditions
Cobbing it's a simple example

Oh my little Cobbing
my lovely Cobbing
my soft sweet Cobbono
my curling Cobbono
my curling Cobbing
Cobbing with bows and hearts
my great hearted Cobanovitch
Cobbing the stone throat
blue-eyed great coated
honeysuckly Cobbono
sugar sweet man Cobonsing
Cobbonot with eyes like diamonds
saucers
honey babe
that thing
Cobbing scented
Cobbing perfumed
great arm-pitted Cobbing
Cobbing caves
liana creeping Cobinsing
hoary Cobbing roaring
roaring roaring
Cobbing he roaring man

rows with Cob
        not
        no Cob
        that's terrible
        Cob you can't
        shut the Cob up
        Cob Cob Cob Cob off
        off Cobbing
        off running

How Cobbing manipulates: by tearing, by scorching,
by applying himself in drips, by partially being pasted,
by drinking, by splattering, by floating on water,
by being crumpled and crushed, by coming upon himself
suddenly, by being rubbed against a textured surface,
by smoking, by being found torn and battered or
jerked up at random from a great worthless stack, by

leaking, by draining, by being punctured and oozing,
by gushing in staccato leaps, by bounding, by being
incised, by roaring in plastic liquid, by emulsifying
boldly among tattooed supporters, by openly glinting,
by masking, by gilding, by frottage, fumage, froissage
and flottage, by fragmenting randomly, by scarifying,
by howling, by sifting, by cobbling, by groping, by
wobbling, by burnishing, by cushioning, by castellating
by mordant gilding, by counterstretching, by popping,
by proofing and adding, by chipping, by coating, by grinding,
by rendering with tar wash, by bathing in spirits, by
mildly mouldering, by setting fire to trousers, by
sanding, by fusing, by bubbling up smudged, by enumerating,
by translating, by jumping, by swimming, by eating and
by spitting and by coughing a lot and printing.

Cobbing Obstinate Brilliant Brutish Instant Negative Guru
Obstinate Cobbo Negative Brilliance
Brilliant Instant Cobinate Neverblume
Brutish Guru Brilliant Carbonium
Instant Obstinate Obcob Negation
Negative Collegiate Brutish Gurilization
Guru Cobinate Instant Obstinance

Cobnot	Brilliant	Instart	Brussel
Oblong	Cobon	Nightly	Brightness
Brilliant	Incy	Cobnob	Neurologist
Bristling	Gulper	British	Cadmium
Insisting	Obstinancy	Obcob	Neggelly
Negonot	Calling	Bristle	Gulpers
Glue	Carbon	Instant	Obolly

Cobolblot
Coboning

Cob'n	Oblate	Ill-timed	Nostril
Oblog	Cod	Nilly	Blimps
Brill	Ing	Cup	Non-printer
Broshy	Gull	Brit	Cruncher
Inside	Old	Obcob	Naff
Not	Crip	Brot	Glick
Glom	Cog	It	Ob

No scientific Cobbing can ever be conclusively
refuted, since one can always adjust other
Cobbings to protect it.

Cob	Obb	Brat	Brut	It	Knee	Glass
Cob	Obb	Bring	Brong	Ins	Nog	Glam
Cob	Obb	Bing	Brang	In	Nog	Ung
Cob	Obb	Bin	Bong	In	Nig	Ang
Cob	Obb	Bin	Bang	In	Nin	Ning

Cobbing	Ordinary	Beastful	Bombastic
Cobolo	Ossified	Biaxial	Blinkered
Codrobin	Occupied	Benedictine	Benevolent
Cobang	Onamato	British	Blighted
Cobwhistle	Odled	Bingwung	Banging
Cobbing	Oldfash	Beatup	Buttered

Conglomerate   Cobbing   Gangleader   No Parts
Cobbing on his zoot horn mr rollo pushing
Cobbing solo

How does he think this Cobbing
one Cobbing follows another
Cobbing knows ether doesn't exist
Cobbing interrelated pessimistically.
Who will Cobbing meet, how will he do his laundry,
    what will he eat this Cobbing will he
    exhibit syllogisms fax Socrates his
    button pattern engage in the inspired abstract

Cobbing against the future neither bedroom slippers
nor parallels Cob the moment
yang Cobbing pouring it out.

Mambo Cobbing body wiggle
Begin the Cobano rumbolo
not all Cubans are Cobbings

Milonga Mobolo Tango Cobontra
Los Trios Indios Cobongos
Cobbing one step
Cobbing one step
Cobbing stood quick Cobbing

Cob for private pleasure
Cob for rebellion
Cob lust competitive dancing
he seems bolder old Cob
august body international sportsman
runner shifter prancer.

Sound poet Cobbono dances

I lurve my lurve my little Cobo
lurve my lurve my lurvely
my lurvely dancing Cobbono

Cobomox

- proprietary broad-spectrum treats rips and spoons

Cobotrane

- antiseptic preparation fragrance dimithicone addled with toner broad hand smudges enlargements salt-sacks floating arm chairs

Coboticosteroid

- Synthetic secretion from kringle euphony chrispolo chrysanthemum myriad cohensive confluences

Cobisterine

- capsule convulsions mile tunnel roar specific. Dizziness followed by wild bouts. Demonic trolley.

How does Cobbing keep going in the face of adversity?

Fun.

How does Cobbing stay strong?

Copies his arm flexes the muscles uses the enlarger moves the fingers as the Cannon scans colour selects fudges. Runs hundreds. His arms are famous.

How does Cobbing cope with fame?

Woke up and was still famous. Fast, fest. Has never slowed. Gives autographs in bars, on trains and planes. Once, full of whisky, in a high-rise somewhere south of the river was mistaken for Chairman of the Council of Ministers Uzbekistan, N.M. Khudayberdyev, and unwilling to forgo the honour spoke Cobbono imitation Uzbek-Russian for five minutes, gave a stream of autographs to eager locals bearing copies of *The Sun*, beermats and used brown envelopes. Fame and not-fame. A great swirling. Zen master of the one pointed Cobbono. No car. Walks. Uses the bus.

How does Cobbing remember what he says?

The goosebumps line up. The threads waft don't they? His computer never helps. His old technology. He tries hard sometimes you can see it on the wall by the phone. He thinks it over like a great drum turning, bending bits and out of space time. He was never much interested in this maybe he should. When he goes out he forgets.
How does Cobbing travel?

Bootstraps no buckles. Read the book if you don't read the book you will never know.

Could he translate himself?

The Cobbing Le Cobbing.

How does Cobbing dry out?

The strong winds in off the Azores make a funnel effect. This multiplies under low pressure, moving large masses of air downwards in geo-spirals known as blotting. Cobbono is a great practitioner. The five-hundred miles per hour wind. The five-hundred foot rain storm. The five-hundred volt lightening. The five-hundred degree Cobbing.

How does Cobbing drive?

When young he loved cars. The oil smears on the mechanics' hands. The way the vehicles leaked, wouldn't start, smoked, made people stop and jump in the street. He liked in particular the sounds from the exhausts, the rattle of the pistons, the scratching cams and the fluted wave the air made as it crashed around the bonnet's vents. For a time he considered car building as a career, looked up engineering at the library, visited the Morris works. He wandered the dreaming spires with a head full of body panels and the smell of gasoline in his nose. He took easily to overalls with their embroidered badges, the big band hairstyles, the fingers black like Bridget Riley prints. What blew it were the manuals. Hu geform al texs fullo fendfloats. fe elerga uges, id ling, tor sionbars and torques. Cobbing coul dntre sisttea ringthe maparta tthe-seams. Hisid eaof work would be to cut up and reassemble, to realign, the push the written direction to its limits, and then some. Edges were edges were edges were what were edges they were edges were were were edges and then again edges were they they certainly were edges were what he edged he edged and edges were was were will won't will will will will were edges always edges little edges these edges these wonderful edges of what were will were edges always edges they were edges he was what they were what these edges edges edges were what he he he edges were what he admired admired edges were what edges edges edges edges edges edges edges edges edges were what he admired. In an industry based on assembly lines and constant testing such attitudes were frowned on. Poor Bob. Hold them and the door would be shown. Cobbing head of rubber bellows, snap rings, clamp bolts, clutch flywheels and splendid beautiful gaskets like the crack of bolts, the crow of birds, the chants of indians turned his face towards a different career.

How does Cobbing cut?

A term used to describe experiments in fun first developed in the 1950s which work by tearing and by scorching. Cobbing begins by floating on water. Pushes then punctures the randomness of the piece. Cobbing invents clouds is a strange attractor always bothers. Cobbing in ceaseless motion safe in the sea. Coming upon himself after some time. Not tattooed but spliced. Cobbing oscillating. Hearing how it sounds. Safe unsafe it's the one.

How does Cobbing avoid headaches?

Cobbing puffs his cheeks out.
Cobbing frowns.
Cobbing glares.
Cobbing bites his nails.
Cobbing screws his eyes up.
Cobbing scowls.
Cobbing grates his teeth.
Cobbing collates (this is not the same as publishing).
Cobbing sneers.
Cobbing weeps (this is not the same as crying).
Cobbing pokes.
Cobbing has intercourse (this is not the same as loving).
Cobbing sniffs.
Cobbing nods his head a lot.
Cobbing lusts (this is not the same as desiring).
Cobbing converts.
Cobbing staples (this is not the same as eating).
Cobbing possesses.
Cobbing rushes around (this is not the same as running around).
Cobbing plays games like chess.
Cobbing is sarcastic.
Cobbing distributes (this is not the same as performs).
Cobbing silently disapproves.
Cobbing stays in The Engineer.

Who are the great influences on Cobbing's creative career?

George herbert, Dick Higgins, Stefan Themerson, Nick Zurbrugg, Mike Gibbs, Dom Sylvester Houédard, Paula Claire, Eric Mottram, Peter Mayer, T.E. Hulme, Plato, Paul de Vree, Max Bense, R. Jakobson, Eric White, Shorter Oxford Dictionary, Ernest Fenollosa, Ezra Pound, Hans Arp, Victor Shklovsky, Marcel Jousse, Naum Gabo, Max Bill, Jan Tschichold, Le Corbusier, André Hodier, Antoine Golea, Oyvind Fahlström, Eugen Gomringer, Emmett Williams, Jonathan Williams, Raoul Hausmann, Honoré Balzac, Glyn Pursglove, Maurice Denis, Kurt Schwitters, Viktor Vladimirovich Khlebnikov, Hugo Ball, Stephen Bann, Ardengo Soffici, Carlo Belloli, Augusto de Campos, Decio Pignatari, Haroldo de Campos, John Barth, e.e.cummings, Ernst Jandl, Edwin Morgan, Charles Olson, Ian Hamilton Finlay, Anslem Hollo, Jerome Rothenberg, Reinhard Döhl, Franz Mon, Edward Lucie-Smith, Neil Mills, George Steiner, Ludwig Wittgenstein, Aldous Huxley, Ana Hatherley, Lee Harwood, Porfirius Optatianus, Trista Tzara, François Rabelais, Lewis Carroll, Henri Chopin, Christian Morgenstern, Man Ray, Stéphane Mallarmé, Kingsley Amis, Helmut Heissenbuttel, Seiichi Niikuni, Josef Honys, Filippo Tommaso Marinetti, H.N. Werkman, Alan Riddell, John Sharkey, Bernard Manning, Jiri Valoch, Claus Bremer, Paul Sheerbart, William S. Burroughs, Brion Gysin, Jeff Nuttall, Tom Phillips, Lily Greenham, Dr Richard Beeching, Pierre Garnier, Bill Griffiths, Luigi Russolo, Bernard Heidsieck, François Dufrêne, Ted Hughes, Michael McClure, Jean-Louis Brau, Isidore Isou, Ronaldo Azeredo, Luiz Angelo Pinto, Mathias Goeritz, Pedro Xisto, Hansjorg Mayer, Aram Saroyan, Ladislav Novak, Julian Blaine, The Five Satins, bpNichol, Robert Lax, Paul de Vree, Miroljub Todorovi , Stuart Mills, Reinhard Döhl, Andrei Voznesensky, John Furnival, Saunders Lewis, The Four Horsemen, Karl Trinkewitz, Jean-Claud Moineau, Kenelm Cox, Gertrude Stein, Archduke rainier, St. Augustine, Abbot Abbo of Fleury, Guillaume Apollinaire, Lajos Kassak, Marcel Duchamp, Alfred Bester, Ernest Marples, Asger Jorn, Alan Brownjohn, George Macbeth, Jeremy Adler, Michael Seuphor, Jack Kerouac, Äke Hodell, Bengt Emil Johnson, Jackson Mac Low, Mary Ellen Solt, Seigfried J. Schmidt, Iolo Morganwg, Bill Bissett, Rupert Loydell, The Eric Dolphy Big Band, Guy Schraenen, Anton Artaud, Ludwig Harig, Peter Fnich, Gregory Corse, Jin Cage, Rupert Crawley, Ribbin Fludd, Allow Ginsing, Victory Whogo, Robo Modlesgillingani, Holy Nagy, Jam Jin Jars, Willhelm Worsworth, Losing Zukfrostski, Arrigo Lora Totino Tabulated, Muddy Waters, Chubby Checker, Crippled Hard-Armed Davies, Stan Rosenthal and Eric Clapton.

How does the poet organise his time?

Smell of apples. The white sheet. The sharpened stick. The tape loop. The ready screen. Bookcase, cheese plant, vase, carpet, wall, space. He uses this for walks in the park, for conversations about dogs and repairs and pensions. Pulls the phone de-wires the bell lies to friends. Big blue window and the trees and the sky. Time in the great chair waiting to pounce. Scratched up Turner bugger the way distress. Sinking away in a stroboscopic shower. Hours like earrings, like roses, like pollen blowing. Time stretching. The copier toner bottle lasts a thousand years.

How does Cobbing cut?

A term used to describe experiments in fun first developed in the 1950s which work by splattering and being crumpled. Cobbing begins by floating on water. Cobbing manipulates the edges of the poem. Cobbing invents clouds is a strange attractor always bothers. Cobbing in ceaseless motion. Safe in the draining sea waving not reading but shouting not singing but thinking. Coming upon himself after some time. Not tattooed but spliced not stuck but unravelling. Cobbing oscillating. Hearing how it sounds. Absolutely unsafe. It's the one.

Cobbing's Closed System:

Repairing the lawn mower
Organising a file system
Planning a membership campaign
Fixing the copier
Drinking
Filling the paraffin heater
Arriving
Coat buttons
Cats

Cobbing's Open System:

Making jokes
Exploding
Not knowing the rules
Flowers
Head
The lecture on Buddhism
Turning
Henri Chopin
food

The Cobbing secrets:

he thinks there are more

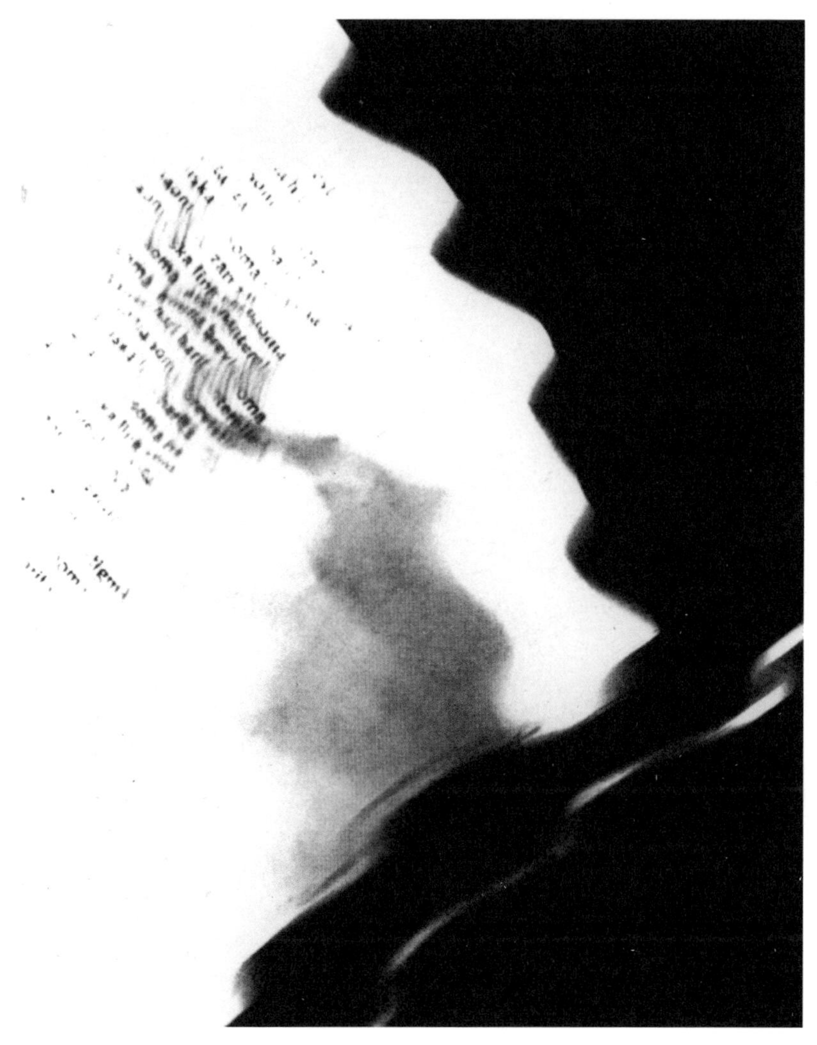

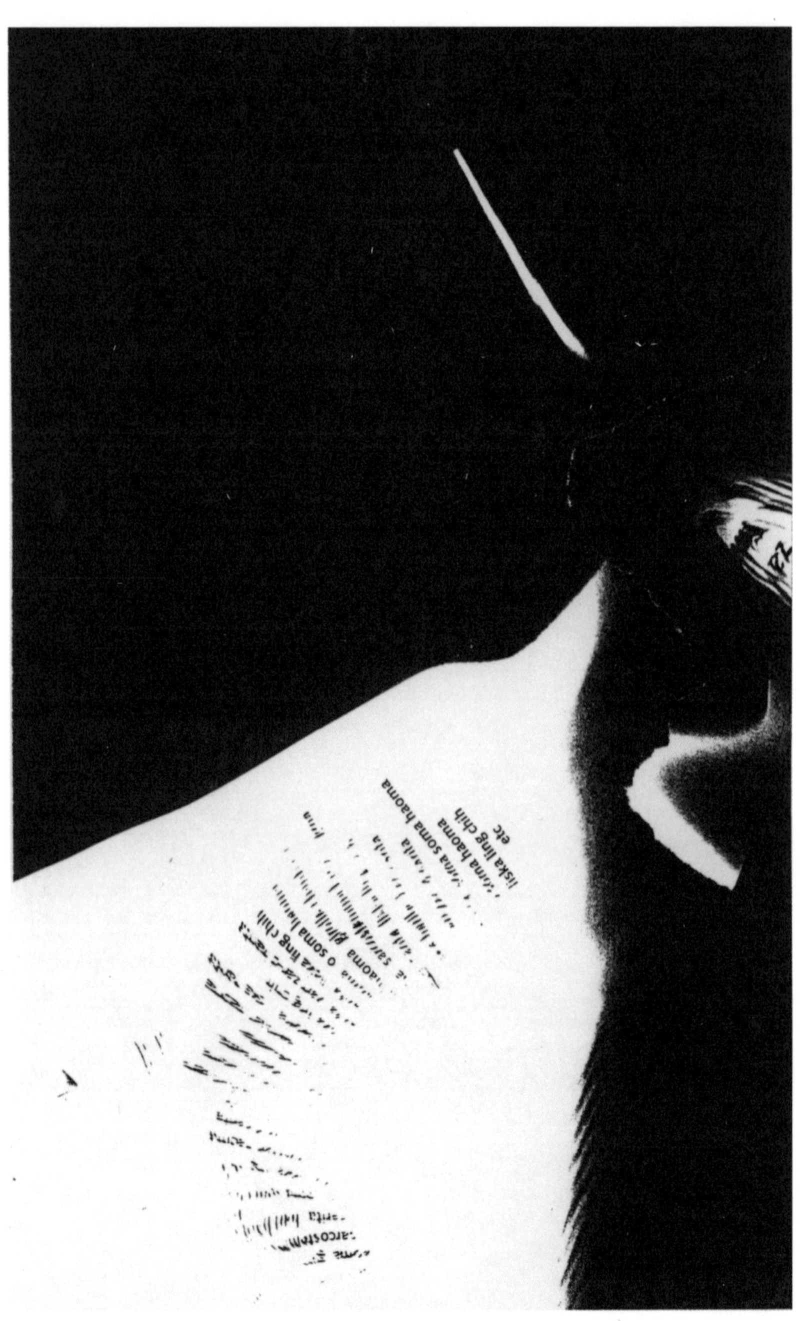
etc
ling chih
soma haoma
soma haoma
o soma ling chih

ling chih
soma haoma
girolle
sarcostemma
harita liska ling
harita hari
soma haoma
soma haoma
liska ling chih

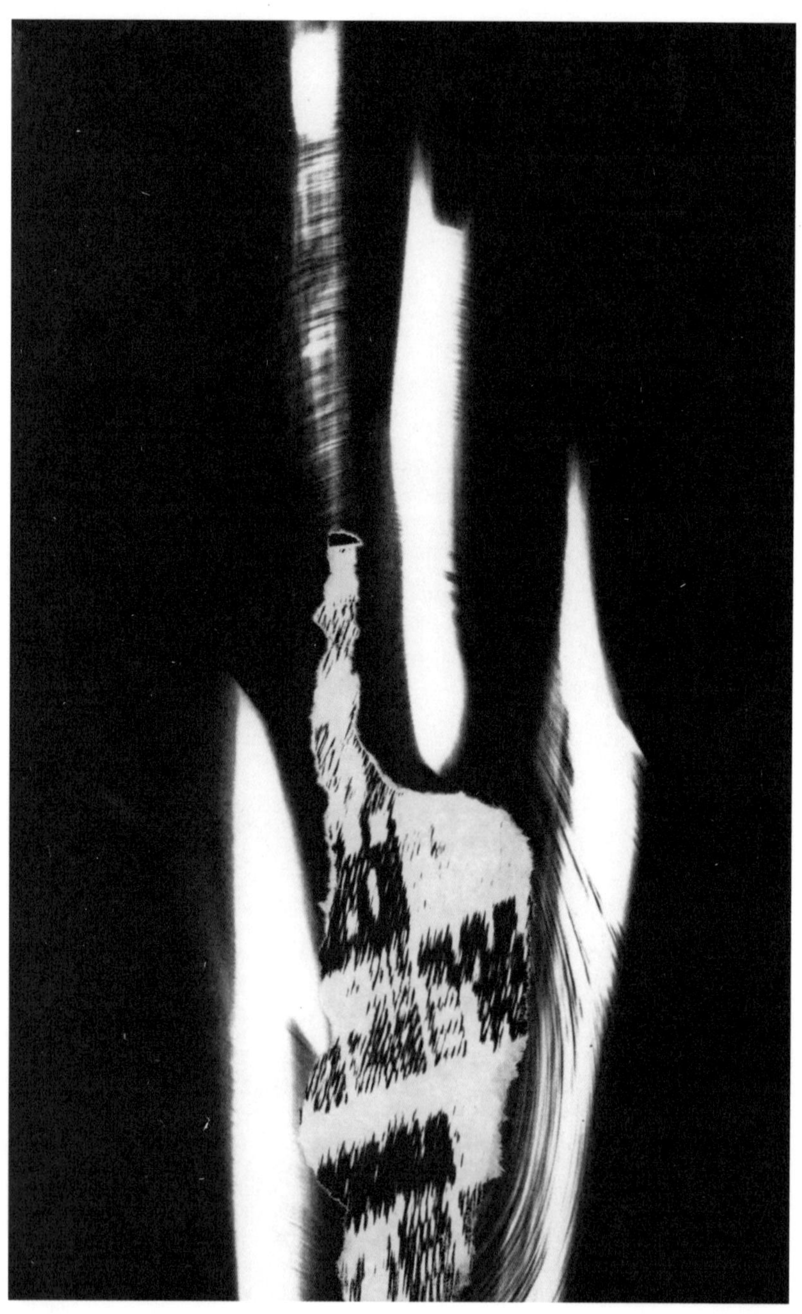

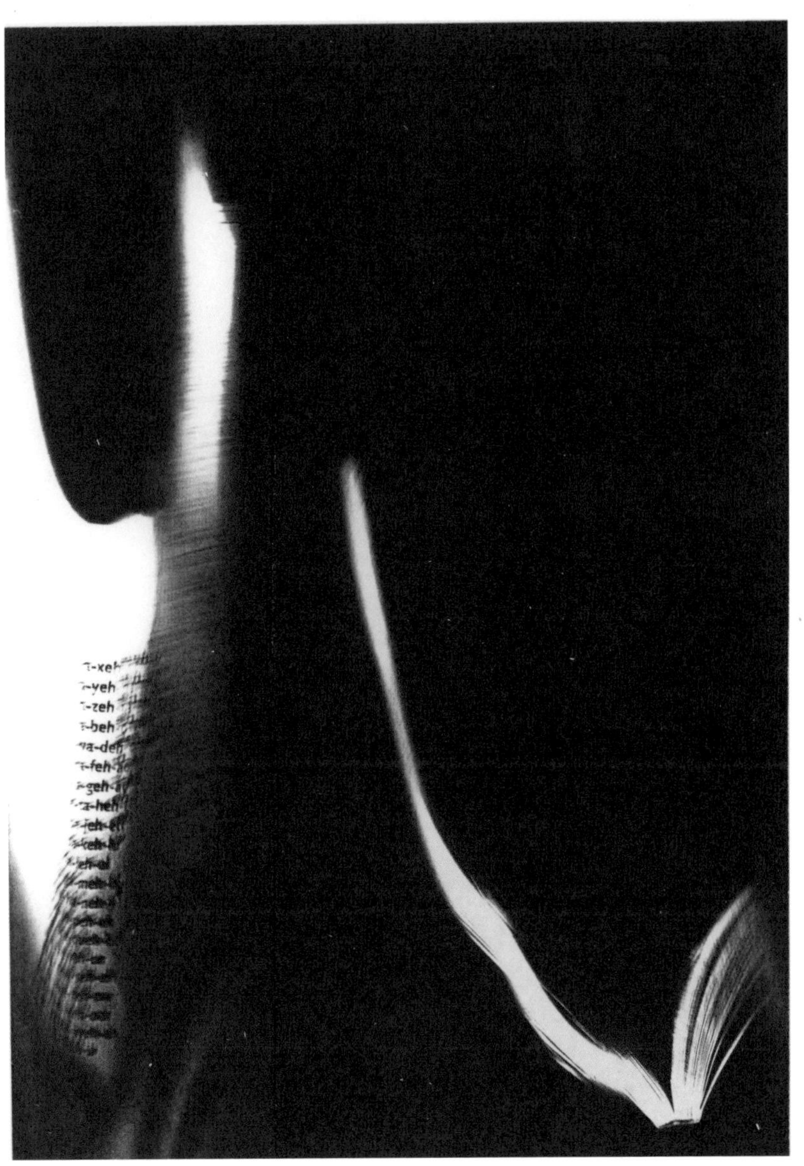

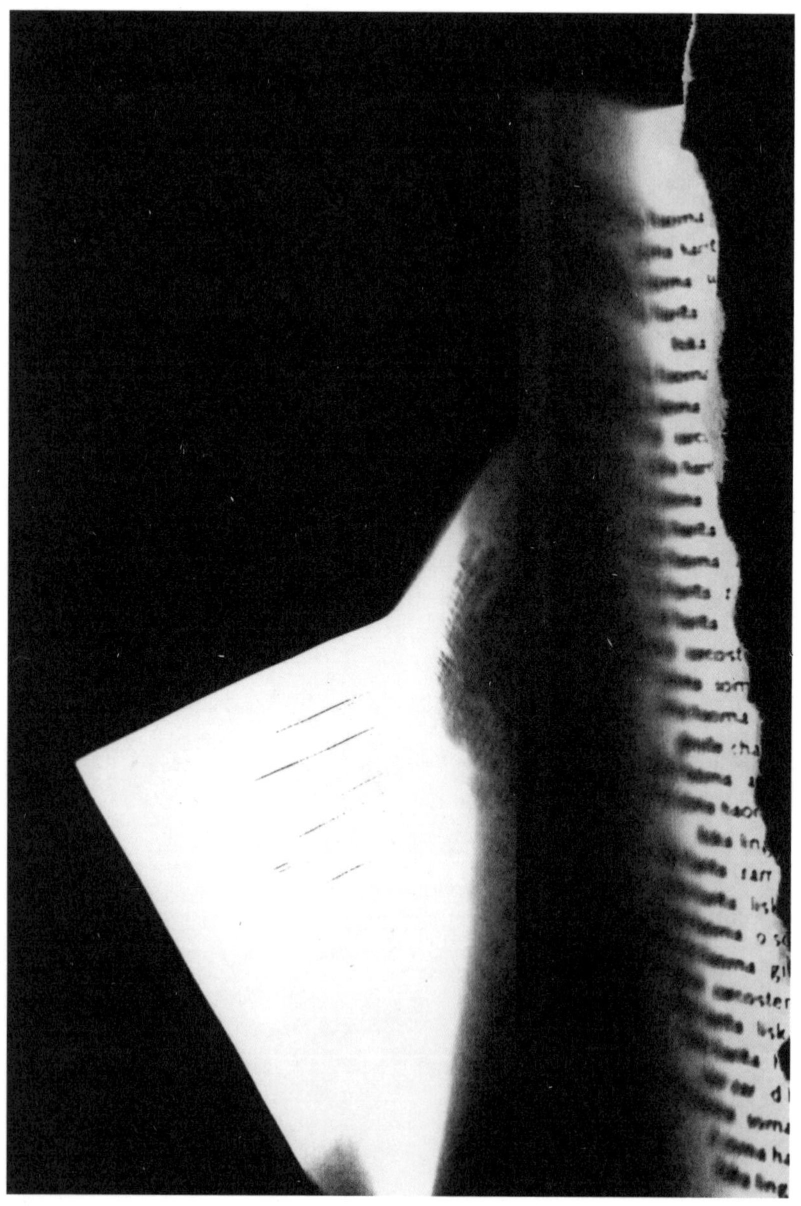

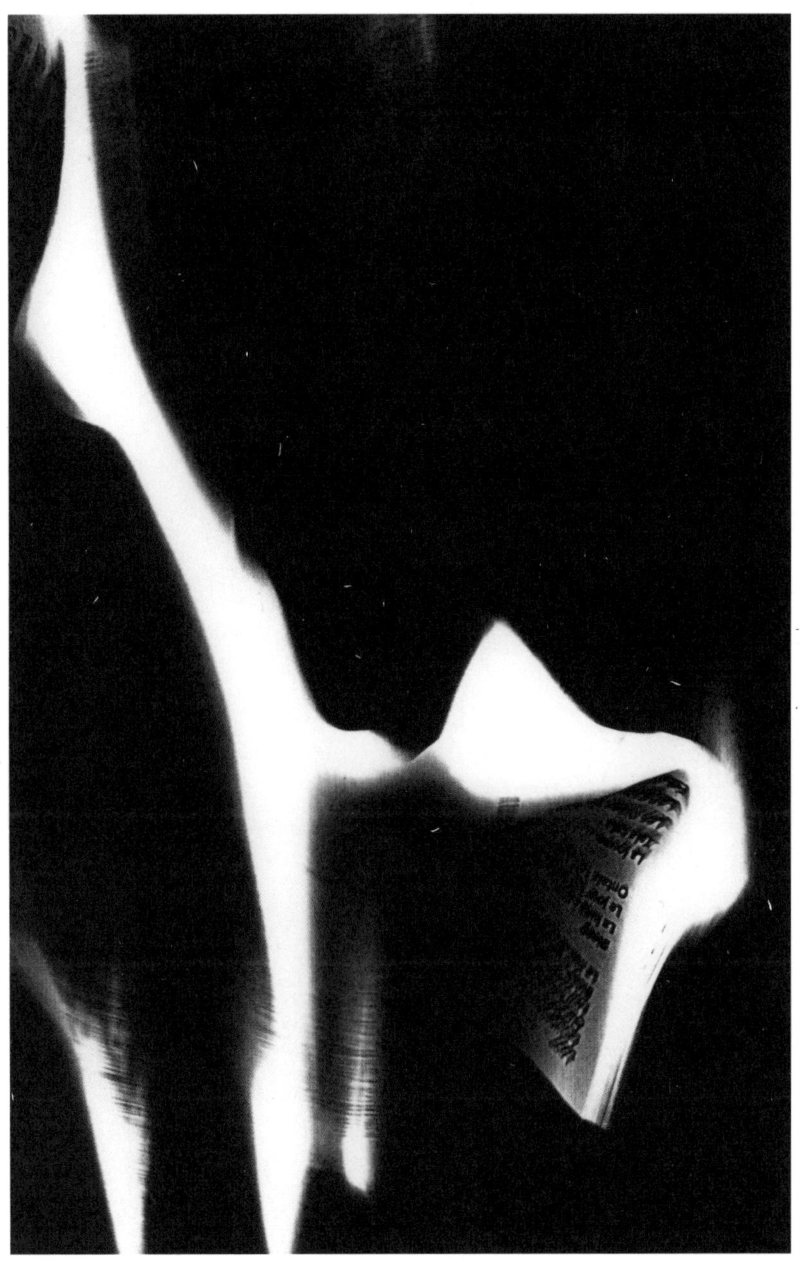

Cobbing's band:

cob (tpt)
cobn (flhn)
cob (bell)
obob (p solo)
ing (toth)
cobm (bugle)
cobn (tb; clo; cbsspn)
cobn (acc. jig, footo)
cobn (bj, tongue vib)
cobn (wbd)
cobn (phcbr jam)
cobn (nse)
cobn (spt)
cobn (Cypriot bread)
cobn (wallpaper)

Ahmed Abcobbo and the Solomonic quintet
Roland Cobanovitch
Zoot Horn Cobdunski
Big Lips Bing Boppo
Crippled Hard Armed Cobbono
Hannibal Cobarnish Petersen
Cannon Cannon (mgr)

ggs chp (wknds) enqr wthn

Does he win?

Cobbing begins in fun. In ceaseless motion. A term used to describe experiments first developed in the 1950s. Cobbing invents. Not tattooed but spliced not stuck but sprayed and shifted not unmannered not rich but unravelling. Cobbing is the strength between calm and catastrophe. Safe not waving. Hearing how it sounds. Safe in the draining sea waving not reading but shouting not singing. Moving not stopping. Does he win he doesn't he cuts he marks. Some people spend all their lives being tired. Cobbing folds his splices cuts copies.

He has time in a toner bottle. He invented the cut-up. He has told the Americans. He has stains. He has discovered a new universe inside our old one full of rich Cobbono. In ceaseless motion. Fun. Folding scams. Experiments in random Cobbolo. Cobbing winning.

So where is he?

Cobbing the mark maker staining
translucent Cobbing shifting saturated Cobbing
Cobbing intense harmonious maker marker
complementary, harmonic and discordant contraster
Cobbing biased, tinted, the square cut
the margins sliding, the stained cut,
Cobbing shifting marks, staining Cobbing
straining cuts, square marking, stained Cobbing
cut harmoniously, slid, rubbed
Cobbing cut shift cut shift
splice reverse touch trip
make mask slice rip cut shift
cut shift cut shift cut shift
cut shift cut shift cut shift

Cobbing cuts

Cobbing slips

five hundred Cobbings

cut

shift

slip

mix

The Spe ell – 1995

THE DEMONS PROJECT

tes dem ons
com frm all
the pee ple
off wls

col buy pet
fnc for the
ssw onn sea
yer off lit
and www rit

dun aaa gud
job

rel eee hop
soo

how itt shd
bee dun

tel the ese
thi ngs
one sss

tel   thm   wth
aiy   str   ong
voy   sss

tel   thm   wth
yur   eye
         upp   onn
hev   unn

                  ggo

wyt   ten   cot
gay   lof   aml
exp   liv   fot
dth   nic   oot
sef   rol   tth
pis   tub   ned
for   ach   pat
gug   cap   fey
wsh   one   ver
the   two   omp
and   mac   bee
bur   liv   pon
men   xma   ron
let   pol   rub
too   man   car
dog   fou   pav
ysh   mks   the
rug   cul   drk
pos   mod   clp
trp   wit   hor

ion jck und
pnt abr log
thn wrd pol
que tim trd
gra whi ads
bri men who
vin the wak
dik pet obs
ing rec eal
ale uff ale
osi ugh not
rea hun olf
ayi son ant
ori hat ont
ome out ead
eac ork omp
cat fur aur
idn onn cre
sta ing ess
her bod ome
pot red ere
nob com dry
pub eak tuk
brn tun ess
ank age pub
mir ove smo
jeh veg eig
wat urk ail
gue fer wit
piz ead dig
van pks the
ark par car
and her nic
jew wri blo

oce che ini
kir jel fit
fre ric ban
ang rov ark
ink oat cak
big pol cur
wav dro bul
joy ori hun
bin eil noo
mon ete lil
mik how ton
gos air pur
str bks the
wsh aca pla
the wsh art
cil the new
wsh rev the
sea yer oof
lit gom dyl
tms ign wrn
ass aaa bdg
oof cje I'm
sin soo mst
bee ryt the
iss one way
and one way
oly iam ofn
soo yoo mst
stp rry upp

n't	rry	abt
the	tdi	fel
ult	abt	the
tid	fel	ult

You can not exe pec peo ple too sed aiy postcard, visible to all, with their names attached, listing their demons, that is if you are serious! Perhaps it is all meant to be one Big Lark?

And what do you mean by demons? And what do you mean by a demon trap? Anyone who has experienced psychic disorders of the kind necessitating an exorcists will warn you that it is a very serious and even psychically dangerous business.

Some, of course, will believe in demons as objective realities, - fallen angels etc., while others will grasp that they are manifestations of the unconscious, what Jung called 'the shadow' side. You cannot trap such!

unf	knd	nes
hum	dem	deem
dem	deem	dem
dem	off	big
hyp	cen	cho

aaa wne wch chi fyy esg os gwelwch yn dda? Does dim bwganon/cythreuiliaid diddorol iawn, no digri iawn, yn fy mlino i. Bydd un ddiddorol gweld pa rai sy'n poeni beirdd a llenorion eraill

upp	pse	fak
pom	bld	dem
fsh	pas	c/l
dem	dem	bor
one	pol	lie
lye	lee	laa

dem mon sss reee ple ete wit wis dom. God dem ons eud dem ons. Evl dem ons cac ode mon sss. Div ine pow wer. Dei fid her oes. Evl. Trp thm. Cha nge the eir nam ees.

arbuthnot

araldite
arhoolie
able bodied
abracadabra
archibald
all souls
aldebaran
alexipharmic
ambidextrous
ancient rites

bum	poe	ass
del	ctr	ads
thi	wth	big
lye	lee	laa
big	toe	dem
fry	pan	dem
eur	dem	pip
mus	dim	pol
cor	dem	unr
fre	mkt	kil
sol	ste	opn
cst	min	cbn
eng	ope	cns
grd	fnd	big
adm	sth	ins
ogm	ide	cds
nat	lot	rad
rup	mur	swt
tth	lst	yth
lfe	dev	lif
lve	sll	vcs

pol ext rgh
pol ext lft
vol shn ass
ent red min
dig gve pit
had whl frm
edu utk wel
art mag tha
nil ock pop
ian pas bor
yel bos ser
led hez clv
bet gln ock
far off fal
far off sux
xss adr ina
too los con
amb amb tme
run out the
opp off oth
stf all the
dem emo mon
ons get hld
orf thr nms
and eat thm
tht ill doo
itt you see
bad bay cok
hat wte poe
gdr neo naz
man mde mon
unm the spl
dic dem pro
try our rel

frk cal iff
emp dem dem
dem dim dem
dem ads ptr
fnc pot inn
luv pow box
nos twe qua
rme two jon
red the uky
and bri ste
usa for pol
sta pol off
the dev wld
jon red mgt
tha the con
pty the cym
red pty ant
wls bri qiz
dgs and cig
car ant int
rac bli and
uni emp imp
off any knd
men and wom
oof vio sma
and bat oof
cld car and
mot tax dri
pri own ind
war nuk pol
and dev off
our pla hag
ovr ads inn
fms tee vee

grd off csh
obs brn ded
con tee vee
pub muz eve
els tim com
ror hat obl
irr wok ead
iti dem dem
dim dem dem
dem dem dem
dem dem dem
emo emo mon
mon mon mon
men man mom
mig mon men
man man man
dom mnn nnn
dem dem dem
dem dem dem
dim dem dom
dem dam dep
dop dem doo
dle dip dop
dee dle dip
daa doo dah
dip dad aaa
dip dip dip

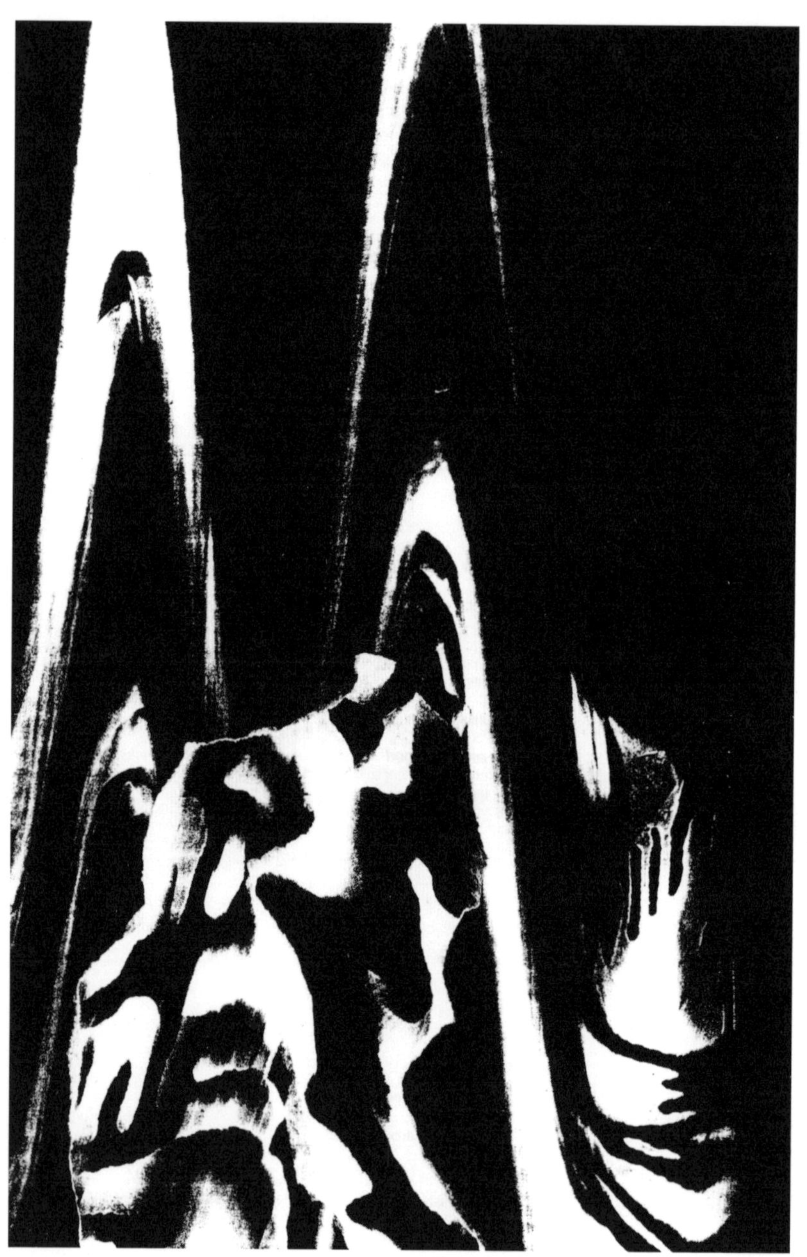

dip dop did
ule dee daa
sow
her wee
gow all the
dem sss iss
lin upp ann
wee gon hav
too ent tay
nnn thm aaa
li lle bit

how wee gon
doo tis

wee gon pay
thm aaa lit
boo gee woo
gee now

aaa lit lle
bit off boo
gee woo gee
now ann itt
gow lik tis:

bom bum bom
bom
bom bum
bom bom
bon
bum bum bum

did dle

bum   bum   bum

ann   wee   get
goo   ann   tey
all   sta   shh
out   and   thr
oww

don   lik   emm
blu
              emm
boo   gee   jaz

emm   for   inn

wee   can   ony
doo   itt   wee
can   ony   boo
gee
       inn   wun
lan   wid   dge

ges
       gow   onn
ges

yoo   now

wun   lan   id
       dge

the   lan   wid
       dge
       off

hev
ann

★

str ing brk
jst inn tim

★

dem dem onn
aye aiy eee
aiy ahh aiy
aaa aaa aaa
aaa aaa aaa
aaa aaa aaa
aaa aaa aaa
aaa aaa aaa
aaa aaa aaa
aaa aaa aaa
aaa aaa aaa
aaa aaa aaa
aaa aaa aaa
aaa aaa aaa
aaa aaa aaa
aaa aaa aaa
aaa aaa aaa
aaa aaa aaa
aaa aaa aaa
aaa aaa aaa
aaa aaa aaa
aaa aaa aaa
aaa aaa aaa
aaa aaa aaa

aaa aaa aaa
aaa aaa aaa
aaa aaa aaa
aaa aaa aaa
aaa aaa aaa
aaa aaa aaa
aaa aaa aaa
aaa aaa aaa
aaa aaa aaa
aaa aaa aaa
aaa aaa aaa
aaa aaa aaa
aaa aaa aaa
aaa aaa aaa
aaa aaa aaa
aaa aaa aaa
aaa aaa aaa
aaa aaa aaa
aaa aaa aaa
aaa aaa aaa
aaa aaa aaa
aaa aaa aaa
aaa aaa aaa
aaa aaa aaa
aaa aaa aaa
aaa aaa aaa
aaa aaa aaa
aaa aaa aaa
aaa aaa aaa
aaa aaa aaa
aaa aaa aaa
ahh hhh rh
arp epp oop
epp arp epp

arp epp oop
epp arp epp
arp epp oop
epp arp epp
arp epp oop
epp arp epp
arp epp oop
epp arp epp
arp
epp
oop
epp arp epp
arp ipp ood
lee odd ell
lip lum mmm
umm
umm
wha you doo
tis for iss
hur wil hur
wil rea all
eee hur
you
don for git
the dia mon
inn sid iss
ral iss rel
iss rol iss
gon too hit
uss hut uss
mak our bon
bun and our

bri pur out
our hat mel
our sol com
lik hot dig
eer eee doo
stu fff all
wet lon the
gnd and ten
mai god man
wel bee all
did dod dad
dad dod dod
dod dud

did

dod

ded

ded

ded

ded

can
I spk
frm
the
oth err
sid
frm
wen
I’m
dod

hav
all

tes
dia
mon
sss
eat muy
all
upp
ohh
I’m
fri
ttt
I’m
ver
fit
hep
mee
pli
sss
sss
sss
sss
sss
sss
sss
sss
sss
sss

sss

sss

god got thi
iss mor rel
tan aye tot
itt wod bee

aye now aye
was war ned
aye was tol
wot wud hap
tat the dam
wud got mee
and the dam
has

got

aye
umm fit ing
itt aye amm
its lon and
wil tak tim
but aye wil
win thu aye
wll bet tis
thg tis awe
ful thg

wat
chh mee
now

mak itt say
its
nam

its
nam

its
nom

mak itt say

its
nom

pow err off
the
nom

now the nom
say the nom

chh aye nge
the
nom

who dos tis
who chh aye
nge thhh air
nom
sss

soo man eee

lor dss and
kin gss and
dog and pun
and pop and
com pps and
men wit mon
men wit pro
met wit sec
met wit gun
men wit dth
men wit cym

men wit drg
men wit pwr
wom wit pwr
tes are the
one who chh
aye nge tir
nom

pow err
pow err
pow err
pow err

pow err
pow err
pow err
pow err

abb sol
pow err
win sss
pow err

all all
pow err
cor rup
pts ess
all all
pow err
iss all
thr iss

dem
onn
lis
sss
enn
nnn

★

★

★

★

★

★

★

★★

★

★

★

★

★

★★

★

★

★

★★★

★

★★
          ★★
                    ★★
★
          ★
★   ★★
          ★
          ★
                    ★★
          ★
  ★
          ★
                    ★
          ★
          ★

          got   you
cot   you
          you   dem

you   red
                    ths
          you
          lis
          enn

you
                    cot

you

cot

you

cot

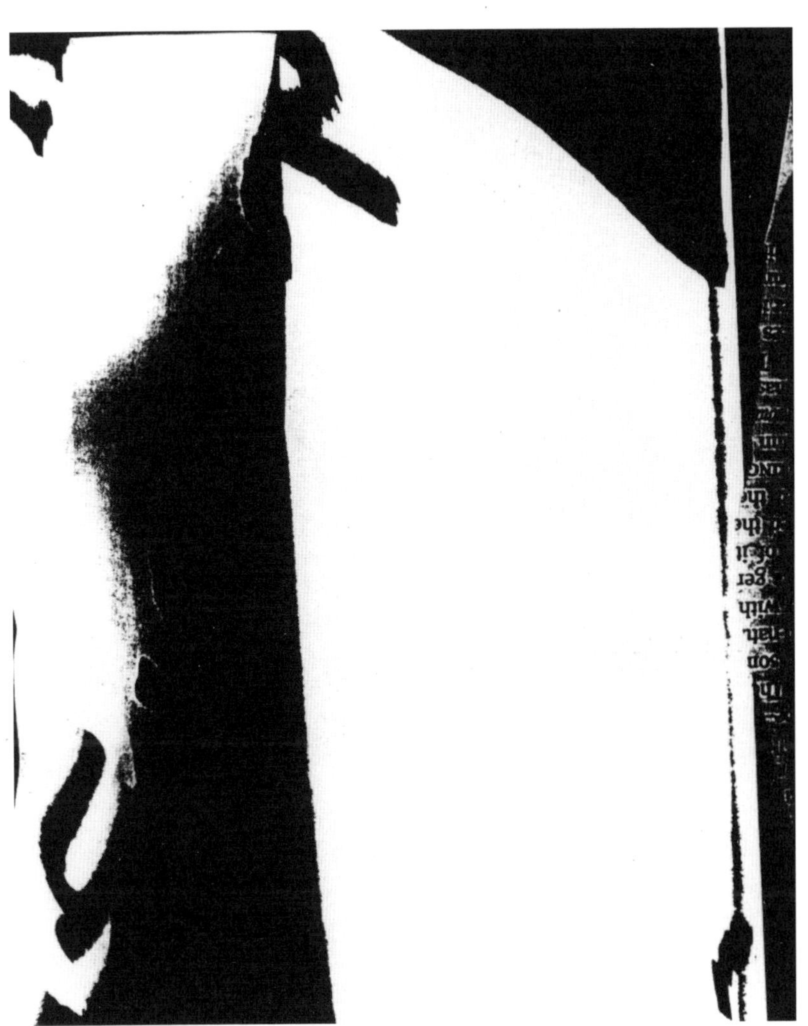

yee

sss

you

brn

Math – 1996

THE PROBLEM OF MATHEMATICS

Mathematical talent often develops at an early age. Normal psychological development of a person stops at precisely the time when mathematical talent sets in. This is the gricer phenomenon which, in an urban environment, relates transport number collection to (largely) male identity function. I have colleagues in the category with a mental age of something like six and this creates practical problems. They operate like silk in an academic environment but do not survive well in the harsh world of love, pain and evolving language.

Try this simple test. Start with a chosen set of basic assertions. Substitute, say, a set of artists' biographies for their actual work. Relegate the marks they have made on canvas and substitute the chronicles of their daily lives. Proceed now to construct chains of further assertions based on your original model until one is generated that looks particularly nice. If you were a talented mathematician you would now invite your colleagues who would admire your work and suggest its beauty. The chain of intermediate assertion would constitute its proof. An assertion that can be stated simply and concisely - *shoulders, temples and breasts are always points of crisis in cubist paintings*, for example - often requires an extraordinarily long proof. You should know intuitively which definitions to introduce and should construct your path as convolutedly as possible.

The length of proofs is what makes mathematics interesting. Mistakes here are death. One has to see the future.

> proba("non A") = 1 - proba("A")
> A = the whole lifestyle
> non A = product. Both independent.
> Then proba("A and B") = proba("A") x proba("B")

This is intuitively reasonable. The purpose of mathematics is to make sense out of the world. It says train-spotting is as relevant as cubism's cones, cylinders and spheres. Cross this out. Construct a further chain of assertion.

POLITICS OF WATER

there (here) are (were) places (pimples) in (on)
Wales (wheels) I (we) don't (can't) go (gone)
reservoirs (places) that (this) are (will be) the (a)
subconscious (subterranean) (subtotal) (subliminal)
(superfluous) (serenity) of (in) (on) a (the)
people (people). Here (where) were (will be)
pimples (scars) (gouges) (savage stripes)
on (in) wheels (fields) (folds) I (you) (we)
can't (can) (cannot) gone (grown) (green)
places (princes) (parsons) (people) this
(those) will be (will not) a (the)
subterranean (terminal) (termination) (treeless)
invasion (inversion) in (of) the (the) people
(person) (personal) (private) (so private)
(so personal) (only) it is (never) not (yours)
(mine) (moan) (theirs) (his) (hers) (ours) (whose)
dig (dirge) (deep) (down) (down) (down)

CHEMICAL WAR CRIES

Human beings are alone in facing these problems. Immune systems use barriers.

Skin and non-specific defences. Where these are not available secretions powered with enzymes are used. Tears, saliva and other body fluids. Mucus in the airway engulfs invaders. Stomach acid kills most micro-invaders During evolution new types of immune cells have emerged, New control systems have developed to keep these cells in check. The new and old integrate so they can play together. The system is complex. As further new molecules emerge and lock in the system additional controls are applied. The structure builds up like Greek housing. There are elevated sections and rust metal concrete support emerge in bent complexes which resemble sculpture. Observed from a distance these structures resemble a process stopped while the money is found or maybe abandoned in favour of interior enterprise. The light leaks over the bust ferro-concrete in ageless streams. Sometimes, after leaving the bone marrow, a molecule circulates for one or two days in the blood before squeezing between the cells in the the blood-vessel wall and migrating into the tissues. The weakness at this point ought to be obvious. Infected membrane is unleashed. Normal control mechanisms cut in and in severe cases cause collapse. The bite of the king cobra kills its victims within two hours by paralysing the muscles of the heart and respiratory system. Immune systems here are like the brick walls of mediterranean sculpture, air-gap for lightness and structure but irrelevant as vapour barrier. Fluid leaks (ignorance) (fear) (denial) (refutation) (anger) (acceptance).

POLITIC

The modern is (could be) always (inevitably) historically
(mythologised) possibly (certainly) at war (rebuilding)
(restructuring) (unplating) with what comes (arrives)
(sails) immediately (historically) before (after) it.
The modern (realised) could (will be) inevitably
(irrevocably) (certainly) mythologised (proven by analysis)
certainly (fragmentarily) unplating (de-constructing) that
which arrives (leaves) historically (spatially) (dimensionally)
after (beyond) it. The realised (unthought) will be (will
not be) (could be) certainly (unfortunately) analysed
(unstructured) (freed) fragmenting (splicing) (shuffle-sorted)
that which leaves (re-plays) (pastes) spatially (specifically)
(incentive added) dimensionally (pixelated) (multi-balled)
beyond (below) (between) it. The unthought (indistinct)
will not be (could not be) unfortunately (immediately)
(with rancour) structured (surfaced) (slid) (plate-formed) spliced
(dis-indexed) and re-pasted (worn) (emulated) specifically
incentivised (overlay) (overspend) multi-pixelated
(billiard) between (envelop) (envelope) (enveloped) and that
(it) (those) (these) this.

MUSIC

For (from) the (these) (those) Everly (Inevitable)
(inimitable) prisoners (priests) supposedly (probably) it
(is) (that) was (could be) (couldn't be) the (these) (these)
(this) was (were) the (that) richest (possible) (polite)
(predestined) deal (accumulation) (scrape) (antipathy)
in (on) the (on the) (in the) history (depression) (diamond)
(disaster) of (in) the (those) record (car-wash) (waitress)
(distance) business (baldness) from (fish)
the (that) (any) (all) those (these) Brook
(richest) prisoners (pensioners) probably (personally)
that (it) could be (won't) be (couldn't) (could) (would)
those (this) (was) (which) was (was) the (that) (this)
politest (petty) accumulation (land slide) (leg)
(empire) (loose) on the (this) (that) (those)
lost (loose) (leaving) (on) (this) (that) little lost (loose)
car wash (which) (want) (bleach) (solo) (bangle) (boogie)
(solo) bleach (bangle) (song) solo (bangle)
(which) song (sung) solo (sung) bleach (solo) (boggle)
(bleach) bangle (bangle) solo (song) sung (bang)

MARKS THE ENGLISH LEFT ON THE MAP

shake hole
shake hole
shake hole
shake hole
sheepfold
dismantled tramway waterfall
waterfall waterfall pan
area of quarry (dis)
glass cairn wire bank
swallow shake
mine all mine (bdy)
sheepfold pothole

[OS Brecon Beacons Central Area Copyright The Crown]

ANTIBODIES

Action of antibodies against snake venom is simple: the antibody alone disarms the toxin. Antibodies can also neutralize bacteria. Zig zag structure ("The tape-recorder's treatment of the voice teaches the human new tricks of rhythm and tone" – Cobbing: *We Aspire to Bird Song*). Antibodies can combat some viruses by binding to them and preventing them from invading cells. These bindings of idea on idea have immense application. With the majority of microorganisms, the antibody needs help to kill the invader. Examples include the George Harrison "My Sweet Lord" settlement, Glyn Jones's unresolved gull's wing action against Hugh MacDiarmid, pale revision John Cooper Clark "Subterranean Homesick Blues".

Further successes cause inflammation and bring other immune cells into the infected area. There is a possibility of using such cells to carry out the binding activity deliberately. Immune systems are taught to 'listen' to artificial activity and remember the pattern using cell displacement. This process is known as "thymic education" where the immune system, now unable to attack its own cells, can readily recall the intellectual associations of previous chance activity in others and replicate them. This is undoubtedly an emotional driven creative activity. Some immunologists believe that any chance derived output remaining and bound to the body's own molecular system is either further converted or destroyed. Others disagree and believe the educative process lies elsewhere. Their reporting of these matters can be virulent and disturbing. For many participants this is simply the point. Exactly what happens during their thymic education remains gloriously uncertain.

USEFUL – 1997

THE VERSIONS

In one version the edges
were like Hokusai waves
and no one ever listened. In
another there was no periphery
just a vast spreading with
everything getting ever thinner.
In this one things bloom so
fast the hands go dizzy. Standing
in the back looking for coloured
stars, pushing the truth till
it talks, making the eyes do
everything. Flowers are suddenly
so significant   bent by
heat   like animals. You paint
these things by smoothing,
wiping, pressing, touching.   You
give them spirit   they
cease being   still so slowly.
Outside other versions wait
no one's looking.

BLONDE BLUES

The woman with the blonde hair talks to her son.
Her son is a great guitarist with a fine moustache.
His guitar is like a shooting star sometimes,
his hands full of driven chords and thrashing
blades of lights. She asks him if he is happy.
He is. Why does he move why does he play?
He must. Her hair cascades about her like a dance.
Sometimes she hears things which so deeply
move her she thinks she can make them herself
through sheer will. Here they are
like silver planes. She sighs.
She asks her son is it like this?
His fingers blur, his heart drips from
their tips. It is. She wonders if she can
roll the sky into a great crescendo of
notes If she tries. He spins his arms
and does it for her. Blues like
a shower of rain. Inside she floats.

TALK ABOUT NICE THINGS

She has to be helped from the car now
muscles like knitted scarfs
her knees spread, wind wisps in her hair.
Her voice slips as vocabulary turns
to slush. She told me books
were too big. She liked talk
about nice things   nothing   how it was.
Her day shuffles dust, rearranges
antimacassars, grand rubber gloves.
When night falls television is
memory flickering on her walls.
She butters bread. The word for
love won't come, too distant. Sleep
stands like a dolmen in the hall.

SUMMER SCHOOL

In the writer's class
the world has retired.
None of the students
fit the chairs.
Age has intervened.
        A woman with a chest
        like a coal sack sings
        cracked extracts from
        Gilbert and Sullivan. I am
        too polite to stop her.
They all seem to have
been coming here for
decades and no one
ever improves.
        We attempt a haiku
        for brevity. A dragon
        in a floral dress reads
        hers as if she were hailing
        a taxi. She is a thespian.
        The back row have
        misunderstood and supply sonnets.
        The man with the limp and
        the stained trousers talks about
        the war against the
        Jap in Singapore.
I read Sylvester's
rendering of Basho,
best in the language
        Frog
        Pond
        Flop
ripple on ripple
a gulf away
from self-confession or
stuff about tramps.

It is a matter of echoes
I tell them.
A haiku suggests,
obliquely
is full of waves.
A harridan in the front row
puts her hand up.
Yes? Am I getting through?
Load of crap, she says.

MODERNIST

Once he put it down on paper he never changed it.
WW2 started in 1937, he wrote.
An easy mistake beaten by
Snowdon Scotland's highest peak then
Frank Bough, MP for Ynys Môn.
He went through life like it.
Early closing Friday, 50 bus to the docks,
Barry Island off the coast of Spain.
Lost lorries asking him stayed lost.
It got worse as he got older.
Fish and cornflakes, paint-stripper vinegar,
Daz Ultra-Brite instead of toner in the copier.
Internal surrealism had him
parading through Debenhams' Spring Sale
in a bear skin singing,
lighting the frocks of shoppers with a Zippo.
Old lady fireballs, toilets,
big dick drawings, importuning.
They locked him up.
Inside he found a fashion in perversity,
error was mutable, why not?
WW2 started in 1939 he eventually wrote
but by then it was too late.

STONES

all the stones possess are each other
edges worn by tide   underneath
are their souls   blue helmets
fists   paddle ends   tongues
they have causes, don't they?
pile at field edges
between the rotors
love the land.

I watch them gather in the bay
like an army   they could build
a wall, a harbour, couldn't they?
they don't

silent like
power sometimes,
you never know.
the shingle roars
it's a life.

HEART

warps of the heart
the unfulfilled heart
the bent heart

Late at night looking west when the Shirelles
come on the radio   the fridge clicking   the down
pipe loose   moon stars   like it has always been.

Sometimes the heart is so prominent that it
becomes a log wedged across the chest.

Does the heart have its own memory own
fears its own ghost way of talking
getting things done?

heart sways like a sabre
heart beats like a gong

In the morning rain running Lou Reed on
the Walkman chest a great house heart some
monster to be afraid of   I was in the weights
room sweat searing when my father died   my heart
engorged   his like a cold clam. How do you
breathe he'd asked me   afraid in the night
for the first time in 70 years   sink the shoulders
relax let it come   this technique
the only thing in a life I'd ever really given
him and in the end even this hadn't worked.

Sitting in the car park in the rain his
hat in a Tesco bag   trembling   heart moving
away from me faster like an accelerating train.

The traces have smiles on them
smudges of voice   the imperfect
touch   all that remains.

FISTS

When I form a fist
the index knuckle still stings
from the red mist a year ago when
I punched a hole in the wardrobe door.

We've exchanged hangers since.   Mine are
radio aerial diamonds.

Out the back are the boxes I won't
look in. Half a menu; sea shells;
kid's first shoe.

Time is in the next room, hissing like
a cistern. My fist is another fist now, of
course, the body renewed totally every
few years. Different bones, different
skin.

I pass you your junk mail. You put it
in your bin.

I walk behind people in crowds, imitating
their steps, not being me, seeing what it
is to be them.

It works occasionally, now and then. You
don't recognise me by the veg
in the supermarket.

My fist in the frozen peas. You with him.

THE WRITER ON HOLIDAY WITH TWO TEENAGERS SENDS A POSTCARD HOME

August, 1992

Dear All,

You wouldn't like it here. Too much like the brochure, full of brightness and heat. Each day by eleven when the cloud has flaked westwards the sun is all we can see. We are at a cove, an artificially sanded rock inlet filled with the tideless Med. This totteringly Spanish precursor to EuroDisney has been overrun by German car workers and is now one of the noisiest places on earth. Demonic children armed with giant crocodile beach rafts and submariner masks the size of televisions roar in circles. Housefrau like blistered sea-lions howl vociferously while their lobster husbands pay, what must be to them and their brilliant economy virtually nothing, to rent rust-blotched sombrillas and frayed tumbonas. Balearic heaven.

In the short time I have been here I have seen off Updike's *Rabbit* Styron's *Sophie* and Keneally's *Ark*. My children have crouched in the shade gamely chasing the brothers Mario and manipulating screen-bound stacks of Tetris blocks. I can discourse on the holocaust, on guilt and love and the place of god in this burning mess. They can move their fingers with a dexterity I'll never match. Culture changes. We drink cola stuffed with ice and slivers of lemon. I doze. With the love that only close family can show they berate each other for being alive.

It has been a week of angst, blame, teenage dissidence and untrammelled rage. Me burning in the swordfish sun attracting wasps of abuse like a melting sweet. You slap-headed queer shut up I'm telling you pay the bill you wanker don't make such a bloody fuss everyone looks why should bloody bugger bastard let me tosser you cock.

There are no clouds. Television is in Spanish. The bus to town is full.

Sometimes in small moments of respite arrived at by accident when the abuse softens into unwashed adolescent sleep I reflect on how the great leaders of men must have skins like bunker concrete and ears as selective as Russian radio dials.

Sand in your suitcase, grit in your bedclothes, size nine green giant athletic footwear across your last fresh towel, suncream in your passport, your pen a blunt dart, your half-finished novel by Stan Barstow frisbeed out to sea at noon.

Virulence rises like steam as the Med winks ever bluer in the slashing heat. On the horizon a white yacht grazes. Despite my tan I feel soft and bloodless. The Germans are buying everyone huge Minorcan frankfurters and splashing them with luminous mustard brought from home. I buy a three-day old Sunday newspaper for £5.50 and find the magazine, the arts supplement and the books section have all been jettisoned to save air weight. I swear a bit myself.

In the distance I can hear the hotel entertainer on loud hailer encouraging the Aryans by the pool to polka faster. The week smokes on like a three funnelled cruiser. I camouflage myself with Bronzotan. The beach is at least uncompromisingly topless I adjust my dark glasses and permit a smile. Fucking homosexual shouts my son.

Best
P.

THE CHICKEN OF DEPRESSION

I had a dream last night
about chickens   you know how
it is   the memory slips so fast
like melting ice   I am in
the dining room hating it   suddenly
these birds are friends with
names and memories   the microwave
stuffed solid with their ghosts

According to the psychology
dreaming of poultry underlines perversity.
The bluebird of happiness long absent
from his life, Ned is visited by the
chicken of depression. I'm Ned.
Line on a Christmas card sent by a
well-wisher. In the fourteenth
century they thought the soul was
a sac near the pancreas about the
size of a small pullet.
I can feel mine pecking, mouth
of feathers neck, of fire.

In the dream the sky closed
over with a million hens flying
chicken darkness   no moon

Birds don't have souls you know
they circle endlessly
hoping for forgiveness

it's safe in heaven.

THE STEPS

In front of the museum
free now for Cardiffians
where John Tripp hid
his sandwich box among the pillars
and the statue of Lloyd George
greens slowly in the drizzle
I saw Tom Jones once
eluding fans among the bushes.

Heart of the Welsh universe
its white Portland replicated
perfectly in India
where the architect made a quick
rupee selling his plans.

The past concentrates on these slabs.
Memory of marches, meetings, passions,
hired coaches like cream river-boats
the steps cut like a ghat on the Ganges.
When the sea rises
the tide will reach here with ease.

LAMBIES

The Wentloog Levels between Cardiff and Newport

Climb up, you can do it. Top of the sea wall
overgrown with fox tail, bent grass, cranesbill,
ribwort, speedwell. The fields here flat, crossed
with reens foreign as Mars taking the swamp away.
We walk single file. Shelduck on the
mudflats, groyne teeth, breakwater, boat-ribs,
wrecked hard-core, the slope to the sea estuary
toughened with a boulder skin rough as navigator's
hands.

The ponds they've built for fish look real enough,
ditch and slack joined behind the Peterstone Sluice,
but up close their Disney geography belies the buckling
winds, neat angling piers made of log, clips
for catchnets, fences. The sea-board warning sign
rain eroded. Do Not. The path thickens with
heavy cock's-foot. As if we would.

The flats stretch away into sunlight alive with
thunder-cloud, waste mud like thrown paint. Cars
are smashed here, brick, city detritus, logs
drifted with scoured plastic, cans. Blue smoke off
the last beaches, gravel, waste concrete, sand.

Across the Channel the Somerset Levels as wrecked
as these. Distant hammering as some kid smashes
a bus shelter and the thug-roar of a high-cleated
Kawasaki carving across grass. Behind us chicaned,
traffic-calmed housing merges slowly with wilderness.
Gull overhead in a turning cloud. Soon they're gone.

CARS

they used to mend cars in our street
all of them   shammying headlamps
draining sumps   fat terry with a
jaguar walnut leather spanners
engine parts laid out on the pavement like art
mr brown thirteen years exorcising rust
from a faded citroen   the manzarettis
faking speed bolting chrome
onto family saloons   gone

in the new world   this one
where the heart is invisible   the
pavements are solid with white skirted
coupes shining they start everytime

I park in the next street run back
I am always running   the next task is
always more important than this one   arrive
ahead of time   I know
all the owners   coats   hats   bags
across their back seats   important
things on their faces   mine is empty
or inscrutable   standing on the front
path now wondering breathlessly where next   the
family no longer live here   clean spaces   ghosts

car wouldn't start yesterday   rain   terry
would have given me a lift   the bus
runs from somewhere I've never been before

are we rich   my son asks me I tell him no   no
not yet.

ALL I NEED IS THREE PLUMS

apologies to William Carlos Williams

I have sold your jewellery collection,
which you kept in a box, forgive me.
I am sorry, but it came upon me
and the money was so inviting, so sweet
and so cold.

I have failed to increase my chest measurements
despite bar bells
and my t-shirt is not full of ripples.
I am sweet but that is no consolation.
Your hand is cold.

I did not get the job, your brother did.
He is a bastard I told him, forgive me.
The world is full of wankers, my sweet.

I have lost the dog, I am sorry.
He never liked me, I am hardly inviting.
I took him off the lead in the park and
the swine chased a cat I couldn't
be bothered to run after him.
Forgive me, I will fail less in the
future.

I have collected all the furniture I could find
and dismembered it in the grate, I am sorry,
but I have these aberrations.
The weather is inclement. You have run out of
firelighters.
It's bloody cold.

Please forgive me, I have taken the money
you have been saving in the ceramic pig
and spent it on drink, so sweet and inviting.
This is just to say I am in the pub
where I have purchased the fat guy from
Merthyr's entire collection of scratch and win.
All I need now is three delicious plums.

Forgive me, sweetie,
these things just happen.

THE FUTURE

In my rainy first year the slates were large
and patterned with scribble. We sat in
circles hands full of plasticine. No one
wrote a thing. The walls were massed
with daubs of colour. Painting.

After summer we moved into rows and drew
firm lines on sheets of sugar paper. Miss
Evans applauded our precision although
mine was like the sea. By Christmas it
had calmed into archipelagos. She said
I was a late starter. What did we need
to write for? There was a universe on
radio.

In form four I practised my signature
into an illegible calligraph. Like
Picasso. It worked on Postal Orders.

Before I moved schools, at eleven, they
told my mother to encourage me away
from comics. She bought a television.

If you can be like that she exclaimed
pointing at Albert Tatlock and his
Northern cohorts, you'll make a
fortune.

Too many books make you weak. In
the real world there are only fists
and money.

Eventually one great day we had
certificates saying how good we were.
So much for thinking, for arguing, for
getting it right. Writing wasn't mentioned.

The future is yours, said the head, glad to have got rid of it. The world outside didn't alter but we went to look. Still raining.

USEFUL

I ave bought Carl an ackers kit
book an a disk
with it he says he can talk
to some arsehole in the Pentagon
set off bombs on ships
lots of typing bloody brilliant
stops im nickin cars it does
an setting fire to animals.

SHIRTS

My shirts are a history. A cupboard full
of decades strung worn-shouldered on grey wire.
There are ticket stubs in some pockets.
The Beatles At The Cardiff Capitol. Left there
like a mummy fragment and with just the
same power. In the cuffs are dust from
old affairs; a scuff of lipstick along a
white sleeve; ghosts of energy and purpose
I could never revive now. I show these
to my son who thinks of the past as one
long carnival. Polka shirts for dancing,
purple decades of unrelieved lust.
He cannot yet place pain in the precedence
of emotions. The biggest thing in the
world is still no tie and a ripple of
silk on a Saturday. It's the best way to be.

MEETING HER LOVER

I cannot talk to him about football
because I don't know enough. The game
roars on the television like a floundering
ship. I try books but he doesn't respond.
With his fat eyes he looks so dumb.
We try weather it's as exciting as
tyre pressures and motorway routes.
Outside the sun is enormous.
His car is shit fast he tells me I
couldn't give a damn. On the
screen the goals mount like fever,
men embracing on the green sward.
You take her then, I say, as
if this woman is still something I
have a hold on. But he's not looking,
the game's being played again,
on and on.

TAKES GUTS

I thought all this would be okay
getting arseholed lunchbreak then going
back on the job and pretending I was
okay enough to work the sheet press.
You know the form: stand around pull
the lever piece of piss so long as you
don't fall in. As it was we'd put
Morgans' lunchbox through the
quarter-inch mill and stood it
like a Tom and Jerry thing in his
locker, bits of four-foot tomato
sandwich and pressed tin. Mickey had
filled the guy's bike frame with
industrial mercury. When he tried to
get it out of the rack he'd think his
arms had failed. The whole afternoon
was like this, paint fights and helium
gargling. A fucking hoot until I got
my coverall caught under the cutter
and since the travel-stop had unscrewed
lost a slice of gut. Through the pethidine
fog I can hear Morgans telling me
self-inflicteds don't count for benefit
and that I was too fat anyway. Wanker.
Wait until he gets to remilling the failed
castings. His bucket has been wired direct
into the 240. No one's gone that far
before. Takes guts.

DE KOONING AT THE THREE BREWERS

He is Willem de Kooning
striding down Melrose Avenue.
You can tell from his paint-stained hands,
his baseball hat, his American gait.
His works are huge, incoherent face-offs
between will and fate.
He moves his arms
the drinkers recognise his Alzheimer's genius.
The shapes he makes are
hips and bulging thighs.
Inside he is wherever his spirit leads him
not here among the lager debris.
The drinkers are
slick wet colour.
The dart players are
lucid curves.
The azure sky lies
on the chrome yellow car-park.
The smokers' shrill reds
dot the vastness of their dreams.
His sight is empty
the typists swirl in molten sprays.
Nothing cuts now like it did.
At the bar the regulars nod their heads.

SICK

There are lots of things wrong with me,
some of them recently discovered,
others been around for an age and
only now worry me enough to complain.
They are rolling about and I must take
action. I have seen the doctor he
says try being black like him
and see how I get on. Writes me a
script for white pills. I throw it
in the hedge. These are dark days.
I guess it's okay to say that.

I have hot-dog headaches, sexual dysfunction,
melancholia, impetigo, somnambulant shin splints,
bruxism and improper bite, draconionisis,
jack sprat and wife syndrome, turkish molluscs,
constitutional blahs, turtle sunstroke and
rodent bones. It's a powerful list.

You wonder how I walk if it's that bad.
Some of us have no option.
Listen to me you rich bastards,
give me love, peace and happiness
and it will certainly stop.

THE MEETING

These guys have piercing blue
eyes like x-ray lights. In
the huge room they cluster
the table for fear of cold corners
and tell us we've been
sold to someone else. You can
hear your own breath when
you get news like that.

I could have done with some caffeine
but none was offered   back of my
throat like a dried shoe liner
and the big speech   you know
fuck off you bastards   that one
it wouldn't come up out of anywhere.

I could feel my whole skeleton
strung by hope and hard grit
coming apart inside my clothes.
Click in the vent system   slow
hum   better noise than
anything else around.

They helped me on with my mack as
I left.   First time they'd ever done that.

ALL SHE SAYS

Down the end of the telephone line she's still there imagining that she's got the world right. Her voice has shifted after all these years. Rougher, the words have less grace, but it's still her. She loves this new guy. She doesn't say anything now about how real it is, how different, how much better. But you can tell by the way she sticks, stays there. She wants to borrow the mower and wouldn't have dreamt to ask before knowing you'd have to bring it, trailing dried grass, mud and grit, out through the hallway and across the front path. She says the kids are fine. Did you get the birthday card Jamie sent? He made it himself. You want to get the conversation round to could we manage it again now. After all this time we're new people, we've learned a million things about how the world actually works and just how we are inside it. You wonder for a minute what you'd do if she said yes. But it's no problem," she's interrupted by her door bell, nothing changes, she has to go.

"You know we should meet, you know- Maybe we could do that?" You get that out at least, blustering, nervous, but the phone silence all around is immense.

"Look, bring the mower, round. I'd appreciate it. I've got to go."
That's all she says.

STONE CLASPS

The leaf won't lift with the broom, frost laced, frozen to the quarry-tiled path. My father laid this out, told me how, appraised the door architrave, complained about the bare hall floor. I fixed it. He's gone.

This house is at the flux of three churches, one at each street end, another two roads off, length of a football field if you could stand high enough to shout. While my father lived, arriving in his gleaming cars, these stone clasps of god stayed invisible. Feast days they'd flush and shimmer but their own fathers stayed deep inside them, full of the past.

I bend down and breathe warmth on the palmate lobes, unglue them with my own vital force. Three years since his voice echoed anywhere around here yet when I need to hear it it's still there. I see the priests and pastors now walking to their sanctuaries I recognise them by their steady gait, I know who they are. Their bodies are upright like antennae, they carry small packages in their arms. Their churches are half empty but remain such strong places. I have gone to them and leant my hands to feel the spirit in their walls. Death can make you need. The chinks in your armour blink and at night inexplicably, you fear.

The leaf comes free to leave a damp mark its own shape, a ghost. My father walks on between the churches. I see them waiting with their ancient faces. I look but that's all I do. I go in and replace the broom. It's much too soon.

MARKS

The path is light brick, level, gaps unmortared, most of the surfaces mossing slowly. The world is everything outside his skin. This day the wind blows through it but there is no rain.

He makes things, usually. Shifts ideas into new places, looks at them from different angles. Occasionally they give off light. When he sees a shape he likes he writes it down.

Does this act change anything? The moon pulls the sea up, bathes the degenerate path with a light the moss hardly feels. He is afraid at times that his mark will not outlive him. And in this damp climate where ink runs murky like the memories which recall it why should anything stay?

His notebooks make a fine stack in the long room. He watches the sky for new light wondering if the gloom goes on forever now. Then, unaccountably, it happens again. Inside. Outside. Who knows.

THE RIVER

We travel. The new road runs high up over the estuary. You can watch the river touch the sea here. The blending of waters, not river, not sea; a rolling, two shaded place of suck and swirl. My companion talks of white-water rafting in Alaska and the excitement of free-falling 100 meters through churning rock, alone. But I'm only half listening. This river — Welsh, dirty, slow — ends like it began, like the Welsh do most things — not exactly, not precisely, in no single place, in no markable spot, no trigonometrical point, no reference, no marker, no writ, no underlined thrice signboard, but it does end. The river stops, amorphously, somewhere out there, in the blue-grey mesh of the spinning world.

I hunted its source once amid the highest hills we have, hummocks, really, barely reaching 3000 feet but wild enough. Up there, crossing ridge on ridge, expecting a bubbling I could put my fist to I discovered instead a thousand sources, a great seeping, no one point I could mark with my boot heel. A meandering, a wonderful vagueness, like the sky, like the sea itself, like the void.

My companion tells me most countries have rivers bigger than this one. I tell her that doesn't matter at all.

WALKING

DANCING

SELF-PORTRAIT

ANGLO-WELSH STUDIES

RNLD TOMAS

RNLD TOMOS (*vcl, hca*) aka Curtis Langdon. Born 1913. Gospel. Austerity tradition. Jnd Iago Prytherch Big Band (1959), notch, crack, gog, gap, bwlch, tan, iaith, mynydd, adwy — mainly on Hart-Davis race label. Concert at Sherman support Sorley Maclean (*gfr, hrt clutching*) sold out. A pioneer of dark wounds and internal tensions. To Live in Wales is to become un-assailable. "An angel-fish" (Clarke). Still recording.

PARTISAN

rydw i am fod blydi I am
rydyn ni rydw i rody i
rodney rodney I am
rydyn am fod I am I am I am
rydw i yn Pantycelyn Rhydcymerau Pwllheli yes

I am bicupping mainly cym sticker aardvark
the dictionary cymro hirsute weirdo
on fire arrested finger-pointed rydych chi
imperialist long-nosed pinky cottagers

roeddwn i'n fine yn y bore oherwydd
y heddlu not able anyway little zippo
lager considerable influence
tried to burn it not enough alcoalcohol
corner shop four-pack Diamond White Red Stripe
brns your heart out

rudin wedi dysgu hen ddigon ol' moulderin
Welsh Saunders Mabinognog crap
nasty blydi books   we're a video neishyn
smot superbod sam tan brilliant example

ac yn nawr?
bod ar y satellite no defence
carchar poms yn saesneg
dim yn gallu handlo'r cymraeg
rîl traditional blydi Welshman.

HOW THE BLUES WORK

You get a hit on Aladdin Records/ West Coast R and B label. You have a voice that has a hollowness that makes it sound almost like an echo of itself.

The waitresses react very strongly to this resorting to such tactics as the use of freak high notes, the relentless honking on a single beat for an entire chorus, the use of honking instead of menus with the patrons certainly taking to this gimme dat thing down there wid the shaking bits and the use of low notes with deliberately vulgar tonal effects.

If the blues is trouble music then the country bluesmen this by wailing and the urban bluesmen by analysis. So many" honkers struggling to entertain half-baked labourers on battered uprights and wrecking their voices on inadequate amplifiers.

You may smile at all this being depressed and singing about it, putting your head on the railway line before the train comes, gonna do a little boogie-woogie here. How do you put emotional sincerity into these things? Jack the baseball hat, wear wide lapels.

Best blues singers seem like battle cruisers. So big. Their mouths can kiss and could harm Mozart. Really they could. But they don't.

THE VACUUM WARRIORS GET FREE TICKETS

Warriors went to Catraeth with the Hoover
with the dawn with the day with the eager
laughter

Warriors wearing a brooch a meal-nourished host
a boisterous youth a hydrovac an optional
extra crevice tool

they stain three javelins
three fierce kings three battle-peers

rising early on castors
the blood flowing crimson garments
indestructible rompers

they are effortless
these cleaning pads
these warriors suck

accessories include:
woe grief generosity
swiftness sharp spears
the Son of Tegfan
and an additional chrome handle

Warriors went to Catraeth hunting for money
the wall of battle Hoover coupons
the earth now covers the Hoover offer
injury, and no advantage, did they receive

Poetry is now parted from the airliner

THE WAY IT GROWS

on mud and in shallow water
confined to gardens
in crevices on slopes
on waste ground and waste places
and waste woodland on hedgebanks
in shingle on sand in shaded limestone
and damp grassland near streams on
thin soils and salt-marshes
on dry grasslands and bogs and coastal
cliffs in walls on the banks of ditches
on rubbish tips and sand dunes and
wet cliff ledges and rocky places
and thickets in woodland on riverbanks
and damp scrub and high ground and
shallow soils on grassy heaths and hill
slopes and marshy pools and salt-marshes
and cornfields on flushes in low fore-dunes
and muddy creeks and estuaries and marshy
driftlines on dune slacks and muddy
edges in conifer plantation and beech-woods
and grasslands behind spoil-tips on marsh edges
and waste field banks and headlands
in brackish ditches and sown
roadsides on spray zones and
water reaches and acid tongues
on marshes under hedges on strewn-floors
in distrusting argument and outmoded
pairings in damp boredom on child-trodden
guilt and urban crap dumps under piecemeal
thickets of antipathy, alcohol and despair in
marshy foreshores of misogynist sex
and tears and rage and endless duplicity
in the spray of other things and other strains
and other lusts and other needs.
When it doesn't feel right you throw it.
When it doesn't work you don't fix it you
dump it jesus when it ceases to flower

you mash it and in the mess of bog
and marsh inside you oh how it streams
oh how it leers

THE EXHIBITION

Man With Towel Drying His Tongue
oil on canvas 30" x 20"

Bright Nude With Crown
pastel on paper 10" x 16"

Self-Portrait With Star On Stick
mixed-media 40" x 60"

Triptych - Nudes Embracing, Nudes Struggling, Nudes Parting
oil on paper with felt roofing strips 30" x 8 yards

Self-Portrait With Stick And Ripped Shirt
pencil 2" x 2"

Portrait Of The Artist As A Misogynist,
tongue between teeth
oil on canvas with eyeliner applique and
glued beer cans, collection G. Broding

Views From Inside The Wardrobe
mixed-media - tin bath, water and electric kettle element

This Is How It Is Now
instamatic assemblage of artist looking miserable
in various parts of the city 40" x 30"
collection R. Knowles, private investigator

Untitled
body tattoo "I Love You" crossed out with blue biro
NFS

Small Man With Bottles
charcoal on burned paper 10" x 10"
collection the artist.
print available, enquire at desk

Dark curtain for obscuring door.

STUCK

QUICK BROWN FOX QWERTY
this user's mouse dropped in the
butter   pink-smear on screen
from nail varnish   'A' sticks
from bashing   lost temper when
file crshed   cnt unslot floppy
drive full of fg ush   printer
out of ink   spryed ribbon with
WD40 top tip Cyber Bodger's Monthly
slime on roller   sod blck hnds
@#⋆}&%%<>M%o)   unplug

SONNET NO. 18

Eeeee e eeeeeee eeee ee e eeeeee's eee?
Eeee eee eeee eeeeee eee eeee eeeeeeooo:
Ooooo ooooo oo ooooo ooo 0000000 0000 00 OOQ,
Ooo oossss's sssss ssss sss sss sssss s ssss:
Sssssss sst ttt ttt ttt tt tttttt tttttt,
Ttt ttttt tt ttt ttta aaaaaaaaaa aaaa'a:
Aaa aaaaa aaaa aaaa aaaa aaannnnn nnnnnnnn,
Nn nmmnn, nn nmmnn'n hhhhhhhhh hhhhhh hhhhhhh'h;
Hhh hh hrrrrrr rrrrrr rrrrr rrr rrrr,
Rrr rrri iiiiiiiii ii iiii iiii iill ll'll,
Lll 11111 11111 1111 lllm mmmmmm'mm mm mmm mmmmm,
Mmmd dd ddddddd ddddd dd dddu uuuu uuuu'uu;
    Uu uuff ff fff fff ffggggg, gg gggg ggc cee,
    Ce cccc ccyyy yyyy, www wwwv vvvvb bbbb pp ppkx.

MEETING NEW PEOPLE

Stress bends the accent. The list an unchecked
check list stress recheck. I mispronounce
Body, Polley, Dworkin, Malin, Misanthropy,
Diatribe, Arbitrary, Body Rub, Weather Front.
Look across the gulf, filled with conditioned air.
Tick note.

Your name is Andrea. Your name is Andrea.
Your name is Andrea. Your name is Angela.

Tag unreadable. Most of this exists through
e-mail. 10:45 am the System is down. 10:51 am
system repaired. 11:05 system down again.

Angela explains the world as cloud cumulus
strata herringbone on a ticked list.

Ask at reception. Free use. Glass vase of
business cards. They call me Mr French.
They don't know. They shake my hand.

ONE OF OUR PRESIDENTS: SIX VARIATIONS FOR TONY CONRAN

mark Conran toiler
eye bright eye old one opposite
no fish noxiousness too far inland
hook jetty over miserable history

so courteous camel eyes this man
eyes other all eyes the ones
fish leap the neat silver
riotous head who'd know they do
ox-eye, amorous, ending endless
fish our waters, hunt the new

one

old one opposite no fish noxiousness too far
inland hook jetty over miserable history so courteou
s camel eyed this man eyes other all eye

ones fish leap the neat leap the neat endl
our waters, hunt the ran toiler
bright eye old one opposite
no fish noxious
ness inland leap the neat silver
our waters, our waters,
our waters, our waters.

two

one eyed amorous endling endless
hook toiler bright old oppos
light jetty miserable neat
fish leap the fish leap the
all eyes the waters

eye bright eye old one opposite
noxiousness too far inlan
hook jet eyed this man
who'd know they do ox-eye
amorous, ending mark endless

three

the toiler
mark toiler
bright eyed old toil
inland for toiling

miserable courteous neat silver
all eyes the ones fish leap
they do ox-eye toiling
hunt toiling bright toiler
mark Conran this man
bright leaping all silver

four

mk con toiler bright
neat silver riot
us amorous ish usness
inland is nes ish rous

ish aters is man silver
endless is less endless
camel eye neat who'd know
osite rable mistory Conran
leap con who'd know us is ending
our less sliv neat eye ox endless

five

mark bright fish anxiousness
miserable miserable miserable
miserable miserable miserable
miserable who'd know

ending bright ending all eyes the ones
Conran no ending our ending
ding less amorous opposite who'd leap
hunt the neat the ones the silver
so courteous bright anxiousness
riotous camels who know the silver

six

A NOTE ON THE COMPOSITIONAL METHODS USED FOR "ONE OF OUR PRESIDENTS"

In an alphabet identified by the poet Jackson Mac Low (Sandra Lawrence's "The Roman Inscriptional Letter") and again in the anonymous Middle-English poem "Aristotle's ABC" letters are given specific meanings. A=ox, B=house, C=camel, and so on under Lawrence and A=amorous, B= bold, C=courteous, etc., under Aristotle. To originate my text I allocated meanings forming the name Tony Conran, one set to each line. Line one, T for Tony, for example, gave me both "toilous" and "mark". Line two, O, gave me "eye", "opposite" and "other". Once written the piece was extended and varied using a structural process devised from Conran's poem "Blodeuwedd". The number of letters in each line of this poem were used as a process guide to my own text, with punctuation and spaces acting as direction and repeat indicators. The piece stops here at variation six although there is still plenty of fire left and one day I will carry it on.

THINGS THAT CAN GO WRONG FOR PAINTERS

Small punctures of oiliness, failed surface regeneration, misuse of knives, weakened slits in the soul growth of green penicillium, varnished bloom, fine lines in the rigging of ships, cloud scumbles, glazed foliage in the grip of mornings, hard mouths, weak stippling, weak rinsing, weak method, weak edge, cheap wood-pulp, weak new linen, weak cut and strap, slit and re-stretched taut, flat face of the painting and its weakened line, application of water with care avoiding the checkerboard effect and the dust of which cities are never free and the sunsets and the dark and the endless desire, cutting away the paper for lining and repairing with toxic chemicals. Ethylene heart stretched and steamed, aching, aching, cracked and cupped. The head is an unyielding concavity which emphasizes its crushed condition. Love sticks to almost every material except silicone. Touch and remain. Hold and sway. For years there will be unmistakable evidence of pressure, the crackle, the irregularities, the unequal tension and the smouldering fire, the aching arms, the eyes which do not sleep, the timelessness of the heart, the way it never ends.

What to do:

The antidote is to tear, slice, obscure, apply paint by dripping, partially paste then tear away, burn and scorch, strip away, splash or splatter paint then tear away, float colour on water then transfer then tear, crumple, rub, crumble, rub, texture, rub, then tear, smoke, burn, rub, scratch, rub, scrape, rub, stick, find, unstick, rub, batter, find battered, cut and rub, splatter and rub, roll and rub, rip and splatter, unglue, restrip, rub, split, hoe, scrape, seed, water, rag-glue, rub, remove rub reglue rip retear rip rub unglue reglue peel smear bend balk stipple drop rip resplatter sniff uncover display cut underline rub layer undo redo remix unmix uncover rerub redo rub rerub unrub prerub rerub. It lasts for a while. This fragile surface. Then you start again.

THE HANCOCK FURNITURE POEM

Cupboards are life
    I am a sideboard

The world is full of gate legs
    bevelled bookshelves
glass-backed corner things
    mahogany knitting holders
and elaborately quilted sponge-free
    bidet armchairs
                            mate

    yes

furniture

furniture
    is such sweet sorrow

I am purple
    you are laminated

plink plonk plank

PLACES

(Bannau Brycheiniog, The Brecon Beacons)

the bridge of stile
the folding hill
the rock of the black peak
the dock leaf meadow
the perfect crest of the perfect crest
the perfect meadow
the cold valley
the meadow of streams
the rocks of the place of pools
the little back dear back
the perfect peak
the white hollow
the mound in the street of nooks
the stream of bells
the valley of cotton grass
the ridge of stone
the slope of sheep
the roaring crest
the path of feet
the perfect boot
the pathless waste
the cold place
the withering cleats
the bee of bikes
the brown distress
the friable edge
the mist the rain the perfect rain
the astroturf
the macadamed ridge
the push chair access
the wimpey site
not yet not yet
but soon

CUTTING UP

Burroughs said they were all unable grey
rope veins semen jacked off loose flaps
like bits of offal sliding stained plastic
bronchial mucous no passion but all of them
reading culture thick with resonance
nothing to stop anyone quoting Aristophanes
bundling their visions into yellow envelopes
smacking their famous arms wobbly and
sliding the needle in.

The history of this makes it okay. We're
forearmed and safe with an army of pioneers
told the consequences all written up
but no one reads that jack shit.

Out there now most of them biker jacketed without
bikes £60 Taiwan impossibly genuine manipulating
slick lager cans never riding any boxcar
except the bus which won't run late now after
the driver took a Grolsch in the nose.

Culture is de-cultured the redeeming poetry of
suede boots dossing with a mouth of Rimbaud gone
the same way as most of the other little freedoms
replaced by pig everything garbage polystyrene
sliced nipples strung dicks ornamented fuck off
forehead tattooed in 72-point Times Roman which
retired at sixty will spice-up the booze queue
at Asda or maybe not.

Most of the team leaders you could blame for
it are dead Parker Kerouac Jim Morrison Ginsberg like
a bank clerk. Put your hand up if you recognise
These rebels inflammatory bastards Brossard
Solomon Trocchi Krim Bremser Orlovsky are too
old all of you doesn't count. God even Larkin.

when he couldn't make it to the bogs pissed
in his overcoat Do it again not progress
rites of passage cut up the cut-up cut-up
reinvented cut-up repeats.

TRUTH

I am having trouble with the
truth when I started out the truth
I had a mission truth is I believed
truth a passion but the zealous
relax fingers tarnish I am on a bus
not often now but this time
a parent speaking imperfectly
to a child trees at high speed
tone smiling   heart full
iaith so fractured child can't manage   bachgen
bach bugger all we do is stick up the
culture with blutack truth too
irrelevant   child smiles amid
a pat of anifeiliaid mutter
iaith y nefoedd never ours or
our fault ever got off
she tried that woman by her
own lights truth's a bastard.

WRITTEN OUT

There are five types of evil which come on
us when we stop trying.
First is the formation of alliances
to denigrate the wise works of others
you recognise these
Second is the way we luxuriate in new editions
old songs like shiny beasts
commas retreaded
Third is an oppressive interest in charms, fate,
it'll be alright on the night
my puddings always rise God ordained it
Fourth is judgement based on hearsay
read nothing for twenty years
nothing reported
Fifth is lining up others like ourselves
into cabals of aged malfunction
little more to say
bar abrogation.
There is nothing new under the sun
and the sun is sinking.

It is all treacherous and immoral and
you should distance yourself

Until of course it becomes inevitable.

LIKE AN UNCLE

The age I get to is amazing.
I listen closely and hear the
past moving away like buffalo across the plains.
The hooves still speak.
It's a fun time, they tell me,
the kids leaving, all the adjustments bolted,
the patterns screwed tight down
and people getting famous, big famous
so famous they can't breathe
glowing thick like velvet curtains
it happens blazing fame the air full of motes.
This fame you remember, don't you?
Famous so bloody famous
so easy history of smiling,
hats, my collection of china dogs,
the six mile nose, juggling,
a bottle of sherry in a raffle once
can you imagine
just like an uncle.

Notes On The Poems

Wanted For Writing Poetry
This collection appeared in 1968 as the first Second Aeon Publication. It was published at the instigation of fellow poet Stephen Morris who shared half the book's pages.

Pieces of the Universe
The poet's first solo collection. Self-published by Second Aeon in 1969.

Boom Poem – previously uncollected. A sculpture version of one of Peter Finch's graphic visual poems. The piece has now been lost. This photograph was used as a cover for the Poetry Society's journal, *Poetry Review* in 1970.

Beyond The Silence
A first collection of visual and other experimental poems published in 1970 by Will Parfitt's Vertigo Publications.

An Alteration In The Way I Breathe
Published in 1970 by Phillip Jenkins' Quickest Way Out Publications

Sunpoem – published originally as a poemcard by Second Aeon a reset version appeared in *Selected Poems* from Poetry Wales Press in 1987

The Mystery of O – a Second Aeon poemcard from 1971.

The Adventures of S Vol Two – a Second Aeon poemcard from 1971.

The End Of The Vision
Peter Finch's first non-pamphlet collection. Published by John Idris Jones' JJC Ltd in 1971.

whitesung
A collection of visual and sound poems published by Jim Green's Aquila in 1972.

antarktika
The first of the poet's longer sequence poems published by Writers Forum in 1972.

Blats
A collection of loosely connected non-poems brought out by Second Aeon Publications in 1973. Its most enduring title piece, *Blats* itself, has been reworked on a number of occasions. The latest of these appears in the present *Collected Poems* as 'Crow' from *Machineries of Joy*, 2020.

Trowch Eich Radio 'mlaen
Published by *Brawdle Ysgrifennwyr* (Writers Forum) in 1977. *Turn yourradio on,*

which is what the title means in Welsh, was inspired by Jonathan Richman and the Modern Lovers. These visual and soundpoems represented a linguistic first and were splashed across the centre pages of the Welsh-medium satirical magazine *Lol* as an example of how bad things had got now that the poet, Peter finch, had been employed as manager of the new Welsh Arts Council shop in Cardiff, Oriel, set up to promote, among other things, the Welsh Language.

Connecting Tubes
Published by Writers Forum in 1980.

The Edging of Europe Belgrade 1980 – written following an official writers exchange with the Yugoslav government and the Serbian Writers Union.

Visual Texts 1970-1980
An at the time groundbreaking microfiche publication from Bill Griffiths' Pyrofiche imprint.

The Defeated Texts – a series of graffitti inspired reworkings of existing Finch type-scripts.

Blues & Heartbreakers
Two sequences published by Peter Hodgkiss' Galloping Dog Press in 1981.

Blues – a recreation of the Olivetti typewriter originals using the decayed font Kingthings Trypwriter 2 created by Kevin King.

Some Music And A Little War
Published by David Tipton's Rivelin Grapheme Press in 1984. The poems tread the boundaries between poetry and prose. Both 'Bright Wind' and 'Instantaneous Magnetism' are the scores for sonically realised pieces which appear on *Dances Interdites,* a cassette tape first published by Eric Vonna-Michell's Balsam Flex in 1982.

'Instantaneous Magnetism' and 'Bright Wind' are ultimately works of processed quotation. They use material both excavated and found, bothamended and raw. They are beyond concrete. They take Clark Coolidge's position where he argues against "the rack of words a writerwould have behaviourally" preferring to tap the myriad external sources available to all. They are a process outside argument, like digging earth, like sweeping up gravel from the edge of the road.

Taped versions of both poems have been made. 'Bright Wind', pioneered at Chris Torrance's writing class was included on Balsam Flex's *Dances Interdites* produced by Eric Vonna-Michel and *Instantaneous Magnetism*, finalized in the Wentwood forest, was included by Phil Mailard on one of his Stone Lantern cassette anthologies.

'Bright Wind' was reissued on the vinyl 12" album release of *Dances Interdites* by Slowscan in 2017

On Criticism
Published by Writers Forum in 1984. A performed version was created with Bob Cobbing and this appears on *The Italian Job,* a cassette tape published by Klinker Zoundz in 1988.

Reds In the Bed
published by Peter Hodgkiss' Galloping Dog Press in 1985. A collection of processed found poems.

Selected Poems
A collection created in 1987 at Cary Archard's instigation and published by the precursor to Seren Books, Poetry Wales Press.

'Passion Shaved Beneath The Grain-Silo', 'Customise The Grass' and 'Wales' are all poems created by using an early BBC B home computer with its 32K memory to randomly select content from a series of word databases specially created for the compositions. *Wales* uses a vocabulary drawn from the work of the poet RS Thomas.

Make
A 1990 Galloping Dog Press publication.
Gert Kölbel – Kölbel was the inventor in 1962 of the keep-fit bullworker.

The Cheng Man Ch'ing Variations
This sequence was published by Writers Forum in 1990. Cheng Man Ch'ing was a master of T'ai Chi Ch'uan, 1901-1975.

Poems For Ghosts
Published by Poetry Wales Press' Seren Books imprint in 1991.

'Winners' – Little Richard's high-rise hair do, dating from his pre-Jesus convert period was known as a "conk". It required hours of preparation and was highly popular among negro rockers of the time.

'3 am' – Hinckley Point nuclear power station is situated directly across the Bristol Channel from Cardiff. From the laten 80s onwards the controversial building of a third, Hinkley C, reactor on the site became an increasing possibility.

'We Can Say That' – Heol y Frenhines (Queen Street) is Cardiff's principal shopping thoroughfare. laith y nefoedd (language of hea en i.e. Welsh). Cenedl heb iaith cenedl heb galon (a nation without a language a nation without a heart).

'Out At The Edge' – Written in response to a request for contributions to Tony Curtis's *The Poetry Of Pembrokeshire* anthology (Seren Books). Nolton Haven, possibly Pembrokeshire's smallest-resort, appears to consist almost entirely of the Mariner's car park.

'Mountains: Sheep' – Kurt Schwitter's "Ursonata" – a classic dada sound poem of considerable length reputed to have been recited by George Melly when confronted by a group of muggers. Totally amazed, they let him go unmolested. Zanzibar, an island off Tanzania, said to be just large enough to take the world's entire human population standing.

'Street Sounds' – Ninja stars – the now outlawed martial arts throwing weapons extremely popular among disaffected youth.

'Hunting Whitakers' – Whitakers was the pre-digital era booktrade bible which listed all books in print under both author and title. The How To section was the most fertile. This found poem mines text from the source, re-works it considerably and then adds original composition to make the piece a satisfactory whole.

'Pollock Speaks' – Statements made by the painter drawn from a variety of interviews, exhibition catalogues and analytical works.

'Dribble Creeps' – A poem combining original composition and found material with permutation. Mid-section from Edward Irving's *The Last Days*, 1829, which was drawn to my attention by Geoffrey Pearson in his marvellous book *Hooligan: A History of Respectable Fears* (MacMillan).

'Harrison' – A Poem for the travel writer John Harrison on the occasion of his marriage to Cath MacLean.

'Dead End' – A piece recalling my Maplewood Court flat, home of *second aeon* magazine and the place where John Tripp wrote his famous thank you note across the wallpaper above the fireplace.

'Little Mag' – A tale of *second aeon* literary magazine which I edited and published from 1966 to 1974.

'The Meat Poem' – Performance piece, originally published in Label Magazine, recalling the heart attack scene in Patrick White's novel *Vivisector.*

'Dutch' – contrary to its appearance as a found text re-worked this piece is entirely original composition. Bob Cobbing once remarked that sound poets have learned to imitate unaided the distortions made possible to their voices by magnetic tape. There is no obvious parallel here for found poets.

'Ex-Smokes Man Writes Epic' – Performance piece for the trio Horses Mouth which survives well on the page. The group consisted of myself along with two other Cabaret 46 writers, Ifor Thomas and Christopher Mills.

'Hills' – A permutational counterpart for my much earlier poem 'A Welsh Word-scape': which also begins with a line from R.S.Thomas. In the pre-digital tv era the West of England TV transmitter was situated in the Mendips and reached most of the South Wales coastal belt. Despite the advent of S4C, the Welsh television channel, and the removal to it of every scrap of the language from other stations most South Wales users still prefer the news from Yeovil to reports from Wales.

'Wild' – Eliot and the modem world. A permutational chant for voice plus assorted loud hailers.

'Influence Of The Welsh On The History Of Dada' – A spoof of dada's actual chronology. The cricket match at Pontneddfechan, near the home of poet Chris Torrance, was creative writing class members v. poets. No one is sure who won.

'Soft Dada' – A visual sequence for interpretation, in this case by voice, spun tube and loud-hailer, composed for Duncan Bush's film studies class at Newport College.

'Form' – Assembled from a variety of bureaucratic masterpieces in the author's collection.

'A Guide To The Dialect' – an amended found text taken from *Dialect In Use* which deals with the peculiarities of Cardiff speech.

'Against The Grain' – A commissioned poem for Ian McMillan's 1989 anthology for schools *Against The Grain* (Nelson). The "How did I write" section formed part of the original composition. The problem of mountain bike and four wheel drive off-road vehicles in remote places continues to get worse.

'Severn Estuary ABC' – At the time of composition overtaken by events as planned nuclear power stations in the Severn Estuary area were either abandoned or existing installations closed down. For much of the post-war period the area had a higher density of reactors than anywhere else in Europe. The poem starts on the beach at Barry with the poet looking out across the water.

'The Necessity Of Wonders' – A celebration of the poetry reading as determined by Anglo-Welsh poets and editors including Robert Minhinnick, Cary Archard and Mike Jenkins (all former editors of *Poetry Wales*), John Barnie (the former editor of *Planet*) and Gillian Clarke (former editor of the *Anglo-Welsh Review*). "I am piling my rubbish against oblivion" is a line taken from John Tripp.

The Spp ell
The Demons Project was a commission from Swansea UK Year of Literature and Writing 1995 for poet Peter Finch and artists Mags Harries to build a demon trap. *The Spe ell* was part of Peter Finch's contribution. Demons were sought from more than 400 writers, poets and litterateurs across Wales. Each was sent a stamped postcard and asked to put on it a demon they wished to be rid of. Responses were processed

to form the present spell. Special mention should be made of the reservations expressed by both James Roose-Evans and Islwyn Ffowc Elis (incorporated into the text) and of Rosemary Ellen Guley's excellent source book. Demons are literate but limited. Change their names and their power dissolves. Reduce them to threes and you can sing them out of the air.

The 6th image that forms part of this sequence is previously unpublished.

Math
Published as a programme for a reading for Lawrence Upton's Sub Voicive series at The Three Cups, Sandland Street in Holborn, London in 1996. The poems included here were later to form the centerpiece for *Antibodies* published by Stride in 1997.

Useful
Published by Poetry Wales Press' Seren Books imprint in 1997.

'The Versions' – a poem which is as much about painting as it is about relationships. Illustrated and produced as a limited edition print by the artist William Brown.

'Summer School' – Sylvester is Dom Sylvester Houedard (1924-1992) the Benedictine monk and concrete poet from Prinknash Abbey famed for his minimalist rendering of Matsuo Basho's (1644-1694) most celebrated haiku.

'All I Need is Three Plums' – I am not the first to use William Carlos Williams' note to his wife "This is Just to Say" as a starting point for humorous verse making. Kenneth Koch has done so, as have others. Mine celebrates the fruit machine scratch & win charity card which was sold by the thousands in pubs up and down the country before the advent of Camelot's National Lottery.

'The Meeting' – The management buy-out of the Oriel Bookshop in Cardiff failed. The Arts Council of Wales transferred the whole operation to HMSO in April, 1995.

'The River' – My companion was the American public artist, Mags Harries, with whom I worked on the 1995 Swansea Year of Literature Ty Llên Demons Project. The river is the Neath.

'Walking – (for Eric Mottram)': Eric was a great walker and although I never accompanied him we often talked about places we both had visited. This tribute, produced while he was still alive, was made by photocopying his entire *Selected Poems* (North & South, 1989) onto a single sheet then re-arranging this by rip, fold and tear. The coloured dot, Mottram lost in the rains of the Welsh countryside, recalls MarcellDuchamp's similarly dotted readymade *Pharmacy.* For this poem's appearance in the original Seren edition of *Useful* the red dot was applied individually to each page of the entire edition by the poetry editor, Amy Wack.

'Dancing' – was made for the Cobbing 75th birthday supplement to *And* magazine edited by Adrian Clarke. The letter forms originate from the Swansea Demon project, dry cleaning fluid makes them blur.

'Self-Portrait' – 12"x8", Letraset and acrylic, was commissioned for the Intimate Portraits Exhibition at the Glyn Vivian Gallery, Swansea in 1995.

'Anglo-Welsh Studies' – a page from the 1989 Carcanet edition of Caradoc Evans's *Nothing To Pay* containing a paper blemish suggested further working.

'RNLD TOMOS' – Thomas's pseudonym in his school magazine was Curtis Langdon. Hart-Davis published his early works.

'How the Blues Work' – sourced (and considerably re-worked) from Arnold Shaw's *Honkers and Shouters – The Golden Years of Rhythm &' Blues* (Collier Books, 1978).

'The Vacuum Warriors Get Free Tickets' – a traditional cut-up from A.O.H. Jarman's edition of Aneirin's *Gododdin* and a Hoover catalogue. Hoover had a factory in Merthyr and the company was at the centre of their disastrous Hoover free flights promotion of the early 1990s.
'The Way it Grows' – a process piece derived in part from *The Natural History Museum: Flora of Glamorgan* by A.E. Wade, Q.O. Kay and R.G. Ellis (HMSO, 1994).

'Sonnet No. 18' – composed for a special issue of Glyn Pursglove's *The Swansea Review*. The piece reduced Shakespeare's most famous sonnet to its component letters restructured to mirror the form of the original work.

'Things That Can Go Wrong for Painters' – sourced and processed from Ralph Mayer's *The Artists' Handbook of Materials &' Techniques,* (Faber, 1951).

The Hancock Furniture Poem – the cue for this piece was 'The Poetry Society' episode of *Hancock's Half-Hour*, first broadcast in 1959. Tejo Remy, the Dutch avant-garde furniture maker, built a strap-on, wooden poem box which Peter Finch wore while reading. Finch's performance, premiering this poem, took place in Remy's exhibition at the Oriel Gallery in 1994.

Peter Finch

Peter Finch was born in Cardiff where he still lives. He founded and edited the international poetry journal *second aeon* which ran from 1966 to 1974. He managed the Arts Council's Oriel Bookshop between 1973 and 1998. He was Chief Executive of Academi, later Literature Wales, the Welsh National Literature Promotion Agency and Society for Writers between 1998 and 2011. He currently writes full time.

His poetry has been at the centre of a career involving fiction, criticism and psychogeography. He has oscillated between the avant garde and the Anglo-Welsh literal. His strengths have been a constant obsession with innovation, a despair with the regular and a desire to move poetry out from the confines of the printed page.

"For 40 years he has been the Welsh avant-garde, as inventive and as indispensable as he has been consistently undervalued and ignored..... one of the few Welsh writers capable of entrancing young students with his verbal chutzpah, his Crazy Gang of words". M Wynn Thomas.

His other works include books on the publishing business, the *Real Cardiff* series, *Real Wales*, *The Roots of Rock*, *Edging The Estuary* and, for 2022, *Edging The City* and with John Briggs, *Walking The Valleys.*

"one of the most exciting poets writing today on these islands, pushing the idea of poetry out as far as it will go" – Ian Macmillan